North American Auto Unions in Crisis

SUNY series in the Sociology of Work

Richard H. Hall, editor

North American Auto Unions in Crisis

in Crisis

Lean Production as Contested Terrain

Edited by
William C. Green
Ernest J. Yanarella

State University of New York Press

HD
6515
A82
I576
1996

Graphic cover (map) designed by John Yanarella.

Published by
State University of New York Press, Albany

© 1996 State University of New York

For information, address State University of New York Press,
State University Plaza, Albany, NY 12246

Production by Cynthia Tenace Lassonde
Marketing by Fran Keneston

Library of Congress Cataloging-in-Publication Data

North American auto unions in crisis : lean production as contested
    terrain / [edited by] William C. Green, Ernest J. Yanarella.
        p. cm. — (SUNY series in the sociology of work)
    Includes bibliographical references and index.
    ISBN 0-7914-2823-0 (alk. paper). — ISBN 0-7914-2824-9 (pbk. :
alk. paper)
        1. International Union, United Automobile, Aerospace, and
Agricultural Implement Workers of America.   2. CAW-Canada.   3. Trade-
unions—Automobile industry workers—United States.   4. Trade-
unions—Automobile industry workers—Canada.   5. Automobile
industry and trade—United States—Management.   6. Automobile
industry and trade—Canada—Management.   I. Green, William C.,
1941– . II. Yanarella, Ernest J. III. Series.
HD6515.A82I576   1996
331.88'1292'097—dc20   95-17213
                                                              CIP

10 9 8 7 6 5 4 3 2 1

To

John, Rachael, and Walker Yanarella

and

William Nathanael Crawford Green

Contents

Contributors

Steve Babson is Labor Program Specialist at the Labor Studies Center of Wayne State University (Michigan) who has participated in training and surveying United Auto Workers (UAW) at AutoAlliance. His books on the UAW and the United States auto industry include *Working Detroit: The Making of a Union Town* (1984); *Building a Union: Skilled Workers and Anglo-Gaelic Immigrants in the Rise of the UAW* (1991); and *Lean Labor* (1995). His studies on lean production labor relations have also appeared in labor publications, including *Labor Studies Journal*.

Carl H. A. Dassbach is Assistant Professor of Sociology in the Science, Technology, and Society (STS) Program at Michigan Technological University. His work has been published in a variety of social science journals, including *Critical Sociology* and *The Insurgent Sociologist*, on the origins of Fordism and the myth and reality of lean production in the auto industry.

Laurie Graham is Assistant Professor of Labor Studies at the Indiana University-Kokomo. Her doctoral dissertation, *Production Control: A Case Study of a Japanese Automobile Plant*, was a participant observer analysis based on her employment at the Subaru-Isuzu plant in Lafayette, Indiana. Her work on lean production labor relations has appeared mainly in sociology journals, including *Work and Occupations*.

William C. Green is Professor of Government at Morehead State University in Kentucky. His research is devoted to the legal dimensions of labor relations, economic development, and contraceptive drug policy. His studies of economic development and labor relations have appeared in *Labor Law Journal*, *Labor Studies Journal*, and *Urban Lawyer*; in Ernest J. Yanarella and William C. Green, eds., *The Politics of Industrial Recruitment* (1990); and in Steve Babson, ed., *Lean Labor* (1995).

Christopher Huxley is Associate Professor of Sociology at Trent University in Ontario. His research on the sociology of work and on comparative studies of union strength in Canada and the United States has appeared in a variety of scholarly journals and in Seymour Martin Lipset, ed., *Unions in Transition* (1986). With James Rinehart and David Robertson, he is a member of the Canadian Auto Workers (CAW) Research Team on CAMI, the General Motors-Suzuki joint venture.

James Rinehart is Professor of Sociology at the University of Western Ontario. His scholarly articles have appeared in leading Canadian and American journals, including *Studies in Political Economy*. The author of the noted study, *The Tyranny of Work Alienation and the Labor Process* (1986, 2nd ed.), he is also coauthor with David Robertson and Christopher Huxley of a forthcoming volume on the CAW and CAMI.

David Robertson is Director of the Research Department at the Canadian Auto Workers and the senior member of the CAW Research Team on CAMI. He has written extensively on the impact of economic restructuring and innovative management techniques upon the Canadian automobile sector. He is the author of *Technological Change in the Auto Industry* (with Jeff Wareham) (1987); *Computer Automation and Technological Change: North Telecom* (1989); *Japanese Production Management in a Unionized Plant* (1993).

Donald Wells is Associate Professor of Political Science and Labor Studies at McMaster University in Ontario. He is the author of *Empty Promises: Quality of Working Life and the Labor Movement* (1987) and *Soft Sell: "Quality of Working Life" Programs and the Productivity Race* (1986). His studies of labor and political economy have also appeared in *Relations Industrielles/Industrial Relations*, *Labor/Le Travail*, the *Canadian Journal of Sociology*, and Jane Jenson and Rianne Mahon, eds., *The Challenge of Restructuring* (1993).

Ernest J. Yanarella is Professor of Political Science at the University of Kentucky. His wide-ranging scholarly interests are reflected in his books and articles on energy, environment, labor, and political economy. His recent studies on Japanese automobile recruitment (coauthored with William C. Green) have appeared in the *Economic Development Quarterly*, *Canadian Journal of Sociology*, *Labor Studies Journal*, and in Ernest J. Yanarella and William C. Green, eds., *The Politics of Industrial Recruitment* (1990).

Acknowledgments

It is a distinct pleasure to acknowledge the support and encouragement of the many people who contributed to the writing and production of this book. Although scholarly work is often seen as a solitary vocation, the larger social context of research belies the stereotypical ivory tower image. This coedited book, perhaps more than other works, enjoyed the company of a wide circle of people whose contributions made its writing and publication possible.

We first acknowledge those individuals, institutions, and programs providing financial support for this project. The costs associated with this volume were underwritten by four grants provided by the Canadian Studies Program, the Quebec Studies Program, the University of Kentucky, and Morehead State University. We gratefully acknowledge the generous financial assistance provided by these organizations which has also supported the coauthors'/editors' analyses of the Canadian labor, community, and environmental participation in Japanese industrial recruitment which have appeared in *Economic Development Quarterly* (1993), the *Canadian Journal of Sociology* (1993), and *Labor Studies Journal* (1994).

These government and university research grants bore much fruit. They permitted the authors to visit Ontario and Quebec in the Summer of 1991, to interview Canadian community, labor, and environmental leaders, and to make initial contacts with Canadian scholars who have contributed to this volume. Subsequently, grants assisted William Green's research for his chapter on the transformation of the NLRA paradigm and Ernest Yanarella's research for his chapters on the UAW and CAW under the shadow of post-Fordism and on worker training at Toyota and Saturn by supporting trips to Saturn (Spring Hill, Tennessee) and Toyota (Georgetown, Kentucky) in 1992 and 1993. These grants also permitted us to organize conference panels for the 1992 and 1995 annual meetings of the Midwest Political Science Association (MWPSA), the 1992 annual meeting of the Southern Political Science Association (SPSA) on organized labor and the crisis of Fordism, and to participate in the 1993 Wayne State University conference on labor and lean production.

We thank the United States and Canadian contributors to this volume whose chapters were commissioned by us. Jim Rinehart brought to our attention Carl Dassbach's essay during our attendance at the "Labor and Lean

Production" conference. We are grateful to Jim for this gift and to Carl for laboring over and revising his original essay in order to integrate Kenney and Florida's recent book into his incisive critique. The other essays were initially presented as convention papers at the 1992 MWPSA and SPSA annual meetings. In addition to offering first drafts of their chapters, Laurie Graham, Steve Babson, and members of the CAW research team on CAMI were generous with their advice and support for this entire project. We would be negligent if we did not acknowledge the support of Don Wells throughout the writing, review, and publication process—especially at a critical stage when encouragement and direction were desperately needed.

SUNY Press, in our humble opinion, is fortunate to have an editor with the energy, insight, and talent of Ms. Christine Worden. Her timely, fair-minded, and sure handling of our book manuscript during the review process made the months of uncertainty and indecision easier to bear. Her care, competence, and quiet efficiency are duly noted and acknowledged with our sincere thanks.

One or more chapters quoted from several sources previously published for which reprint permissions were required. We wish to acknowledge those journals for granting permission to use these quoted materials in this work. They are: *Work, Employment & Society*, for quotations from K. Williams, C. Haslam, and J. Williams, "Ford versus 'Fordism': The Beginning of Mass Production?" Vol. 6, No. 4 (December 1992); and Sage Publications for quotations from Martin Kenney and Richard Florida, "Beyond Mass Production: Production and the Labor Process in Japan," *Politics and Society*, Vol. 16 (1988), pp. 121–168.

Closer to home, we are grateful for the tireless efforts of Rob Aken to assist us in the many library and bibliographic needs associated with completing this work. Robin Mullins, staff assistant in political science at the University of Kentucky, was absolutely giving of her time and talents in seeing this work through its many drafts. Efficiency, good cheer, and sometimes sheer determination marked her many gracious contributions to the production of this work. We also owe a debt of gratitude to Sandy Barnett, whose timely assistance at key points helped bring the final draft to fruition.

We are grateful to our respective wives, Rowena Green and Elizabeth Yanarella. While they can fully stand on their own in their respective professional lives, we hope that the ebb and flow of mutual support we offer one another in making family and professional lives together and apart has not been too heavily weighted to our side in this latest book venture. Insofar as Freud was right in claiming that the meaning of life is to be found in love and hard work, we feel blessed by the boundless gifts that their love and support contributed to the production of this work in small ways and large.

To our children, also gifts of love and hard work, we dedicate this book. As they, like we, negotiate the local and global processes explored in this book

that are transforming our lives, we ask them to consider this book and its dedication as tokens of hope for a better future for them and their generation.

William C. Green and Ernest J. Yanarella

Introduction:
Building Other People's Cars:
Organized Labor and the Crisis of Fordism

Ernest J. Yanarella
_____William C. Green

Japan's rising economic prowess in the 1980s and the reaction of the United States and Canadian governments to its penetration of the North American automobile marketplace prompted Honda, Nissan, Subaru-Isuzu, and Toyota to construct six auto assembly plants across the North American industrial heartland from Smyrna, Tennessee to Alliston, Ontario. At the same time, it led the 'Big Three' auto makers to negotiate joint ventures with three Japanese firms: NUMMI (General Motors-Toyota), Diamond-Star (Chrysler-Mitsubishi), and CAMI (General Motors-Suzuki). Then by the decade's end, this environment moved General Motors to build the Saturn in response to the Japanese challenge.[1] This common American and Canadian experience also involved a transformation in industrial production methods and a reorganization of work defined in terms of Japanese lean production methods and cooperative labor-management relations. This triggered a crisis for the Fordist or mass production regime, its adversarial system of labor-management relations, and organized labor.

The eight essays in this volume provide a comparative cross-national perspective on the implications of the crisis of Fordism for organized labor. They focus on the serious challenges which lean production recruitment, training, "cooperative" labor management relations at the Japanese automobile transplants, their joint ventures with the Big Three auto firms, and GM's Saturn pose for the United Auto Workers' (UAW) and Canadian Auto Workers' (CAW) traditional Fordist organizing, collective bargaining, and shop floor representation practices. In this regard, these essays examine how these two unions have responded to lean production's dilemmas and challenges at the unionized Big Three plants and their Japanese joint ventures. Then they scrutinize the

1

implications of nonunion lean production transplants for the limits of worker resistance and the possibilities for worker skills training and development. Finally, these essays explore the reasons for the UAW's and CAW's failure to organize the transplants; the nature of the collective agreements these two unions have negotiated with the joint ventures and Saturn; and prospects for organized labor in a changing international and hemispheric political economy increasingly dominated by lean production.

This opening essay draws upon these themes to introduce this study of organized labor and lean production in the United States and Canada. First, it examines the Japanese transplant recruitment phenomenon and the ensuing debate over lean production. Then it turns to the social, economic, and legal perspectives on organized labor and lean production in the United States and Canada; the divergent national paths the UAW and CAW have taken in response to lean production at the unionized Big Three-Japanese joint ventures and Saturn; and the common challenges both unions confront at the nonunion Japanese transplants. This essay draws to a close with a glimpse at organized labor's future in an era of lean production.

Industrial Recruitment, the Transplant Phenomenon, and the Debate Over Lean Production

Initial North American scholarship on the Japanese transplant phenomenon largely focused on industrial policy and on federal, state, or provincial experiences with the recruitment of these foreign automobile transplants and joint ventures with American auto makers (Bartik, 1984; Blair and Premus, 1987; Chernow, 1979; Dubnick, 1984; Fox and Neel, 1978; Glickman and Woodward, 1989; Goodman, 1979; Grady, 1987; Lind and Elder, 1986; Milward and Newman, 1988; and Yanarella and Green, 1990). Studies of the politics of industrial recruitment explored the use of state or provincial tax and financial incentives to attract these assembly plants; the competition between the states and provinces and the escalating incentive packages they offered to have one of their communities chosen as the plant site; the constitutional issues generated by these state incentive schemes; the economic, social, and environmental impacts of these foreign assembly plants on the greenfield communities; and the episodic opposition they generated from environmental, labor, and community groups.

The economists and business management scholars who provided the major themes in the study of this transplant phenomenon and its impacts brought to these studies their economic growth agenda and boosterist biases (Blair, Endres, and Fichtenbaum, 1990; Blair and Premus, 1987; Fox, 1990; Fox and Neel, 1987; Gelsanliter, 1990; Miller, 1988; Shook, 1988; and Williams and Brinker, 1985). When United States and Canadian auto workers began building other people's cars using Japanese production methods (JPM) or lean production techniques, economists and management gurus who had studied these techniques and their application extolled their virtues in epochal terms. According to James Womack and his fellow researchers (Womack, Jones, and Roos, 1990) at MIT's International Motor Vehicle Project (IMVP), lean production techniques heralded the resolution of the Fordist crisis and the appearance of a "post-Fordist" regime synthesizing mass and craft production.

Critical studies on the transplant phenomenon and the crisis of Fordism have rejected this managerial perspective. Scholars from labor studies, critical sociology, radical (Marxist and post-Marxist) geography, and political science have begun to expand the theoretical and strategic horizons of the post-Fordist/lean production debate as it relates to organized labor and life on the shop floor (Babson, 1993; Bradbury, 1989; Carroll, 1990; Dohse, Jurgens, and Malsch, 1985; Drache, 1991; Drache and Glasbeek, 1989; Graham, 1993; Green, 1990; Hansen, 1990; Harvey, 1989; Holmes, 1988, 1989, 1991; Jenson, 1990; Jessop, 1990; Lowery, 1990; Mahon, 1987, 1991; Mair, Florida, and Kenney, 1988; Parker, 1990; Perrucci and Patel, 1990; Robertson, Rinehart, and Huxley, 1992; Sayer and Walker, 1992; Williams, Cutler, Williams, and Haslam, 1987; Yanarella and Green, 1993, 1994a and b; and Yanarella and Reid, 1990). In so doing, these second-wave social analysts have tapped into wider theoretical discussions and debates in England, Germany, and Italy and have placed their concerns over lean production's alternative to Fordism within continental and global theoretical frameworks generated by the French regulationist school led by Michel Aglietta, Alain Lipietz, Michel DeVroey, and Alain Noel; by the spectrum of European and Australian post-Fordist schools represented by Michael Piore and Charles Sabel, Stuart Hall, and John Mathews; and by the German neo-Fordist and post-Fordist schools organized around the work of Knuth Dohse, Ulrich Jergens, and Thomas Malsch, and Wolfgang Streeck, Arndt Sorge, and Horst Kern, respectively. As a consequence, this latest phase of scholarship in the United States and Canada promises to take earlier, more traditional disciplinary interests and foci and to replace them with a more theoretically sophisticated and globally grounded agenda which opens up the Fordist/post-Fordist controversy to new actors, larger issues, and more complex local-state-global interactions.

The American and Canadian scholarly debate, which is now beginning to feel the impact of these critical studies, is still largely shaped by the vocabulary and outlook of the high priests of the lean production school. James Womack and his IMVP colleagues in their *The Machine That Changed the World* (1990) and Martin Kenney and Richard Florida in their *Beyond Mass Production* (1993) have been the most notable champions of this new economic regime and its accompanying mode of production and consumption. While the epochal claims of the lean production school have been carefully scrutinized and exhaustively criticized on theoretical, conceptual, and empirical grounds, the post-Fordist variation offered by Kenney and Florida has yet to be critiqued in the growing literature on the Fordist/post-Fordist controversy.

In the first chapter, Carl H. A. Dassbach begins to fill this lacuna by subjecting this lean production literature to sustained critical analysis. From a neo-Fordist perspective on JPM, he raises serious questions about Womack's work and Kenney and Florida's arguments. Since the MIT study's bold and uncompromising advocacy has been an easy mark for critics, Dassbach turns to a much more demanding task: Kenney and Florida's copious study and qualified endorsement of lean production as a putative alternative to Fordist mass production. In dissecting their major claims for lean production's purported benefits, he provides evidence of its daily impact upon workers on the shop floor and documentation of its failure to give any meaningful attention to workers, organized labor, and their role in its transformation of industrial production. Rejecting Kenney and Florida's counter arguments, he joins Philip Garrahan and Paul Stewart (1992) in exposing how hegemonic control in so-called lean production facilities is produced and reproduced through a series of interlocking and precisely orchestrated strategies which suffuse the entire work organization of the typical Japanese automobile assembly plant. The result, Dassbach argues, is a neo-Fordist factory regime that closely approximates nonunionized Fordist practices by cleverly camouflaging them in subtle and advanced forms of human resource management. As a consequence, critics like Dassbach point to the need to design a labor relations model which preserves a critical function for unions in steering changes in labor-management relationships, in shop floor work reorganization, and in labor union identity and rank-and-file relationships.

The politico-strategic framework informing Dassbach's and other essays in this volume is the concept of ideological or cultural hegemony. Antonio Gramsci (1970), an Italian Marxist philosopher, formulated the concept of hegemony to help understand the dramatic changes in the shape and character of power in advanced capitalist societies since the early twentieth century. In a series of highly sophisticated theoretical works grounded in a rich understanding of economic and historical developments in his day, Gramsci defined hegemony as the rule by an alliance of class factions based on a subtle mixture of coercion and consent. Class power, he argued, was always backed by coercive instruments, but had increasingly become masked and fortified by methods of securing the consent of the underclasses to the ruling group's world view.

Carl Dassbach and Ernest Yanarella, in his chapter on the UAW and CAW under the shadow of post-Fordism, critically appropriate Gramsci's hegemonic analysis to explore the operation of lean production in Japanese transplants and joint ventures. Interpreting the elements of lean production as either the forms of hegemonic control or as a hegemonic system itself, these chapters seek to demonstrate how post-Fordist practices are grounded in a subtle inter-weaving of mechanisms of coercion and consent which are designed to win over workers' allegiance to the reigning corporate world view and its supporting values and to harness, not merely the worker's body to the production process, but the worker's intellectual capacities and shop floor knowledge as well.

Other chapters, including those by Laurie Graham's and by James Rinehart, David Robertson, and Christopher Huxley explore the forms of work-er resistance to the pace and intensity of lean production techniques and show how these hegemonic processes have either set the outer bounds of obstruction-ism in nonunionized plants or have been modified in the face of collective action, including a strike, at a unionized plant. As these and other chapters reveal, lean production as a hegemonic system shows great resiliency and com-mands grudging support from many workers, even as they oppose some of its more overtly exploitative features. As chapters by Steve Babson and James Rinehart et al. acknowledge, in the absence of new strategic vistas on work reorganization by organized labor in the United States and Canada, the legiti-macy and integrity of lean production systems may actually become stronger with modification and reform.

In sum, hegemonic analysis overcomes the bipolar tendencies of most Fordist and post-Fordist theoretical formulations and opens up a political space for long-term strategic programs and short- to mid-range tactical actions that avoid approaching the politico-economic world with either antiquated Fordist assumptions or illusory post-Fordist dreams. Instead, it situates the quest for counter hegemonic tactics and strategies within the interstices of Fordism and post-Fordism and calls for collective forms of action by organized labor within the shifting balance of forces, changing relations of coercion and consent, and fluctuating space of blockage and maneuver in the conflict between capital and labor.

Social, Economic, and Legal Perspectives on Labor and Lean Production in the United States and Canada

The United States and Canada have intrigued Louis Hartz (1964), Seymour Martin Lipset (1989, 1990), and other leading historians and sociolo-gists because of the status of these countries as "liberal fragment societies" spun off from Great Britain. In spite of their shared heritage and the homogenizing influence of the American economy, salient differences in their constitutional frameworks, political institutions, party structures, and public policies have also been equally influential. Canada's lack of a revolutionary break with the British Empire, akin to the United States, has created a red Tory tradition where a more conservative state and political culture have created a governing elite more committed to social welfare and government transfer programs, provided a more fertile political ground for social democratic movements and parties, and generated a legislative climate more predisposed to national and provincial labor law supporting strong and militant union representation of the working class (Horowitz, 1968). By contrast, the thoroughgoing liberal political culture and constitutional framework of the United States, shaped heavily by Locke, Montesquieu, and Hobbes, have produced a political system characterized by a powerful, yet often intolerant, liberal mainstream, a two-party structure gravitating toward the political center, a federal system where sovereign power is divided between a national government and often contentious states, and a political economy skewed toward corporate capitalism and against working class interests.

How did these two North American polities respond to the restructuring of the global political economy, the internationalization of automobile production, and the increasing penetration of their national economies by Japanese cars? In the early 1980s, the Reagan administration took action on the international trade front to pressure Japanese auto makers to reduce imports and to locate auto assembly plants in the United States. At the same time, the Reagan economic team adopted a series of macroeconomic programs designed to bring inflation under control through the severe tonic of recession. In combination, these two federal policies put the states in a position of seeking dramatic relief from 'Reaganomics' strong fiscal medicine by intense interstate competition to woo and win Japanese auto transplants.

The Canadian government, feeling similar pressures, also attempted to limit Japanese auto imports and encourage Japanese auto firms to build assembly plants in their country. The Canadian politics of industrial recruitment was also characterized by sub-national competition but the recruitment game had fewer players, principally Ontario and Quebec. On the other hand, provincial competition made up in intensity what it lacked in numbers, principally because of the deep cleavages and bitter jealousies between Anglo-Canadian Ontario and French-Canadian Quebec. This said, the stronger state tradition flowing from its non-revolutionary Tory past, led the Canadian competition for Asian auto transplants to follow a more technocratic or top-down model, than the American case, with federal leaders and administrative officials in various ministries playing a strong hand.

The entrance of the Japanese auto transplants and joint ventures into the North American auto marketplace had two manifest impacts on the dominant political economy of the United States and the largely branch-plant economy of Canada. In the first place, it exacerbated the problem of overcapacity in the continental economy and threatened the economic security of both the Big Three automakers and the UAW and CAW, the two national unions representing American and Canadian auto workers. Secondly, the introduction of new management strategies based on lean production techniques, first refined by the

Toyota corporation, provided a direct challenge to older Fordist assembly plant operations and their traditional labor-management relations. In this crowded marketplace, the market share of the Big Three declined because their older American and Canadian plants were threatened with closure from the newer, more efficient Japanese transplants which were able to produce automobiles with high consumer demand.

This North American experience at these lean production auto assembly plants has led a few scholars to doubt that JPM has had a deep impact on UAW and CAW organizing, collective bargaining, and shop floor representation. In his chapter about the transformation of the NLRA paradigm, however, William Green shows in stark detail how lean production operations at these plants have attacked the legal foundations of Fordist plant operations and traditional labor-management relations on the shop floor. These so-called post-Fordist auto plants, in his view, have provoked a crisis for the National Labor Relations Act (NLRA) paradigm, the foundation of Fordist labor law in the United States and Canada. In fact, this legal framework for union organizing, contract negotiations, and workplace representation has been undercut along two dimensions. The NLRA paradigm's public law side has been effectively eroded by the success of Japanese auto transplants in relying upon narrowly construed labor statutes to engage in union avoidance strategies. On the paradigm's private law side, the traditional collective bargaining protections have been diluted by contracts at the Japanese-American joint ventures and the Saturn plant to fashion cooperative labor accords modeled after JPM. In response to this assault on their legal rights, the UAW and CAW have faced a common challenge at the nonunion Japanese transplants, but they have taken divergent paths at the unionized Big Three-Japanese joint ventures.

Lean Production and the Divergent National Paths of Organized Labor at the Unionized Big Three-Japanese Joint Ventures and Saturn

The divergent national paths of the UAW and CAW can be traced to the early 1970s. At that time, UAW national leaders looked to evolving strategies of work participation modeled on the Swedish example as one way to develop an independent union vision of workplace reorganization. As Ernest J. Yanarella shows in his chapter on the UAW and CAW under the shadow of post-Fordism, leading UAW officials like Don Ephlin and Irving Bluestone used their strategic positions in the union and on its international board to promote quality of life, jointness, and other worker involvement proposals. In contrast, the UAW's Canadian wing, owing in part to its stronger tradition of union militance, resisted the lure of worker cooperation programs and, rejecting UAW acceptance of corporate calls for concessions and givebacks, broke away from the international UAW in 1985 and formed the Canadian Auto Workers (CAW) union. Since then, the UAW's response to lean production has, in decided contrast to that of the CAW, abetted the weakening of the NLRA paradigm.

In Canada, native cultural, political, and legal assets have facilitated the CAW worker mobilizing and organizing strategies and permitted the national union to make a tactical compromise with General Motors and Suzuki by negotiating a pre-hire lean production contract at the CAMI plant while continuing to honor its syndicalist heritage of shop floor adversarialism. As the CAW Research Team on CAMI makes abundantly clear in the chapter entitled "CAW, Worker Commitment, and Labor-Management Relations Under Lean Production at CAMI," the commitment of the CAMI's unionized workforce to the company's lean production philosophy has ebbed considerably since 1988 when the CAW negotiated the CAMI labor agreement. The lofty ideals extolled in the CAMI training manual have run aground on the harsh truths of a lean production workplace. In fact, flagging worker commitment and growing corporate work intensification efforts, the CAMI Research team concludes, provided the impetus for the Local 88's strike call in 1992 and its ultimate success in negotiating a contract which allows the local an expanded role in shaping the terms of joint programs on the shop floor.

In the United States, the comparatively weaker political and legal environment has largely transformed the UAW into a union with a national organization and decentralized locals pulling in sometimes convergent, sometimes contradictory directions. In this setting, union locals at Big Three Fordist plants continue to pursue adversarial labor relations, but lean production locals are divided. The Japanese-Big Three joint ventures have become deeply divided over labor relations strategies and tactics while Local 1853 has become deeply committed to the Saturn Way. One reason for this intra-union pluralism has been the UAW national's willingness to negotiate, as exceptions to its Big Three national agreements, pre-hire lean production agreements with the Japanese-Big Three joint ventures and GM's Saturn division which permit the national union to advance its labor-management cooperation agenda by appointing a local's leadership committed to the practice of lean production principles.

At AutoAlliance (formerly Mazda), the UAW's national appointed a local leadership committed to Mazda's participative management philosophy, but once the cooperative environment promised during the recruitment process and in training center classroom met the realities of fast-paced full production, labor relations became increasingly combative and local union politics more contentious. In this setting, Local 3000 members replaced the national UAW-appointed pro-Mazda local leadership in 1989 with the leaders of militant caucus linked to the UAW's New Directions movement. In preparation for the negotiation of a new agreement the following year, the new local union leadership conducted a membership survey. The results, as Steve Babson recounts in his chapter, disclosed that the AutoAlliance workers decisively rejected the lean production truths of participatory decision-making, consensus norms, and team dynamics. Any doubt that the workers took these issues seriously was dispelled in February 1991 when Local 3000 members supported a strike authorization vote and then engaged in eleventh-hour bargaining which produced a new agreement containing significant modifications of the lean production model akin to those the CAW won in the CAMI strike.

The UAW national leadership also hand-picked the local leaders at Saturn, but, until recently, Local 1853's leadership has not encountered any meaningful opposition from its membership. Not because labor-management cooperation has provided for a more formally democratic decision-making process within the company's strategic councils, but, as Ernest Yanarella argues in his chapter on worker training at Toyota and Saturn, the union local's leadership has simultaneously become isolated and buffered from the rank and file, its administration more authoritarian, its policies almost indistinguishable from the corporation's, and its almost evangelical commitment to generating loyalty and enthusiasm for the Saturn Way more well-focused and determined. In spite of this united corporate and union elite level strategy, the 1992 local union election witnessed the appearance of opposition candidates who challenged the incumbent leadership on the issue of union democracy even though they did not differ from the incumbents in their commitment to Saturn's lean production system. After an intensely fought election campaign, the incumbent leadership was returned to power by a narrow margin. Still, as Ernest Yanarella observes, Saturn's success in the marketplace may require GM to recruit UAW members from its other Fordist plants who, if less committed to the Saturn Way, may weaken the hegemonic strategy jointly forged by corporate and union local leaders.

Yet there is considerable room for doubt. At Big Three-Japanese joint ventures and Saturn, a multistaged recruitment process has been carefully designed to screen in future employees whose native skills, attitudes, and temperament predispose them toward corporate lean production values. The UAW's involvement in screening and recruitment processes at NUMMI, AutoAlliance, and Saturn has moderated and blunted the impact of these processes as hegemonic agencies, but the strength and impact of other components of lean production's hegemonic system, particularly orientation and initial training, have partly compensated for labor's involvement by reinforcing hegemonic values, practices, and behavior on the shop floor.

Orientation and initial training is jointly-directed, but it has remained largely a management-led operation whose fundamental purpose is less to hone new skills for the so-called multiskilled worker than to inculcate the dominant values of the corporate culture and to enlist the assembly workers in willingly giving over their tacit knowledge and self-generated shop floor skills to manage-

ment for its use in tightening and speeding up production. Drawing upon
Garrahan and Stewart (1992), Carl Dassbach reveals how the application of
teamwork principles on the assembly line institutes a new form of worker surveillance and control which relieves management of this direct responsibility by
imposing supervisory functions on the worker. At Saturn, where GM and the
UAW have devised a virtually pure post-Fordist model, the deployment of a
sophisticated worker training and retraining program integrated into the auto
production process has, as Ernest Yanarella observes, appropriated the workers'
shop floor knowledge and tacit skills, enmeshed the work force in plant management decision making, blurred the distinction between labor and management interests, and, thereby, fragmented the potential for worker solidarity and
collective voice.

In sum, a local union, like CAMI Local 88, provides the opportunity to
mobilize workers behind an independent vision of work reorganization that
restores the balance between management prerogative and union power. The
UAW locals at NUMMI and AutoAlliance also demonstrate how a local union
may provide the opportunity for rank and file insurgency and the achievement
of a democratic renewal of union structure and governance. Still, Saturn provides a cautionary tale about the impediments to union regeneration and
renewed strength in lean production plants. Here union pressure on management will originate in the gulf between professed corporate ideals and hard realities of the lean production shop floor, but local union efforts to push management to fulfill its promise of a democratic workplace will be set by the language
of the lean production and may, over the long run, also heighten employee loyalty to lean production objectives. In this setting, only refortified union power
and solidarity and an autonomous vision of workplace reorganization can overcome the formidable advantages enjoyed by lean production management. This
is the chastening lesson of the UAW and CAW successes at AutoAlliance and
CAMI.

Lean Production at the Nonunionized Japanese Transplants and the Common Challenges of United States and Canadian Organized Labor

The UAW and CAW represent workers at the Big Three auto plants and
at Big Three-Japanese joint ventures, but not at the six transplants in the
United States and Canada operated by Honda, Toyota, Nissan, and Subaru-
Isuzu. The failure of the UAW and CAW to organize the Japanese transplants
can be traced to American labor unions' dramatic membership decline since
the 1950s and their plummeting impact on national politics. UAW representation of automobile workers, 90 percent or more during the glory years, has been
substantially higher than union representation of the nonagricultural work
force, but the influx of nonunionized Japanese transplants helped to reduce

UAW membership from 86 percent in 1979 to 68 percent in 1991 (Slaughter, 1992) and to produce a similar, but less dramatic decline in the Canadian auto union membership.

Traditional UAW organizing advantages have been further weakened by the decision of Japanese firms to locate in greenfield sites far from the UAW and CAW's urban power bases, by state and provincial government recruitment monies used by Toyota, Honda, Nissan, and SIA to select employees with minimal industrial and union work experiences, and, as William Green shows in his chapter, by the ability of the United States and Canadian transplants to use a NLRA paradigm diluted in favor of corporate union avoidance strategies to defeat UAW and CAW organizing campaigns.

The UAW's and CAW's failure to organize the Japanese transplants may also be explained by the daunting forms of hegemonic control integral to lean production's chief elements and exercised by transplant firms over their workforces and in their neighboring communities. In her chapter, Laurie Graham focuses on the manifestations of worker resistance at the Subaru-Isuzu Lafayette, Indiana plant and in the process also highlights many of the components of the hegemonic processes which SIA and other transplants build into the operation and management of their plants in order to win the hearts and minds of their nonunion work forces. SIA begins with a multistage employee recruitment process that weeds out union sympathizers, uses the initial orientation and training programs to socialize new workers into the plant's guiding philosophy and corporate world view, and then organizes the shop floor lives of their nonunion worker into a web of assumptions, commitments, and outlooks that extends beyond the plant to the worker's family life and community relations.

Toyota Motor Manufacturing's (TMM) Georgetown plant, explored by Ernest Yanarella in the chapter entitled "Worker Training at Toyota and Saturn: Hegemony Begins in the Training Center Classroom," is the classic example of the power of the hegemonic system incorporated into lean production. At TMM's nonunion greenfield plant, the worker recruitment process garnered over 100,000 applications for an initial recruitment and screening process to choose 3,100 employees. This recruitment experience, common to all the nonunionized transplants, has meant that management could mobilize an enormous pool of applicants, take them through a multistage testing and interviewing process, and select corporate-tailored employees who reflect the widest mix of male-female ratios, minority percentages, and background attitudinal and skill profiles.

Once Toyota and other Japanese transplants have selected their corporate-tailored employees, their training assumes a crucial importance. TMM and other transplants used significant federal, state, and provincial incentive package monies to construct training facilities and to design and implement worker training programs. Once in operation, these training programs, epitomized by

TMM's at Georgetown, emphasize soft or interpersonal skills over hard or technical skills, cultural or attitudinal training over skills training, and multitask training over genuine or in-depth skilled trades training. As both Laurie Graham and Ernest Yanarella suggest, the lean production ideal of the multiskilled worker is largely a myth at the transplants where their lean production practices reconfirm the passing of the skilled trades person and the ascendancy of the multitasked worker.

Once these carefully selected and trained employees begin to work on the shop floor, the absence of a legally authorized agency to promote their collective voice and represent them through collective bargaining and grievance arbitration has meant at least two things, as Laurie Graham observed at SIA. First, worker resistance to the negative, exploitative features of lean production, has produced minor, often temporary ad hoc managerial accommodations, but it has not been able to institutionalize permanent changes. Secondly, the individualizing and fragmenting consequences of lean production's hegemonic processes upon workers have been able to continue with impunity unobstructed by union mediation. As a result, a differential wage scale, corporate awards, and other employee recognition programs which elevate individual achievement have further splintered the work force and contributed to the corporate goal of using the production process to galvanize a sense of team identity and corporate loyalty as the only alternative forms of identification beyond the individual.

Lean Production, Organized Labor's Future, and the Prospects for Labor Law Reform

Clearly, the incredible success of the Japanese transplants and Big Three-Japanese joint ventures in institutionalizing lean production, in defining the terms of academic and labor debate, and in establishing an innovative management model for other industries demonstrates the extent to which the crisis of Fordism is at once a crisis of Fordism as a regime of accumulation, a mode of production and consumption, a mode of regulation, and an ideological or legitimation system. As such, this multiple crisis presents labor union forces with the need to rethink their identity as agencies of interest representation and as progressive forces for political change, as well as their political strategies for reshaping post-Fordist management and production techniques in a democratic direction.

The UAW's strategic ambivalence toward the transplants and joint ventures is partly a reflection of its organizational structure and the outlook of its national leaders who have produced work reorganization policies marked by local pluralism. At the same time, the UAW national has encountered enormous problems and witnessed a substantial diminution of its influence, power, and maneuver due to the Japanese penetration of the North American auto market, the global and continental restructuring of auto production, the declining economic fortunes of the Big Three, the managerial assault on traditional union rights, and the greater success of American auto makers in defining a corporate-led vision of workplace restructuring. Still, the lack of the necessary internal ingredients for a more effective response to the transplant challenge constitutes the major impediment hobbling the UAW, but apparently not the CAW.

The UAW has gained entree at NUMMI, AutoAlliance, and Diamond-Star by virtue of the participation of the Big Three auto firms in these joint ventures, but the national UAW's lean production agreements at these plants have not created a cooperative work environment. They have led to combative labor-management relations and contentious local union politics defined by pro-company and militant opposition caucuses whose interactions have produced modified lean production agreements. But the UAW's strategic program for gaining union certification at the Honda, Nissan, SIA, and Toyota transplants, as Ernest Yanarella observes in his chapter "The UAW and CAW Under the Shadow of Post-Fordism," has been characterized as "weak, wavering, and without consistency" and has failed at Nissan, in spite of an intense unionization drive partly because of the transplant's superior in-plant resources, its greenfield workforce, and its legally-sanctioned union avoidance strategy.

The Canadian experience, on the other hand, demonstrates that a national union which adopts a proactive stance toward the transplants, one more consistent with maintaining its collective identity and more intent in marshaling its political power and its rank and file resources, may be able to go farther in reshaping lean production labor-management relations, as the CAW Local 88 has at CAMI, and may be able to mobilize worker grievances and dissatisfaction to the point of transplant unionization as the CAW had apparently done at Hyundai. Together these two CAW experiences suggest that mobilizable issues abound in the transplants and joint ventures and can serve as a basis not only for advancing labor's interests at unionized plants in creating the democratic work place promised by JPM, but also for building the foundations for union certification at nonunion plants.

There is, in other words, room for maneuver at both union and nonunion lean production plants, but a word of caution must be voiced. At one Canadian and four United States auto assembly plants where the UAW and CAW represent production employees, the collective agreements negotiated by the unions remain deeply enmeshed in the managerial framework and language of lean production and their meaning is found in lean production practices in the training center classroom, on the shop floor, and in management-labor councils. After several years of experience, however, renegotiated agreements at NUMMI, AutoAlliance, and CAMI appear to be pulling these post-Fordist labor accords back toward more traditional procedures and rights. On the other hand, it appears likely that collective bargaining will never return to an earlier Fordist era of arms-length, adversarial labor-management relations. Post-

Fordism has progressed too far and the prevailing hegemony of lean production has too deeply permeated economic organization and political regulation to be easily excised.

In the face of the corporate advantages generated by global restructuring, lean production techniques, and internationalized auto production, the task of organizing the nonunionized transplants remains daunting. Despite the CAW's apparent success in unionizing the Quebec Hyundai plant, arguably the weakest and most vulnerable of the North American transplants, the Japanese transplants will prove to be more difficult targets. Toyota, Honda, and Nissan have a long legacy of opposition to American-style unions, and each has developed powerful methods to obstruct union certification. Aware of how thoroughly their lean production processes are permeated by hegemonic control mechanisms, the transplants have recruited pliable workers, used orientation and training to further their attitudinal adjustment and cultural integration, and involved them in teamwork and *kaizen* processes to advance line speed-up, to appropriate their knowledge, and to advance their corporate loyalties by remolding their identities on the basis of individualistic values of wage differentiation and internal mobility.

The UAW's declining political capital and the CAW's growing alienation from even the Ontario New Democratic Party, combined with their common participation in a North American marketplace dominated by the Big Three auto makers under siege from Japanese competitors, suggest a pressing need for internal debate and sobering reflection on new beginnings. To this end, a counterhegemonic strategy counsels the UAW and CAW to undertake a militant program that works through these new production relations to create a union identity and role in the interstices between Fordism and post-Fordism. Both unions need to critically examine alternative labor-management models, including Germany's IG Metall auto union, in carving out an autonomous, labor-driven vision of work reorganization while remaining cognizant that neither the United States nor Canada is Germany.

Organized labor's future alternatives, will, after all, lie not in the dualist poles of Fordism and post-Fordism, but in the many permutations and combinations that will be forged out of the political struggle to create a better and more democratic future in the world of work and in the wider political community. Organized labor has historically been a major progressive force in the national politics of liberal democracies in the United States and Canada, tempering the excesses of their capitalist political economies. At a time when the globe seems to be in the process of being turned upside down, the hope and promise of labor is that it will find the means to put its house in order, to fortify its political and economic power by reaching out to other progressive groups and movements, and to employ their resources to realize the dreams of productive work, a decent standard of living, and a just commonwealth for all.

Note

1. There is some misunderstanding about which auto assembly plants are transplants and which ones are joint ventures, a situation perhaps made more difficult by the fact that one transplant became a joint venture and one joint venture became a transplant. To minimize confusion, here is a current status of the transplant and joint venture auto assembly plants.

The Honda plants in Marysville, Ohio and Alliston, Ontario, the Toyota plants in Georgetown, Kentucky and Cambridge, Ontario, the Nissan plant in Smyrna, Tennessee, and the Diamond-Star (Mitsubishi) plant in Bloomington-Normal, Illinois are sole venture Japanese transplants. The Hyundai plant in Bromont, Quebec was the only South Korean transplant in North America. The Subaru-Isuzu plant in Lafayette, Indiana is a joint venture Japanese transplant. All of the transplants are nonunion, except Diamond-Star, which began as a Chrysler-Mitsubishi joint venture, but became a wholly-owned Mitsubishi plant in October 1991.

The NUMMI, AutoAlliance, and CAMI are the three joint venture plants. The NUMMI plant in Fremont, California, is a General Motors-Toyota joint venture; the AutoAlliance plant in Flat Rock, Michigan, is a Ford-Mazda joint venture; and the CAMI plant in Ingersoll, Ontario is a General Motors-Suzuki joint venture. Workers at all of the joint ventures are represented by the UAW or CAW including AutoAlliance which began as a union Mazda transplant. Mazda became AutoAlliance in June 1992.

PART
I

THE CRISIS OF FORDISM
Theoretical, Legal, and Strategic Challenges
for Organized Labor

Lean Production, Labor Control, and Post-Fordism in the Japanese Automobile Industry

Carl H. A. Dassbach

Much of the discussion and debate about post-Fordist production has focused on a specific country, Japan, and on a specific industry, the automobile industry. In a marked departure from previous attempts to explain the Japanese advantage in world markets, it is argued that this advantage can be attributed to the Japanese organization of production which emerged out of the unique political and economic conditions of postwar Japan.[1] It should be noted however, that not everyone who advances this claim uses the term 'post-Fordism' to characterize the Japanese organization of production. Another frequently used term is 'lean production' while others simply point to the existence of a unique social organization of production in Japan (Wood, 1987; Womack, 1987; DiLorenzo, 1988; Lipietz, 1987; Kenney and Florida, 1988 and 1993; Cusumano, 1988; Krafcik, 1988 and 1989; Business Week, 1989b; Brown and Reich, 1989; Womack et al., 1990; Florida and Kenney, 1991; and Yoshida, 1992).

The single most important factor in drawing attention to the organization of production in Japan has been the ability of Japanese automobile companies to establish 'transplants' in Europe and the United States.[2] Even though these transplants are located in a highly competitive industry, long characterized by contentious and adversarial relations between labor and management, they can produce automobiles with a non-Japanese work force which are comparable in quality to those produced in Japan (Business Week, 1989a; Rowand, 1983; and Walsh 1983). The generally acknowledged reason why transplants can produce these high quality vehicles is that they have managed to recreate the Japanese social organization of production (Institute of Social Science, 1990; Oliver and Wilkinson, 1988; Womack, et al., 1990; and Kenney and Florida 1993). Transplants have thus proven that Japanese methods can be successfully transferred/replicated in other nations and are not dependent, as 'culturalists' such as

19

Lee and Alston (1990) argue, on unique aspects of Japanese society such as an administrative state or the persistence of feudal relations.

From the perspective of management, the superiority of lean production over conventional, or so-called 'Fordist', methods is well documented by substantial differences in productivity, space utilization, in-stock inventories, and product quality (Womack, et al., 1990; and Cusumano, 1988). Less is known, however, about the impact of these techniques on workers or the quality of working life. Despite this paucity of information, we find that many are heralding lean production as promoting a significant improvement in the quality of working life, especially when compared to Fordist methods. Some of the strongest proponents of this position are Kenney and Florida (Florida and Kenney, 1991; Mair, Florida, and Kenney, 1988; and Florida and Kenney, 1988, 1993) followed closely by Womack et al. (1990). Similar, if somewhat more circumspect claims can be found in Piore and Sabel (1984), Wood (1987), Womack (1987), Lipietz (1987), Toyoda (1987), Brown and Reich (1989), Yoshida (1992), DiLorenzo (1988), and Adler (1993).

These claims have not gone unchallenged. Several (Sorge, 1982; Dohse, et al., 1985; Klein, 1989 and 1991; Junkerman, 1982 and 1987; Burawoy, 1985; Parker and Slaughter, 1988a and 1988b; Wilkinson and Oliver, 1988; Garrahan and Stewart, 1992; Marsh, 1992; Robertson, et al., 1992; and Graham, 1993) have either raised doubts about the supposed positive impacts of lean production on the quality of working life or asserted that all is not as it appears in these factories. While these challenges are important, they have not been especially forceful for a variety of reasons.

Some authors rely on limited sources. For example, Burawoy (1985), Dohse et al. (1985), and Sorge (1982) base their discussion on Kamata (1982). Klein's (1989 and 1991) observations about the negative impact of lean production on workers are based on studies of non-Japanese factories which adopted methods such as JIT (just-in-time). Marsh's (1992) work reinterprets a survey of Japanese firms originally undertaken in 1976 and 1983. Others (Junkerman, 1982 and 1987; Robertson et al., 1992; Graham, 1993; Garrahan and Stewart, 1992), draw their conclusions from the study of one plant or transplant. As a result, it is not clear if their conclusions pertain to just that plant or to the Japanese auto industry as a whole. The two studies which rely on considerably more evidence, Parker and Slaughter (1988a) and Wilkinson and Oliver (1988), are, for differing reasons, less conclusive about the impact of Japanese techniques on working life. While Parker and Slaughter repeatedly emphasize the negative impact of Japanese techniques, their criticism of these techniques is often obscured by their primary concerns: educating workers and proposing strategies for resistance. On the other hand, Wilkinson and Oliver (1988: 162) are ambivalent about the impact of Japanese techniques on working life. Although they point to the heightened pressure, accountability, visibility of performance, and stress associated with Japanese techniques, they state that Japanese practices "seem to hold out the opportunity for an improved quality of working life" (p. 102).

This chapter has three objectives. The first objective is to examine the claims about the positive impact of Japanese methods on workers, especially as viewed by Kenney and Florida, and to show that most of these claims are, in fact, false. The organization of work in the Japanese auto industry as a whole, and not simply in one or two transplants, does not improve the quality of working life. Instead, it serves to further degrade working life.[3] The second objective is to examine how labor control is achieved in Japanese factories. I will argue that labor control occurs through a set of far more subtle and carefully contrived strategies than in Fordist factories and that these strategies permeate every aspect of working life in Japanese plants. The third objective is to analyze specific Japanese practices and compare these to Fordist practices in order to show that lean production is not, as Kenney and Florida (1993: 9) claim, a radical break with Fordism but merely a more advanced form.

The Ideology of Lean Production

According to Kenney and Florida, the Japanese organization of production has the following characteristics and consequences. First, "production in Japan replaces the fundamental characteristics of fordism—functional specialization, task fragmentation, and assembly line production—with overlapping work roles, job rotation, team-based work units, and relatively flexible production lines" (Kenney and Florida 1988: 131). Second, "[w]ith work teams, work roles overlap and tasks can be assigned to groups of workers and then reallocated internally by team members" (Kenney and Florida 1988: 36, 132). Third, "[t]he cornerstone of [lean production] lies in the harnessing of the worker's intelligence and knowledge of production . . . as a source of continuous improvement in product and processes, of increased productivity and of value creation" (Kenney and Florida, 1993: 15–16). Fourth, "[m]ulti-skilling is absolutely essential for this strategy to be successful . . . Rotation within teams allows workers to familiarize themselves with various aspects of the work process . . . This rotation scheme extends to the entire plant. Workers subsequently master the different tasks and grasp the interconnectedness among them" (Kenney and Florida, 1988: 133; also 1993: 38). Fifth, "[t]oday, 'just-in-time' is the distinguishing feature of Japanese production" (Kenney and Florida, 1993: 38). "The objective of the JIT system is to increase productivity not through the super-exploitation of labor but rather through increased technological efficiency" (Kenney and Florida, 1988: 136). Sixth, "most importantly: the social organization of Japanese labor is not simply a better or more advanced version of Fordism, it is a distinct alternative to it" (Kenney and Florida, 1988: 137). "We see this model as a fundamental supercession and potential successor to mass-production fordism . . . [a] new stage of capitalism" (Kenney and Florida, 1993: 9–10). "[Japan] has reached a level of development that is post-fordist, and we refer to this new and unique social organization of production as 'postfordist' Japan" (Kenney and Florida, 1988: 122).

Certainly, this is a compelling image for management, caught in the bind of the lagging productivity and the inflexibility of Fordism, and for labor, caught in the trap of boring, repetitive work. From Kenney and Florida's characterization one could only assume that both management and labor will benefit—the so-called 'win-win' situation—from the adoption of Japanese methods. Management will benefit through increased flexibility, improved quality and productivity, and the reduction in "certain aspects of worker alienation that result in high rates of absenteeism and sabotage under fordism" (Kenney and Florida, 1988: 132). Workers will benefit from enhanced skill levels and more meaningful and satisfying work. In other words, an industrial utopia is finally at hand! Without a doubt, if Owen or Pullman were alive today, they would join the pilgrimage to Japan.

But when one leaves the rarefied air of generalizations (and the prospects of healthy consultancy fees from firms seeking enlightenment), work in Japanese factories looks markedly different than the glowing picture painted by Kenney and Florida.

Self-Managing, 'Intelligent' Teams?

Teams in Japanese plants are not the autonomous, self-managing units which are assigned work roles, "reallocate work internally," and harness the intelligence of workers. Instead, the primary objective of team based organizations is to create smaller units which can be more closely supervised and more completely exploited. Even while praising team based organization in Japanese factories, Kenney and Florida admit that "[t]he team is a simultaneous source of motivation, discipline and social control for team members, driving them to work harder and more collectively . . . Teams are the microorganizational solution to the problem of extracting both knowledge and physical labor from workers. Workers are thus made to 'voluntarily' mobilize their own intellectual resources" (Kenney and Florida, 1993: 39–40). Team leaders do not resemble, as advocates of Japanese production would have us believe, information 'transmitters' or 'expediters.' Instead, they bear "an uncanny resemblance to the old straw bosses" (Lichtenstein, 1988). The primary function of team leaders is "control, surveillance and exploitation" (Garrahan and Stewart, 1992). These are achieved through the detailed supervision of workers, constant pressure to meet production goals, and the implementation of management's directives (Monden, 1983; Kamata, 1982; Parker and Slaughter, 1988a; and Robertson, et al., 1992).

Even the most cursory reading of Kamata's (1982) description of work at Toyota's Japanese plant reveals that team leaders represent management and not the workers.[4] In his first three months at the factory, the quota for his line was raised several times without consulting the team or adding additional workers. Although the team protested to its leader each time the quota was raised, its protests were ignored with the reply "it's an order from the section. manager" (Kamata, 1983: 47).

At the Mazda plant in Flat Rock, Michigan, whatever power teams and team leaders had to make even the most minimal alterations in production was eliminated after production began. Salaried unit leaders took control of several teams and began making changes without informing workers (Fucini and Fucini, 1990). Keller (1991) notes that teams in Japanese factories have very little input into changing or organizing production and March (1990) reports that most of the important decisions regarding the organization of production in Japanese factories are made by upper level managers.

The ability of workers to reallocate tasks within the team or even have a true input into how tasks are to be performed is almost nil. In his definitive work on Toyota (generally recognized as embodying the best Japanese practices), Monden is quite clear on who determines work procedures and allocates tasks: management via foremen or team leaders.

> Standard operations [are] aimed at production using a minimum number of workers . . . A standardized order of the various operations to be performed by each worker, called the standard operations routine, is important in facilitating this goal. The components of the standard operation are determined mainly by the foreman (supervisor). The foreman determines the labor hours required to produce one unit at each machine and also the order of the various operations to be performed by each worker (1983: 85–86).

All Japanese companies use standard operations routine and discussions of this aspect of Japanese production, including Kenney and Florida's, agree that foremen or team leaders determine standard operations and assign tasks to workers (Parker and Slaughter, 1988a; Kenney and Florida, 1993; Robertson, et al., 1992; and Garrahan and Stewart, 1992).[5] According to Babson "team members can not alter their programmed Work Sheets without supervisory approval, and casual deviation from the programmed job sequence is strongly discouraged" (1992: 7). Not only do Japanese companies use standardization to control working behavior, they also use standardization to control nonworking behavior. All workers who have 'empty' time during a job cycle are instructed to remain absolutely motionless (Dohse, et al., 1985). This quickly reveals the "pores" in a worker's tasks so that these can be eliminated.

Japanese companies may "harness the intellectual capabilities of their workers" by encouraging them to suggest improvements or modifications in their work routines but this pseudo-participation occurs within an environment that is rigidly and autocratically controlled by management. Individuals cannot innovate on their own, management and team leaders decide which work procedures will be modified and how they will be modified, and all changes must be cleared by several layers of management before they are implemented (Graham, 1993; Garrahan and Stewart, 1992; Robertson, et al., 1992). Transplants in the United States have also gone to great lengths to protect management's direct control over work. In the case of Mazda at Flat Rock, "the Management Rights Clause in the collective bargaining agreement establishes the company's exclusive right to direct and control . . . the methods, process and means of handling work" (Babson, 1992: 6).

Theoretically, both Wilkinson and Oliver (1989; and Oliver and Wilkinson, 1988) and Klein (1989, 1991) have argued that self-managed teams and worker autonomy are inconsistent with the constraints and demands of Japanese production methods, especially JIT. Because JIT is extremely vulnerable to disruptions and requires the close coordination and synchronization of work operations, departures from precisely planned routines can not be permitted. Wilkinson and Oliver (1989: 53) also maintain that Japanese managers go to great lengths to "prevent the utilization of this power capacity" and workers in Japanese factories have less autonomy and are subject to far more direct control than workers in traditional factories. Even one of the strongest advocates of lean production, Womack, has admitted that there is little room for creativity or worker autonomy in Japanese factories: "[e]ach task is worked out—indeed choreographed—with excruciating care through classic time and motion studies" (Womack, 1987: 11).

Multiskilling and Job Rotation?

Unlike workers in Fordist automobile plants who are restricted to a limited series of tasks because of rigid job classifications, workers in Japanese plants perform multiple tasks. However, it is another matter whether workers in Japanese plants are truly multiskilled. Consider Monden's description of the work routine of what Kenney and Florida would surely call a 'multiskilled' worker:

> Toyota prepared a new workplace layout . . . so that each worker could handle several different types of machines at the same time. In the gear manufacturing process, for example . . . each worker attends to 16 machines . . . which perform different types of operations: grinding, cutting, etc. The worker . . . first picks up one unit of a gear brought from the preceding process and sets it onto the

first machine. At the same time, he detaches another gear already processed by this machine and puts it on a chute to roll in front of the next machine. Then, while he is walking to the second machine, he pushes a button between the first and second machines to start the first machine. He performs similar operation on the second machine, and then he moves to the third machine pushing a button again to start the second machine, and so on, until he has worked on all sixteen machines and finally returned to the initial process (1983: 69-70).

There are, in fact, very few skills involved in the multiple tasks which this worker or most multiskilled workers in Japanese factories perform. Most critical observers would agree with Parker and Slaughter's observation that: "[t]he essence of 'multi-skilling' is actually the lack of resistance, on the part of the union or individual worker, to management reassigning jobs whenever it wishes, for whatever reason . . . Once hired, the worker does not benefit by learning more marketable skills. Instead, she learns how to carry out a large number of extremely 'job-specific' tasks" (1988a: 25).

Kenney and Florida's claim of the centrality of job rotation in the Japanese automobile industry is questionable on a number of grounds. In their 1988 article, the implicit assumption in their discussion of job rotation is that they are referring to the automobile industry but their primary source is Koike (1984) who focuses on the steel industry. In their 1993 book, *Beyond Mass Production*, there is no indication nor any reference to one interview or discussion with a Japanese automobile worker about rotation.[6] In fact, they document their discussion of rotation in Japan by citing another article by Koike and two books by other authors. Second, information from Japanese transplants indicates that job rotation is not a universal practice. While there is some evidence that Honda, NUMMI, Toyota, and Diamond-Star rotate workers between cognate jobs (Adler, 1993; Kenney and Florida, 1993; and Brown and Reich, 1989) rotation does not appear to be common in other plants. At Nissan's United States plant, job rotation was abandoned as a general policy after fourteen months of operation. Afterwards, it was used to punish disgruntled workers by assigning them the most demanding jobs in the factory for months at a time (Junkerman, 1987). At Mazda, job rotation was scrapped once the plant was at full production, even among skilled workers who had been cross trained in different manufacturing operations (Fucini and Fucini, 1990; and Babson, 1992).

Although Kenney and Florida (1993: 103, 104, 108, 117, 267–268, 269, 287, 288) frequently attribute this lack of rotation (as well as other problems) at transplants to what they call "unreconstructed" American managers who resist the complete implementation of the Japanese system, there is a more fundamental explanation. Quite simply, rotation is practically inconsistent with the organization of production, especially the JIT system. A fully operating and stressed JIT system requires a close coordination of tasks while the continual elimination of the "pores" in the system means that only the most adept workers can perform a given task (Fucini and Fucini, 1990; and Garrahan and Stewart, 1992). While other workers might be able to perform these tasks in theory, when tasks have been rationalized or kaizened to the point where they require sixty seconds of every minute to complete, only highly experienced workers can repeatedly perform these tasks in a satisfactory manner within the allotted time.

Super-Exploitation or Increased Technological Efficiency?

Super-exploitation is a central issue in the discussion of Japanese manufacturing techniques. Kenney and Florida take the "greatest issue" with Dohse et al.'s thesis that the Japanese organization of production is a form of superexploitation (1988: 23). According to Dohse et al. (1985: 141), the sum total of Japanese methods of production, or what they call "Toyotism" is simply the practice of the organizational principles of Fordism under conditions in which management prerogatives are largely unlimited. While Kenney and Florida admit "that Japanese factories are not a workers' paradise" (1988: 23) and acknowledge that "[l]ong hours and high stress are the defining features of Japanese manufacturing" (1993: 10), their position on the question of superexploitation is, to say the least, inconsistent.

In *Beyond Mass Production* (1993), Kenney and Florida write: "Far from being romantic or naïve, this view recognizes quite explicitly that the new industrial revolution exploits workers more completely than before" (17). "The core of the new model of . . . production lies in its ability to get workers to . . . increase their own rate and pace of work . . . [and] in the way it extends its reach to the worker's intellectual capabilities and uses group social pressure to increase the total work accomplished" (270–271). They also devote Chapter 9 of the book to moving their analysis in the "new direction" of exploring the "underlying tensions . . . between [lean production's] powerful ability to unleash human creative and intellectual capabilities and the use of forms of corporate control which . . . function to align the individual interests of the workers to broader corporate interests" (264).

At the same time, they minimize the meaning of their "new direction" with comments such as: "It is important to point out here that we are principally concerned with developing an objective theory of the Japanese production system and of the new stage of capitalism it represents. We do not consider the normative question of whether this model is 'better' or 'worse' than fordism or other Western economic arrangements" (10). They also repeat, almost verbatim, the same apologies for Japanese production (25) that they offered in their 1988 article.

"[C]onditions in Japanese factories may not be much worse than the widespread loss of skills and the high levels of discontent found in U.S. manufacturing plants . . . Moreover, an inefficient system of industrial organization that both wastes human labor power and poorly integrates workers into production (such as U.S. fordism) is not necessarily less onerous than one that effectively harnesses and integrates labor" (1988, 123).

As a consequence, it remains unclear where Kenney and Florida stand. They admit that the "new industrial revolution exploits workers more completely than before" but somehow this is "less onerous" than "an inefficient system that both wastes human labor power and poorly integrates workers into production" (ibid.). Such logic would confuse even a scholastic philosopher!

One way to determine whether Japanese production represents super-exploitation or what Kenney and Florida (1988: 137) have called "increased technological efficiency" is by examining the practices of Japanese production. What these practices reveal, in no uncertain terms, is that workers are exploited both physically and mentally.

The continual heightening of physical exploitation is ingrained within the system because the overriding imperative of lean production is to reduce the size of the workforce. Monden is quite clear on this point: "Remember, the first purpose of any improvement is to reduce the number of workers" (1983: 123). "[A] reduction in the man-hours required to produce a unit (*shoroyokuka*) is not the same thing as a reduction in the workforce. For this reason, a true reduction in the workforce is called *shoninka* to distinguish it from *shoroyokuka*. Only *shoninka* can reduce the cost of an automobile" (124). Monden is aware that reducing the number of workers means that the remaining workers must work harder and faster. But, despite his attempts to argue that this is not the case by advancing a variant of the well-worn 'smarter but not faster' argument as well as platitudes about 'Toyota's respect for humanity,' he cannot escape the fact that the primary function of job improvement is: "to eliminate . . . wasteful action and use the time instead to perform net operations with added value, thus reducing the total standard operation time and the number of workers" (124–125). One could call this a search for constant improvement, rationalization, or 'increased technological efficiency' but Kamata grasps the heart of this matter when he bluntly observes: "The other side of rationalization is compulsory labor" (203).

What dictates both the pace and duration of work in Japanese factories is not 'respect for humanity' but meeting the production quota.[7] As a result, overtime is a regular occurrence because the low levels of staffing make it almost impossible to produce the quota during the normal working hours. If a worker is absent, there are no replacements. Instead, his or her team members must either work faster or, if they are working at their limit, longer to meet the quota.

According to Kamata, overtime is a normal part of the working day in Japan. Moreover, overtime does not simply take the form of an extension of the day. A considerable part of overtime is worked at the expense of paid personal holidays and vacations. Neither overtime nor the lack of vacations are voluntary: they are compulsory. Monden states that overtime is used to "smooth the workload" and it is compulsory (1983: 59). Yamada (1985) places the average number of hours worked in Japan, at its lowest point in the postwar period, 1975, at 2,100 hours per year or the equivalent of fifty-two weeks of forty hours with no vacations. Large enterprises have the highest average number of overtime hours and certain types of enterprises, such as vehicle manufacturing, were well above the average of 223 hours a year in 1984. Yamada also confirms that overtime is worked at the expense of vacations. Japanese workers only take 60 percent of their entitled leave and work, without any extra compensation, during the remaining 40 percent. Kenney and Florida (1993: 10) report that workers in Japanese industry work from 200 to 500 hours longer than their American or European counterparts, 60 percent of the members of the All Toyota Union suffer from chronic fatigue, and *karoshi*, or death from overwork, is a major social issue in Japan. "A good Nissan man," according to a worker at Nissan's factory in Zama, Japan "is one who is never late, never takes a day off, and never complains" (Junkerman, 1982: 23). In 1990, the average auto worker in Japan worked 2,300 hours a year, or fifty-two weeks at forty-four hours a week, and did not take "three consecutive days off once a year without feeling that they were burdening their fellow workers" (Maskery, 1991 and 1989; and Helm and Edad, 1985). A 1990 survey of 10,000 of the 750,000 members of the Confederation of Japan Auto Workers Union found that 86 percent of those surveyed complained of "an increase in production quotas, a decrease in the number of factory workers, and more compulsory overtime and holiday shifts" (Solo, 1990).

The human consequences of 'increased technological efficiency' are even clearer in Japanese transplants. Parker and Slaughter (1988a) characterize the NUMMI system as "management by stress" and report that workers "say their jobs are like eight hours of calisthenics" (Parker and Slaughter, 1988b). Workers at Nissan describe their work as "eight hour aerobics" and even a Japanese advisor commented on the intensity of the work when he noted that seventeen workers in Nissan's Smyrna plant did the same work as twenty-four in Japan. Reportedly, Nissan's management even asked workers to restrict their intake of fluids during the day so they would not have to go to the bathroom during their shifts (Junkerman, 1987).

The Health and Safety Administrator of Honda in Marysville, Ohio admitted that accidents are common and cuts, sprains, and strains are a daily occurrence. Accidents are common because the heightened tempo of production causes workers to rush around the factory and take unnecessary risks. Cuts, strains, and sprains are frequent because of the great deal of material handling associated with the JIT system (Kendall, 1987: 50). In 1988, one in five workers at Nissan suffered an injury (which is higher than most other auto plants) and Nissan refused to allow workers to inspect the plant's injury logs.[8] Fucini and Fucini (1990: 175) report that occupational illness or injury caused Mazda to lose 42.6 days for every 100 workers during the first year of two shift production, compared to an average of 33.9 workdays per 100 workers at other body and assembly plants in Michigan.[9]

Central to both physical and intellectual exploitation is the practice of *kaizen*, or constant improvement. In theory, the kaizening of work processes has two basic objectives: reducing the amount of time required to complete a process and 'line balancing,' i.e., eliminating inequalities in the distribution of work so that all team members are operating at the same level of effort. An example of the latter would be a situation where there are four workers, one working at 70 percent and the others working at 90 percent and their work is kaizened so that everyone is working at 85 percent.

In reality, *kaizen* is merely a means for constantly increasing the pace and intensity of work. Workers whose work is kaizened so that they can perform the same operation in less time, cannot use the extra seconds of nonwork to assist others or pause before the next work cycle. Instead, they are either assigned additional tasks or the duration of their work cycle is shortened. Line balancing is not used to more equitably distribute work between team members but to eliminate workers and increase the load on the remaining workers. If for example, there are four team members, one performing at 40 percent and the others at 80 percent, work is redivided so that three team members perform at 90 percent or more and one is eliminated (Flint, 1989).

As Fucini and Fucini (1990: 162–163) point out, in a JIT system which holds intermediate inventories to a minimum, reducing the amount of time needed to complete one work process through kaizening increases the work tempo in other, related processes.[10] If for example, installation of gas tanks is kaizened so that it takes less time to install tanks, the workers fabricating the tanks must produce more tanks in less time, even if their work process has not been kaizened. These workers are also forbidden from creating a buffer inventory by fabricating additional tanks during their breaks in order to maintain what Mazda calls "the will to *kaizen*."

Kaizen exploits the intellectual capabilities of workers by enabling management to acquire whatever new skills or capabilities workers develop in the process of completing their tasks (Graham, 1993). According to Garrahan and Stewart:

[E]ven despite strong de-skilling imperatives, workers still acquire new skills which can and do present management with numerous

> headaches. *Kaizen* meetings are all about the need to continue to appropriate from workers new ways of doing things . . . [T]he detailed know-how that each worker accumulates [is] made accessible . . . and disinvested of its private or specific skill content. This process is one of constant attrition on individual know-how . . . [which] is continually being transferred to management through *kaizen* (1992: 75-77).

Workers are not simply expected but required to improve product and process and, in general, they receive little or no compensation from their employers.

Is this super-exploitation or increased technological efficiency? One need not be familiar with the theory of relative surplus value to answer this question. Instead, consider, as the final word on this question, Fucini and Fucini's observations about Mazda's Japanese and American factories.

> The workers . . . at Hofu [Mazda's Japanese plant] were actively engaged in a production activity close to 60 seconds every minute. At the non-JIT American auto plants...workers maintained a 40 to 50 second work pace . . . The 10 to 20 second-a-minute difference would not give Hofu a significant productivity advantage had it applied to only a handful of workers. But when even a 10 second differential is applied to a plant with 2,000 workers, the productivity gain will add up to 2,667 worker hours over the course of an eight hour shift, and 13,335 extra worker hours over a five day week. Assuming that every worker at the plant works a 40-hour week, the 10 second productivity gain is equivalent to hiring 333 extra workers (1990: 37, emphasis added).

> Because workers at Flat Rock [Michigan] were actively engaged in their work for 57 seconds out of every minute, compared to the 45-second-a-minute average pace of the Big Three auto worker, a Mazda workday, in essence, included more work than a Ford or GM workday—12 seconds more every minute, 12 minutes more every hour, 96 minutes more every eight hour day, and one eight hour day more every 5-day week (1990: 148, emphasis added).

The Dynamics of Labor Control

Fordism subordinates workers through high wages and controls them primarily through the technical organization of work, although unions have become an important ancillary mechanism in the post World War II period. Despite these mechanisms, Fordism has repeatedly confronted problems of effective labor control and product sabotage (Dassbach, 1991). In the Japanese system, labor control is achieved through conventional methods as well as some extremely subtle and unique mechanisms resulting in what Garrahan and Stewart have characterized as a new "Regime of Subordination" (1992).

Conventional methods for labor control include line pacing, high wages, and intentionally locating plants in rural areas to tap workers who have no experience in industrial production (Kamata, 1982; Cusumano, 1985; Ishi, 1988; Kertesz, 1988; Rubenstein, 1992; Graham, 1992; and Garrahan and Stewart, 1992). In addition, Japanese companies employ at least two mechanisms for labor control which are either not found or poorly articulated in Fordist factories. The most important, identified by Kenney and Florida (1993) in one of the few places they are critical of the Japanese system, is the establishment of a 'corporatist hegemony' over work life. The second is peer pressure.

Although the careful screening and selection of applicants is the first step in establishing hegemonic control, "[h]egemony," as Yanarella's chapter in this volume points out, "begins in the training center classroom." While training ostensibly provides instruction in work skills, its most important function is to socialize employees into corporate values and norms. In addition to training, Japanese companies use several other mechanisms or practices to ensure their hegemony over workers by minimizing what Oliver and Wilkinson have called "goal heterogeneity" (1988). These include:

> . . . giving employees long time horizons . . . seniority based payment systems . . . [and] recruiting people raw from college, at least for the core workforce. In addition, employees' opportunities to encounter goals and values other than those promoted by the company are, as far as possible, minimized. If a core worker marries someone inappropriate or associates with 'unsuitable' groups . . . his lifetime employment is liable to come to an end . . . . [H]eterogeneity from internal arrangement [is] countered by an emphasis on a single status (reinforced by everyone wearing the same uniform), internal promotion system, [and] the Japanese industrial union. Being enterprise based and incorporated, rather than craft or occupation based and independent, unions in Japan are far less likely to have goals which are at odds with those of the company. (Oliver and Wilkinson, 1988: 40–43).

Some companies, such as Toyota, extend their hegemony to the local community with sizeable financial contributions, joint programs with schools, and cultural events creating "a total and 'hegemonic' sociocultural sphere . . . that envelops a worker's entire existence" (Kenney and Florida, 1993: 291).

In its most elemental forms, peer pressure is used to ensure attendance and compliance with work routines. Because staffing levels are extremely low and Japanese companies refuse to hire replacement workers for absent workers, team members and leaders resent absences because these increase their work load (Brown and Reich, 1989; and Parker and Slaughter, 1988a). As a result, they exert pressure on co-workers not to be late or miss work.[11] With short cycle times for jobs and the fact that an individual's task is often predicated on another team member completing his or her task properly, workers and team leader pressure other workers to properly perform their tasks. In Nissan's English factory, an official policy of 'Neighbor Checks' requires workers to report fellow workers whose work is deficient (Garrahan and Stewart, 1992).

Peer pressure also takes more subtle and indirect forms. Whenever the assembly line is halted at Subaru-Isuzu, a computer determines which team stopped the line and plays 'their' music over the company loudspeaker system, thus informing others which team stopped the line (Graham, 1992). In both Japan and the United States, Japanese companies employ temporary workers who are promised permanent employment if they 'prove' themselves in their temporary positions. This promise of a permanent, high paying job is a powerful incentive and temporary workers who aspire to these jobs will drive themselves and their co-workers in order to impress team chiefs and section supervisors who make the hiring recommendations (Kamata, 1982; Fucini and Fucini, 1990; Kenney and Florida, 1993).

Although Japanese companies have been unable to implement all of these practices in the United States, many can be found in either their original form or a modified version in most transplants. All transplants promise and provide their core workers with employment stability, award raises based on job tenure, offer wage and benefits schemes comparable to the Big Three, and provide special perquisites such as low priced car leases. Recruitment is highly selective, companies prefer workers who may not be raw from college but, as already noted, have little or no industrial experience. Transplants consciously attempt to socialize employees into the firm's 'culture.' Workers are censured for what is considered inappropriate behavior, e.g, speaking with the press. Internal homogeneity is enhanced in most transplants by practices such as requiring all employees, whether salaried or hourly, to wear uniforms, eat in common dining rooms, and use the same parking lots. Although Japanese companies have not introduced enterprise unions—they have done the second best thing: they have strenuously attempted to keep out the UAW, usually by casting the issue in terms of the opposition between 'us' (the company and its associates) and 'them' (the UAW) (Moskal, 1988; Hampton, 1988; Fucini and Fucini, 1990; Parker and Slaughter, 1988a; Junkerman, 1987; and Business Week, 1989a).

Many of the questions about why Japanese companies and transplants have lower rates of absenteeism and superior product quality can be answered by referring to these strategies of labor control instead of the supposed greater worker satisfaction and empowerment resulting from the organization of work.

Work in Japanese plants is neither more 'rewarding' nor 'satisfying' than work in conventional plants. Instead, the Japanese have created subtle and sophisticated strategies for labor control which serve to make workers neither more willing nor more cheerful accomplices in their own exploitation but—most important from the management's perspective—far more silent, obedient, and compliant.

Post-Fordism and Post-Fordist Japan?

Kenney and Florida are certainly not alone in their use of the term post-Fordism, but they further confuse the entire Fordism/post-Fordism discussion by adding another meaning to the term post-Fordism. Clearly, they accept the original 'narrow' meaning of Fordism as a social organization of production, based on moving assembly, and created at the Ford Motor Company between 1910 and 1914 (Gramsci, 1971; Dassbach, 1991; and Clarke, 1992). They also accept a more recent understanding of Fordism, originated by Aglietta (1976), as a macro-social mode of regulating—maintaining the institutional, economic, social, and political stability—of an intensive regime of accumulation. As such, Fordism has several characteristic features; the two most important are: the 'charmed circle'—the linkage of production and consumption—and automatic increases in wage levels to keep pace with the growth in productivity and thereby to maintain a relative equilibrium between production and consumption.[12]

The problem is the three different meanings they assign to post-Fordism. In various places, they argue that Japan embodies, a new, i.e., post-Fordist, mode of regulation, which they call "fujitsuism." Its distinguishing features are a greater "resilience" than the Fordist mode of regulation and "micro-mass consumption" (Kenney and Florida, 1988: 146–147; and Kenney and Florida, 1993: 54, 316–324). But, in response to the question of whether Japanese production and industrial organization are post-Fordist, Kenney and Florida introduce two different meanings for post-Fordism: "a new model that comes 'after' fordism," which will be abbreviated as PF1, and a model of production which is "a direct progression from and [bears] a strong genealogical link to fordism," abbreviated as PF2 (Kenney and Florida, 1993: 9).

The question of whether Japan embodies a new post-Fordist mode of regulation will not be addressed here. Instead, the concern will be much narrower: what type of post-Fordism, i.e., PF1 or PF2, does the Japanese organization of production represent? According to Kenney and Florida (1993, 1988) and Lipietz (1987), the organization of production in Japan is PF1—"'something' markedly different from both Fordism and Taylorism"—"a distinct alternative" and not PF2, a "more advanced form."

The evidence demonstrates that Kenney and Florida are wrong: Japanese production is not PF1. It is not an alternative to Fordism and Taylorism but, as Dohse et al., point out, an extension of both, i.e., PF2. For example, Monden writes on the first page of his book: "It (the Toyota Production System) follows the Taylor system (scientific management) and the Ford system (mass-assembly line)" (1983: 1).[13] Of course, Monden's statement" does not disprove Kenney and Florida's assertion that the social organization of Japanese production is "a new model that comes 'after' Fordism"—it merely shows that the author of what is generally considered to be the most authoritative work on the Toyota's production system sees a direct linkage between lean production and Fordism/Taylorism, in other words, PF2.

Kenney and Florida's claim that lean production represents "a distinct alternative" to Fordism (PF1) can only be examined by identifying the unique practices of Japanese production and comparing these with Fordist practices. Obvious differences between the two would suggest that Japanese production is, as Kenney and Florida assert, PF1, but clear similarities between Japanese production and Taylorism/Fordism would indicate that Japanese production is, at best, "a more advanced form" or PF2.

Three Japanese practices which have been repeatedly identified as diverging from Taylorist/Fordist practices are extreme selectivity in hiring, extensive training of workers, and cooperation between labor and management (Shimada, 1986; Wood, 1987; and Institute of Social Science, 1990). These practices are described in the following passage as: "[T]he selection of the best worker for each particular task and then training, teaching, and developing [them]. . . . [T]he development of a hearty spirit of cooperation between the management and the men in the carrying on of the activities." Certainly, this is an apt description of key elements of the Japanese system even though this passage was written in 1907 by one of Taylor's employees, Carl Barth. In other words, selectivity, training, and cooperation are not Japanese innovations. Instead, they are three of "Taylor's four great underlying principles of management" (Barth, 1917: xvii).

Two other practices that are considered unique to Japanese production are multiskilling and work force flexibility. As I have already argued it is highly doubtful whether workers in Japanese factories are truly multiskilled because they do not learn new marketable skills but merely a set of cognate tasks.[14] In fact, a much more accurate characterization of multiskilling at these plants is Parker and Slaughter's (1988a: 80) observation that "[m]ultiskilling every worker means deskilling every job." On the other hand, work force flexibility, or the ability to deploy workers to different tasks in the plant, is a not a Japanese innovation but a central aspect of Fordism. In reducing tasks to simple, repetitive functions, the Fordist organization of production creates a highly flexible workforce. Barring restrictions imposed by unions, workers in Fordist factories can be easily deployed to different assignments because these can be quickly and easily mastered.[15]

Monden (1983: 80) has suggested that a unique Japanese manufacturing practice is sequential machining. Unlike a typical machining plant where parts are transported in large lots to separate sections for processing, Japanese factories have different types of machines physically arranged in an order which corresponds to the order of operations to be performed on a given part. A rough casting enters one end of the line, is machined and treated as it moves along the line and emerges as a finished piece at the other end. But sequential machining is not unique to the Japanese. This is a well-established Fordist, or actually pre-Fordist, practice introduced into the Ford Motor Company by Walter E. Flanders in late 1906, seven years before the introduction of the moving assembly.

Kenney and Florida assert that JIT and *kaizen* are unique Japanese innovations. Williams, et al. (1993) study of the Ford Motor Company during the 1910s shows, on the other hand, that JIT and *kaizen* were, in fact, fundamental principles of Fordism. On JIT, they write:

> [r]esearch confirms that [the Ford Motor Company's] stock levels [in 1914] were maintained at nearly Japanese levels . . . At company levels, Ford's best achievement was stock equal to 6.5 weeks sales in 1914; this is more or less exactly the level of stock cover which Japanese manufacturing as a whole has been operating at for the past twenty years . . . The implications are clear: Ford in Detroit discovered the benefits of so-called "lean production," which is falsely assumed to have first been invented in Toyota City in the 1950s (1992: 8).

While the Ford Motor Company certainly never used the term *kaizen*,

> the real dynamic at Highland Park . . . was the continuous improvement in workflow, . . . the reduction of walking and waiting time in-process, . . . [t]he elimination of indirect stock handling, . . . [and] reductions in work travel, stock levels and indirect labor requirements . . . Ford [was] never really satisfied with any given layout and expected to achieve continuing cost reductions. [This is] an eloquent testimony to the culture of "Kaizen" inside the Ford Motor Company which Sorenson aptly described as "an organization which was continuously experimenting and improvising to get better production" (Williams, et al., 1992: 9–15).

So far, an examination of 'uniquely' Japanese practices has only shown the continuity between Taylorism and Fordism and the Japanese organization of production (PF2). It is still possible, however, that Kenney and Florida's Japanese post-Fordism (PF1) can be found at a deeper level than practices, Japanese practices may appear to be a more advanced form of Taylorism and Fordism, but the principles underlying these practices reveal, in fact, a distinct alternative to both Taylorism and Fordism.

It might be argued, for example, that a crucial difference between the underlying principles of Taylorism and Japanese production is that the former separates "conception" and "execution" while the latter "unifies" them. "[T]he key element of the Japanese industrial system," Kenney and Florida (1992: 39) write, "lies in its ability to harness worker's knowledge as a source of value directly at the point of production." Clearly, one of the most important means for harnessing this knowledge is expecting/requiring workers, instead of industrial engineers, to *kaizen* production. But despite the role of workers in rationalizing their work and the work of others, "the Taylorist principle remains dominant. In other words, while the process of restructuring jobs constitutes a departure from traditional industrial engineering practices, the outcome of the process conforms to the Taylorist dictates of tightly timed, standardized, repetitive tasks" (Robertson, et al., 1992: 103).

Taylorism, as Monden already acknowledged, is one of the underlying principles of Japanese production. Is Fordism, as Monden also pointed out, another? Consider what Simon Clarke has identified as the underlying principle of Fordism: "the decomposition and recomposition of the labor process as the basis for the generalization of industrial production methods and the internalization of the sources of technological dynamism. In this sense, Fordis[m] . . . . is synonymous with the technology of the capitalist labor process, in which the social organization of production is subordinated to the minimization of labor time" (1992: 18–19). If Fordism is, as Clarke asserts, "synonymous with the technology of the capitalist labor process in which the social organization of production is subordinated to the minimization of labor time," then Fordism is clearly the second, and perhaps the most important, principle underlying Japanese production. It is "most important" because Japanese production raises the principle of "minimizing labor time" to its first principle, superseding even the drive to increase productivity through the substitution of labor with capital.[16] One need only be reminded of Monden's (1983) statement, "[r]emember, the first purpose of any improvement is to reduce the number of workers" or consider the tremendous importance of continually reducing the size of the work force to see the centrality of this Fordist principle in Japanese production.

The Japanese Organization of Production Reconsidered

Kenney and Florida's (1988) assertions that the Japanese production is post-Fordism, as a "distinct alternative" to Taylorism and Fordism (PF1) cannot be sustained at the level of either practices or underlying principles. Instead, the Japanese organization of production is post-Fordist only in the sense that it represents "a direct progression from" Taylorism/Fordism and exhibits "a strong genealogical link to fordism" (PF2). Japanese production, in other words, is not a break from either Taylorism or Fordism, but merely an advanced version of both. Neither Fordism nor Taylorism are transcended either in Japan or in the transplants. Instead, they are exceeded in what is, for workers in these plants, an inhuman parody. The only aspect of Japanese production which represents a break with Fordism are certain mechanisms for labor control, but this is hardly a positive break with Fordism. Beyond these mechanisms for labor control, the only other Japanese practices or principles which break from Fordism or Taylorism are those imagined by authors such as Kenney and Florida who lack the most basic understanding of the historical development and organization of production in the automobile industry.

While Dohse, et al.'s (1985: 141) characterization of Japanese production methods as "simply the practice of the organizational principles of Fordism under conditions in which management prerogatives are largely unlimited" is an oversimplification, it is certainly a far more accurate description of Japanese methods than anything offered by Kenney and Florida. The inescapable conclusion is that compared to Fordist factories, there is no substantial improvement in the quality of working life in Japanese factories. In many ways, work in these factories may actually be worse because the tempo of work is much more intense than in Fordist factories. This heightened work tempo increases the likelihood of being maimed or injured. Worker autonomy is not enhanced, it is restricted and management's direct control is not circumscribed, it is extended. Work is repetitive and restricted to a limited number of tasks and multiskilling is a sham. Whenever and wherever workers participate in making decisions, the process is tightly controlled by management. The only significant difference between Fordism and the Japanese production is that under the Japanese system "management prerogatives are largely unlimited" because of the weakness of labor organization in Japan and in most Japanese transplants (Dohse, et al., 1985; and Treece, 1985) and subtle and clever strategies of cooptation and control.

The social, as opposed to technical, rigidities of Fordism, especially the complex system of job classifications which limits the ability of managers to deploy workers wherever they see fit, is not inherent in Fordism. These so-called rigidities were, in fact, the result of a hard and bitter struggle waged by labor against the unlimited management prerogatives of 'pure' Fordism in the 1920s and 1930s. In the era of economic crisis and the inability to compete with the Japanese, it has become fashionable to 'blame' organized, high-waged, labor for these rigidities and, more generally for the economic malaise of the United States.

The truth is that management must bear the lion's share of the responsibility for both the inflexibility of production and the economic malaise of the United States. The social rigidities of production were the result of concessions granted by management to labor during the 1950s because of record levels of profits in the auto industry. At that time, these 'rigidities' were a crucial element in continued accumulation and the fact that they became an obstacle to accumulation in the 1980s merely demonstrates the contradictory nature of capital-ism: every solution to one contradiction engenders a new contradiction.

Management must also accept the bulk of the responsibility for the eco-nomic malaise of the United States. Here, I agree with Kenney and Florida (1993: 216) when they write: "the real underlying causes of America's manufac-turing decline [are] short term, myopic investment horizons [and] a lack of rein-vestment in manufacturing plants, equipment and technology . . . ."—in other words, those areas of enterprise which are the exclusive province of manage-ment. Moreover, as Kenney and Florida show, Japan's success in the latter por-tion of the twentieth century is a result of Japanese management behaving in the opposite fashion.

As a final word on Japanese production, consider Gramsci's discussion of the 'new' man required by Fordism: "Ford's industry requires a discrimination, a qualification, in its workers, which other industries do not yet call for, a new type of qualification, a form of consumption of labor power and a quantity of power consumed in average hours which are the same numerically but which are more wearing and exhausting than elsewhere and which . . . the wages are not sufficient to recompense and make up for" (1971: 311–312). Without a doubt, the same could be said about Japanese production. Gramsci then raises the question whether Fordism is "rational: whether, that is, it can or should it be generalized, or, whether, on the other hand, we are not dealing with a malig-nant phenomenon which must be fought against." This question is equally valid for Japanese production. Gramsci replies that "the Ford method is rational . . . and [with several qualifications] should be generalized . . . ." (Gramsci, 1971: 312). Had Gramsci lived until today, he probably would have withdrawn this statement and considered both Fordism and Japanese production as 'malignant phenomen[a] which must be fought against.'

Notes

1. This argument emphasizes the unique aspects of Japanese culture, 'statism,' higher capital intensity, significant differences in business practices and management philosophies, and a more docile and involved work force, but these explanations will not be reviewed because they are summarized in Akoi, 1984; Dohse, et al., 1985; Lincoln and McBride, 1987; Lee and Alston, 1990; and Kraus, 1992.

2. In North America seven Japanese automobile manufacturers are involved in either wholly-owned and operated plants or joint ventures with other Japanese firms or United States firms. Honda has two plants in Ohio and one in Ontario; Toyota solely operates one plant in the United States and one in Ontario and runs a third plant, NUMMI (New United Motor Manufacturing, Inc.), as a joint venture with General Motors; Mazda has one plant in Michigan, now a joint venture with Ford; Mitsubishi and Chrysler formerly operated a joint venture in Illinois; Subaru and Isuzu jointly oper-ate a plant in Indiana; and General Motors and Suzuki operate a plant in Ontario.

In Europe, Nissan, Toyota, and Isuzu have solely owned plants while Honda has two solely-owned plants as well as a joint venture with Rover in England; Nissan and Suzuki have plants in Spain; Toyota has a plant in Portugal; and Suzuki has a plant in Hungary.

3. In many ways, the claims presently advanced in support of Japanese production methods are similar to claims for industrial robots during the 1980s, but there is little difference between the impact of Japanese methods in the 1990s and the impact of industrial robots in the 1980s. See Dassbach, 1986.

4. Both Ronald Dore in the introduction to the English version of Kamata's book and Kenney and Florida (1993: 25), attempt to minimize Kamata's account of conditions in Toyota by claiming that his account describes an unusual period in the Japanese automobile industry, i.e., the early 1970s. While it may be true that conjunctural conditions such as labor shortages, rapidly rising wages, and lagging productivity during this period influenced the conditions at Toyota, this neither explains nor excuses the fundamental conditions of work described by Kamata. Moreover, as Kamata points out in his last chapter, written in 1980, the conditions at Toyota were neither different nor better than in the early 1970s even though, according to Dore, the general conditions in the Japanese automobile industry had improved markedly.

5. Still, Kenney and Florida report that workers at Honda and Toyota's United States plants have a "significant input in the design of their jobs" (1993: 106). One wonders about the veracity of this statement given their previous observations that "team leaders are the first line of supervision and play crucial roles in organization, design, and allocation of work on a daily basis" (105) and the fact that they cite interviews with manufacturing executives at Honda and Toyota and not workers as the source for this statement.

6. This is, in fact, a major contradiction in Kenney and Florida's 1993 book, *Beyond Mass Production*. The first part of the book which discusses the organization of work in Japan is based on research they conducted in Japan which consisted of roughly 60 site visits to factories, R & D labs, and corporate headquarters and more than 120 interviews with executives, R & D scientists, engineers, workers, and government officials (1993: 326). In the first part of the book, however, they do not refer to any statements made by Japanese workers. This is surprising given their claim in the appendix that they spoke with Japanese workers and used material from interviews with several American workers in their discussion of Japanese transplants in the United States. One can only assume that, despite the appearance of the word "worker" in one passage in the appendix, Kenney and Florida never spoke with one Japanese automobile worker.

7. In this context, see the comments made by Tatsuro Toyoda, President of NUMMI in Toyoda, 1987.

8. Legally, these records are open to inspection by all workers. Nissan's refusal resulted in a $5,000 fine by the Tennessee Occupational Safety and Health Administration. (Business Week, 1989c: 65).

9. Even more interesting is the fact that the most common injury reported by Mazda workers were CTI (cumulative trauma injuries), especially carpal tunnel syndrome. This is a fairly common occupational injury in the automobile industry. At most of the Big Three plants, those afflicted with the problem are generally older workers who have been working in the plant for several years. At Mazda, however, workers suffering

carpal tunnel syndrome were far younger and had worked at the plant, at most, for a year and a half. See Fucini and Fucini, 1990: 178–180.

10. Hill (1989: 469) points out that the JIT system even allows core companies, such as Toyota, to determine the pace of work at its quasi-independent suppliers.

11. Apparently, peer pressure is quite effective: unscheduled absences at NUMMI are about 2 percent a year while unscheduled absences at General Motors are 8.8 percent a year (Parker and Slaughter, 1998a: 21).

12. There may be a linkage between mass production, high wages, and mass consumption in the more 'narrow' sense of Fordism. Henry Ford, for example, wrote: "I believe in the first place that, all other considerations aside, our own sales depend in a measure upon the wages we pay. If we can distribute high wages then that money is going to be spent and it will serve to make the storekeepers and distributors and manufacturers and workers in other lines more prosperous and their prosperity will be reflected in our sales" (1922: 124).

13. Those versed in the dialectic, such as Kenney and Florida, might claim that Monden has missed an important example of the transformation of quantity into quality; namely, that the intensification of Fordism and Taylorism has not resulted in their extension, but, rather, their sublation.

14. Nissan, according to Garrahan and Stewart's account, rejects "the traditional notion of skill" and defines skill as "the ability to do the job correctly . . . . The company's own definition of skill . . . renders 'skill' synonomous with a form of work which is really the opposite of what skill means" (1992: 60–61).

15. An important factor leading to the development of mass production at the Ford plant was the high rate of turnover, the costs involved in retraining workers, and their initially lower rate of output. Mass production solved these problems because it made large groups of workers virtually interchangeable, or in modern parlance, created a flexible workforce (See Dassbach, 1991).

16. Monden (1983: 124) is quite clear on this point. While *jidoka*, or the introduction of automatic machinery, may reduce the number of worker-hours needed to manufacture a component, if it does not reduce the size of the work force, it should be avoided.

The UAW and CAW Under the Shadow of Post-Fordism: A Tale of Two Unions

Ernest J. Yanarella

The breakaway of the Canadian wing of the United Automobile Workers in 1985 was a signal event in the politics of the North American automobile industry. Although frictions between the two wings had been simmering for at least six years, the origins of the divisions that ultimately precipitated the international union's breakup have been traced to their differing history, traditions, cultures, and ultimately strategic outlooks on unionism (Gindin, 1989; and Holmes, 1990).

Since the formal split-up of the UAW, both North American automobile unions have had to confront a series of challenges rooted in the restructuring of the global and, by implication, continental political economy and the internationalization of automobile production (Robertson, et al., 1992, 1993, and this volume; and Yanarella and Green, 1990, 1993, 1994a and b). This common experience coincided with a crisis of the Fordist regime of industrial production and capital accumulation that has refracted through the North American automobile industry, posing new dilemmas and new problems for the UAW and CAW leadership and rank and file membership (Mahon, 1991; and Holmes, 1989, 1991).

Against this background of industrial restructuring and the crisis of Fordism, this chapter examines the continuing and growing gap between UAW and CAW responses at the national strategic and local tactical levels to tendencies increasingly associated with the Japanization of the automobile industry. To accomplish this, it will first examine the sources of the growing infatuation of elements of the UAW national leadership with work reorganization schemes dating back to the early seventies before corporate management in the United States began to assimilate more directly aspects of Japanese Production Management (JPM) techniques. It will then explore the implications of the

GM-Toyota joint venture, the Saturn experiment, and the Japanese automobile transplants for the political space for maneuver in developing an independent union vision toward workplace reorganization distinct from the JPM model.

The chapter will then turn to an examination of the post-1985 direction taken by the CAW in dealing with the issues and challenges of the arrival of Japanese and South Korean automobile transplants onto Canadian soil, looking in particular at the active involvement of the CAW in the recruitment to Ingersoll, Ontario of CAMI, the GM-Suzuki joint venture, and the collective agreement it struck with Suzuki to represent the workers. It then highlights the problems and dilemmas the union leadership has faced in organizing and representing workers in a lean production facility governed by a modified Japanese management style. From there, the chapter explores the challenges the union has yet to overcome in organizing the three other East Asian automobile facilities (Honda in Alliston, Toyota in Cambridge, and Hyundai in Bromont). The chapter concludes with certain grounded speculations on the possible future course and direction for organized labor in the North American marketplace in its attempt to negotiate the uncertain political terrain between Fordism and post-Fordism.

The UAW, Work Reorganization, and the Japanese Challenge

The crisis of the North American automobile industry in many ways recapitulates the trajectory of the crisis of Fordism. Because the era of mass production was ushered in by the supplanting of craft production and the integration of assembly line techniques associated with Henry Ford and the scientific management practices of Frederick Winslow Taylor, it should occasion little surprise that the fate of Fordism and the automobile industry should be inextricably intertwined.

With the mounting crisis of the Fordist mode of production and consumption beginning in the decade of the seventies, the UAW found itself in the throes of a rapidly changing political and economic environment that eroded the foundations of the New Deal industrial relations model and sent its leadership ranks in various directions in search of modifications in that old model or ingredients for a new model of labor-management relations. That model—also known as the NLRA paradigm—was characterized by a system involving: collective bargaining over wages, hours, and working conditions; a pattern bargaining process for setting agreements on common standards within and across industries; job control unionism expressed in highly detailed and formalized contracts specifying wages for each job and assuring job allocation by seniority; and quasi-judicial grievance procedures where the union served as the union worker's advocate (Kochan, Katz, and McKersie, 1986; and Green, this volume). Grounded in the key assumption that the conflict of interest between management and labor was fundamental, but manageable, this industrial relations model secreted a political model institutionalizing worker rights to representation through unions and legitimating union rights in the bargaining process. In this political model, the state assumed responsibility for overseeing and enforcing those rights and protections.

As national economies in the West driven by mass production systems sputtered and stalled and as Fordist production methods came under attack by the leaner and arguably more efficient JPM techniques advanced by Japan and Newly Industrializing Countries like South Korea, the rippling effects of crisis and challenge began to weaken the New Deal model achieved through the labor-management peace accord instituted by the 1948 contract negotiations in the North American industry, as that accord and its underlying system started to unravel.

The 1979–1983 economic doldrums in the North American economy and auto marketplace, exacerbated by increasingly fierce competition from foreign competitors and heightened in market demand, contributed to the erosion of the auto industry's traditional collective bargaining system. It also put on the agenda for labor-management debate the issues of cost reduction and increased flexibility in human resource allocation (Katz, 1985: 49). Unlike previous cyclical downturns in the industry, the sharp decline begun in 1979, given its depth and duration, suggested that the global auto industry long dominated by the American Big Three and its Canadian branch plants was undergoing a major restructuring. This severe economic recession prompted increased corporate efforts to modify, then seek to transform, the old labor-management rule book.

As these developments began to cut into Big Three sales and profits, the status quo in the auto sector was challenged by a corporate assault on union labor both in the United States and Canada and took the form of auto maker demands for union givebacks and other concessions on worker wages and benefits. As opposed to contrary pressures and strategic and tactical proposals from the Canadian wing, the American-dominated leadership of the international union approached this serious economic and political situation by considering a combination of contract concessions and quality of work life or other so-called worker participation schemes as means of lowering production costs, responding to its foreign rivals at the low end of the market, and stimulating consumer demand.

The UAW on the Defensive:
Concessions and Worker Participation Programs

The significance of the UAW turn toward concessions over wage and benefits reductions and changes in work practices was at least threefold. First, the 1979 concessions exacted by government demands to save Chrysler from bankruptcy and the 1982 wage rule modifications and givebacks in the contractual agreements with General Motors and Ford precipitated a bitter contestation between the American and Canadian wings of the UAW over the tactical wisdom of the concessions policy, thus laying the groundwork for the UAW's eventual split in 1985 (White, 1987: 199–218). A second outcome of concessions was the negotiation of several new income and job security programs—including a new guaranteed income stream benefit program, a profit sharing plan, and a joint employment training and development program—that had the symbolic effect of making the wage and fringe benefits reductions more tolerable for the union rank and file. In addition to making the concessions more palatable, their further significance lay in planting seeds of a new industrial relations model which, for example, linked auto worker pay to economic performance of the firms and contributed to a divergence in employment terms across auto corporations (Katz, 1985: 60, 63).

With wage and benefits reductions came corporate pressures upon union locals to modify work rules as an alternative to management's decision to out source parts from foreign suppliers. As Katz notes, such changes in local work rules frequently implicated union locals in complex interactions with management in joint committees and worker participation programs. In the process, another facet of the connective bargaining structure of the traditional model was undercut from "shifts away from the traditional job control focus in bargaining" (71).

If wage and work rule concessions began to chip away at the UAW's commitment to control, the trend toward worker participation or quality of work life programs in labor and management policies after 1979 threatened to jettison this keystone of the American auto labor relations system. A creature of corporate management's concern to constrain union rights and prerogatives and American labor's willingness to accept a form of business unionism within the framework of American capitalism, job control unionism produced an adversarial system of collective bargaining that focused on wages, benefits, and workplace rules within a legalistic negotiation process yielding lengthy and explicit contracts connecting worker wages and rights to a detailed job classification scheme. With the introduction of various worker participation, employment involvement, job enrichment, and other worker participation programs beginning in the early 1970s, the labor relations paradigm guiding labor-management relations and contractual negotiations began to give way to modifications and alternative practices that threatened its integrity.

The origins of the UAW's effort to forge an independent and union-driven vision of work reorganization in the United States go back at least to 1973 when a letter of understanding was appended to the national UAW-GM contract and subsequently to agreements with Chrysler and Ford. The purpose of the auto industry's early Quality of Work Life (QWL) experiments was, according to the letter (cited in Ephlin, 1986: 137), to: "improve the quality of work life, thereby advantaging the worker by making work a more satisfying experience, advantaging the Corporation by leading to a reduction in employee absenteeism and turnover, and advantaging the consumer through improvement in the quality of the products manufactured." As these experimental programs began to be instituted, they drew upon the spirit and content of the Swedish model of work reorganization.

The stimulus to UAW interest in QWL projects during this early period was the eruption of shop floor militancy, symbolized by the 1972 GM Lordstown strike. Despite overwhelming coolness or opposition within the UAW International Executive Board toward such programs, widely varied worker participation programs at GM were enthusiastically endorsed and promoted by Irving Bluestone, who was then vice-president of the UAW and director of its GM department (Kochan, Katz, and McKersie, 1986: 42). These cooperative programs involving team-style production, however, had a checkered record and were generally short-lived. In general, the union interest in less traditional, softer workplace issues represented by these early QWL projects were viewed as amendments or supplements to the more conventional collective bargaining approach. Even Bluestone, who would later become a leading advocate of the new industrial relations, argued that QWL activities must remain distinct and autonomous from the normal collective bargaining process (Katz, 1985: 75).

Such worker participation programs did not gain new currency within the industry until the economic slump of 1979–1983. Even then, the proliferation and impact of such projects among the Big Three were uneven. Bluestone's early support for QWL endeavors at GM was augmented after 1979 by heightened managerial enthusiasm with the appointment of Alfred Warren, Jr. (Warren, 1986), to the post of corporate vice-president of labor relations. Don Ephlin's assumption to the position of UAW vice-president and director of its Ford department, coupled with Pete Pestillo's appointment as Ford's vice-president of industrial relations, brought to parallel posts two vocal and long-term supporters of what became known at Ford as the employee involvement (EI) program (Ephlin, 1986). Only at Chrysler was significant elite support on either side lacking.

Studies of this later wave of worker participation projects by Kochan, Katz, and Mower (1984) point to the great diversity of experience by Big Three plants and the widely varying views of management, local union officials, and workers toward workplace changes spawned by these endeavors. Yet, at the national level, these projects gained new attention among UAW leaders and set in motion new and more powerful tendencies on the shop floor that had the cumulative effect of further weakening the hold of traditional anchor points—especially the role of shop stewards, committee members, and other union officers—in the collective bargaining system. With the growth and proliferation of these programs, the union was increasingly faced then with a new development posing itself not merely as an addition to, but as an alternative to, collective bargaining procedures and rules. Moreover, since these programs increasingly encroached upon terrain formerly defined by the collective bargaining system, it also put the UAW in a position of needing to articulate its own vision of these worker participation activities.

The UAW Confronts the Joint Ventures, Saturn, and the Auto Transplants

With the expansion of QWL programs and their evident, though uneven, rootedness on the auto industry landscape, the stage was set for further inroads into the traditional industrial relations model by innovations connected with JPM and the Japanese challenge. That challenge not only took the form of the influx of foreign, largely Japanese, imports into the North American auto market. Sparked by American and Canadian political pressures to limit these imports and the rising yen in the international money market, it was also manifested in the appearance of United States-Japanese joint ventures and Japanese automobile transplants across the industrial heartland of the United States and Canada.

The UAW response to these developments was a complex one not reducible to a single, monolithic organizational stance. In part, the pluralism of the UAW was a consequence of its organizational structure and its internal debate process. Although a fairly centralized national union with historically active, democratic unions, the UAW is governed by a president and an International Executive Board whose members come from peak posts of different departments overseeing union policies and activities of each of the major automakers (and, until 1985, from their counterparts in Canada). Moreover, given the degree of power delegated to or assumed by incumbents at lower organizational levels, the latitude of especially regional directors tends to foster regional variations to national policy directions set at the Detroit UAW headquarters.

In addition to particularities of its organizational structure, Herzenberg (1993) has pointed to a second shaping influence: the favored approach among union leaders toward channeling and containing internal debate within the UAW. Noting the deep splits and divisions within the UAW over how to respond to management initiatives in work reorganization during this period, Herzenberg emphasized the extent to which the union's national leaders "relied heavily on their institutional power to marginalize their critics" (321). Herzenberg attributes this to the perpetuation of union leadership practices instituted at peak levels in the late forties seeking to prevent the eruption of a viable opposition unionwide so as "to pursue its centralized bargaining agenda, and [contain] rank-and-file pressure for more emphasis on shop-floor issues" (322). This strategy of elite control and containment also had the effect of alienating top union leaders from local and regional activists who would be instrumental in forging close relations with progressive groups and movements in this country and alliances with auto workers in other nations.

During the early to mid-eighties, much of the political action bearing on joint ventures fell into the province of the UAW heads of the GM and Ford departments—i.e., union leaders like Don Ephlin and Irving Bluestone whose sympathies toward QWL-type programs would predispose them toward aspects of JPM. When the GM plant in Freemont, California was closed in March 1982 as part of a wave of plant closures and negotiations between GM and Toyota led to an announcement eleven months later that the plant would be reopened as a joint venture, Ephlin, who was then UAW director of the GM department, played an instrumental role in working out the letter of understanding between the parties leading to the agreement on the union's role in the New United Motor Manufacturing, Inc. (NUMMI) joint venture (Ephlin, 1986).

For each of the major participants, NUMMI represented different things. For GM, it provided a laboratory for studying Toyota's much-vaunted production methods and seeking out lessons to be transferred to other GM plants (Keller, 1989: 134–135). For Toyota, it provided a mechanism to circumvent the voluntary import quotas, since domestically produced foreign vehicles were not counted as imports. To union supporters of the philosophy of joint partnerships like Ephlin, GM-Toyota venture gave the UAW an opportunity over a three-year period to hammer out a cooperative union-management relationship with a foreign partner that had been historically antagonistic toward unionization.

On the positive side, the union was actively involved in the hiring process which created a NUMMI work force that was more than 75 percent former GM/Freemont workers and included the local union's militant leaders and rank and file activists (Turner, 1991: 56). This old militant core has also kindled local union democracy, manifested in a People's Caucus within the local that has competed with the cooperation-oriented Administration Caucus. On the other hand, the terms and shape of the workplace reorganization that has been institutionalized on the shop floor has been founded upon the Toyota Production System and its underlying production and training philosophy. All but the residues of the UAW's apprenticeship approach to training have been eliminated by Toyota's individualistic/human resource development philosophy. (On this issue, see the chapter entitled "Worker Training at Toyota and Saturn.")

Even the more critical and activist People's Caucus has been unable to forge an alternative to Toyota's team system and other work reorganization model. In the absence of this contrasting vision and the political backing to sediment it into production relations, the best that can be hoped for by the ascendancy of the People's Caucus within the NUMMI local is a more active and democratic union dedicated to old-style adversarial relations which still leaves the Toyotism virtually intact. Turner's overall assessment of the scope and limits of the militant opposition's critique and alternative agenda is compelling:

High productivity combined with outsourcing (both domestic, as for seat production and cafeteria work, and foreign, as for engines and transmissions from Japan) means fewer jobs at the plant than before, and this also means fewer unionized auto industry jobs in the United States than might otherwise be the case. Substantive training opportunities for production workers remain limited as the wide cleft between skilled and production groups stays unchanged. Cycle time is short (around one minute), and there is great pressure to maintain high work standards, to work fast and intensely . . . . In perhaps the opposition's most telling critique, the merging of labor and management viewpoints does raise the danger of an American version of enterprise unionism, stripped of its strong independent base (1991: 61–62).

Increasingly, the price being paid at NUMMI for involvement in managerial decision-making at all levels except for management's strategic prerogatives has been the loss of power, the erosion of union solidarity, and work intensification (Robbins, 1983; and Marsh, 1992). Lacking an independent path, the UAW seems caught in an eddy whirling between the Charybdis of home-spun adversarialism that seems outmoded in the era between Fordism and post-Fordism and the Scylla of jointness or cooperative labor-management relations that puts in jeopardy its identity as an independent union.

The experience at the other notable joint venture—the AutoAlliance plant at Flat Rock, Michigan—reveals similar ambiguities regarding the JPM model, but greater activism and halting steps to work through the democratic facade of "post-Fordist" production methods (see Babson, this volume). With the increased participation of Ford in this Mazda venture, this transplant (MMUC) cum joint venture (AutoAlliance) has been marked by the least smooth adaptation and organizational transfer of Japanese work principles to American soil (Florida and Kenney, 1991). The experience of work intensification and worker exploitation on the shop floor, combined with the linkage of the dissident caucus with New Directions, the national democratic movement within the UAW, quickly precipitated intense local and regional union politicking over the gulf between Mazda's professed and actual production methods and labor-management philosophy and led to the unseating of the president of Local 3000 and replacement of the director of Region 1A by Phil Keeling and Robert King respectively, challengers and critics of Mazda work organization model (Fucini and Fucini, 1990).

Yet, while the victory of the opposition caucus at the Mazda/Flat Rock plant has seen the nativizing of the JPM model and the movement toward a "third culture" (Fucini and Fucini, 1990), the terms of the political conflict still tend to be defined by the vocabulary of Toyota-inspired Japanese production system and are fueled by efforts to make real or concrete the failed promises of the plant management in implementing the system. For example, the latest AutoAlliance contract, stemming in part from the legacy of the dissidents' belief that the plant's high injury rate among production workers was due to management's failure to properly cross train the work force as avowed in Mazda's philosophy, has produced several strides in augmenting the training program and the constructing of a separate training facility. On the other hand, while the training function is to be overseen by a joint labor-management committee, actual responsibility for this activity is completely left in the hands of management and professional trainers (UAW-Mazda, 1991: 144–152, 123–124).

If joint ventures like NUMMI and AutoAlliance reveal a union caught between an adversarial labor relations model resting on crumbling Fordist foundations and a cooperative Japanese labor-management model grounded in solidifying post-Fordist ones, the Saturn experiment discloses a model built upon principles and aspirations merging the joint philosophy of leading union cooperationists and the human resource development philosophy of GM's corporate supporters (Yanarella and Green, 1994a; and Yanarella, this volume). A combination of GM President Roger Smith's vision of a paperless factory of the future and GM's enduring technological compulsion, this bid to restore GM's leadership in the small car segment of the American auto market was given substance and shape by a joint study group called the Committee of 99—55 from the UAW and 44 from GM—jointly selected by GM vice president Alfred Warren, Jr., and UAW GM department head, Don Ephlin (Ephlin, 1986: 144).

As detailed elsewhere in this volume, the Saturn contract eliminated the managerial rights clause in traditional union contracts and recast decision-making—from shop floor rules to strategic policies—into a joint union-management committee framework based on consensus. Despite the recent eruption of rank and file restiveness, the trajectory of Local 1853 over its brief tenure at the Saturn plant suggests that the toll exacted by the new industrial relations model founded upon cooperative labor-management relations and thoroughgoing union participation in every facet of company decisions and policies has been a heavy one on local union democracy and national union solidarity.

Far from ushering in a new era of workplace democracy, Saturn's approximation of what Bluestone and Bluestone (1992) call the new Enterprise Compact has been extremely corrosive of local union representation and local-national and inter-local unity and support. Indeed, the more formally democratic the corporate culture and union-management relations has become, the more autocratic has grown the local union authority vis-a-vis its membership and the greater distance the local union leadership has tried to put between perceived local plant interests and concerns and larger, more transcendent inter-local and national interests.

The formalization of an equal union 'voice' in the corporate decision-making process at Saturn has thus been achieved by Local 1853's officers at the expense of the local membership. Its president Michael Bennett has created a two-tier buffer of some 400 personally appointed work unit counselors and business unit coordinators between himself and the rank and file members in order to more smoothly carry out the joint partnership program. Opposition from the dissident caucuses, especially the 'Members for a Democratic Caucus,' has derived largely from members brought in from the more traditional GM/Norwood plant near Cincinnati, Ohio.

The direction and long-term fate of the Saturn experiment may, however, rest on the outcome of the decision of Steve Yokich, currently UAW vice-president of the GM Department, to reopen the Saturn contract for negotiation with corporate officials in order to reinstitute more conventional components of union-labor relations (Chappell, 1993). In the light of Yokich's apparent aspirations for the UAW presidency, this move may signal a significant change of course in Saturn's industrial relations system. Given the local president's remolding of Local 1853 into a model bordering on an enterprise union, this ploy by Yokich appears to be a clear bid to reassert national direction to an errant local.

The UAW strategy for winning union certification at mid-American auto transplants remains weak, wavering, and without consistency. Despite periodic proclamations of new campaigns to gain union representation of the work force at TMM, Diamond-Star, and Honda, these organizing efforts have failed to gain momentum locally and, as a rule, have petered out without evident progress. At Honda, where a vigorous campaign was mounted, the results were disappointing for the near- to mid-term prospects of success. Post-mortems on the Honda unionization effort attributed the 2:1 defeat to the absence of a mobilizable issue at the plant and Honda management's greater resources within the plant for implementing an intense union avoidance strategy (Kenney and Florida, 1993: 284–285). A deeper reason for the UAW's tepid response to the transplants, in contrast to the CAW's more militant and proactive stance toward Canada's GM-Suzuki joint venture and the three East Asian transplants, has to do with the power, collective identity, and real and potential resources of a national union over time, which "hinge on [the] union's past choices and practices, its analysis of society and organized labor's place within it, and those organizational structures which facilitate or impede a union's ability to effectively mobilize its membership" (Gindin, 1989: 75).

What the preceding analysis suggests then is that the strategic equivocation of the UAW—manifested in its blurred and confusing organizational and political identity, its past decisions and actions toward contract concessions, new production processes, and new directions generated within its leadership ranks, and its contradictory relations with and approaches to its locals on these and other developments—has contributed enormously to its general incapacity to work through the many-faceted problems and dilemmas posed by the shadow cast by the rising sun of Japanese production management and labor relations over America's industrial landscape.

Canada Auto Labor Confronts Industrial Restructuring and the Crisis of Fordism

The problems and challenges that the Canadian automobile industry and its workers have come to confront since the eighties may be viewed, as John Holmes (1988) does, as aspects of a double crisis: an earlier crisis of the Canadian auto industry in the late 1950s and 1960s and a later crisis of the North American auto industry from the early 1980s onward. Until the mid-sixties, tariff protection legislation had the effect of structuring the Canadian and American auto industries into two separate operations. While dominated by the Big Three Detroit automakers, auto and auto parts production and sales were largely organized along national lines with only limited trade in assembled automobiles across the borders of these friendly neighbors. Eventually, Canada's smaller market for cars and trucks limited its productivity, causing the Canadian auto industry's competitive position to deteriorate vis-a-vis the United States (Wonnacott, 1987).

As Holmes (1988: 35) argues, the policy "solution to this crisis lay in rationalization of assembly and parts production in Canada and its integration with production in the U.S." The 1965 Auto Pact (Canada-United States Automotive Products Trade Agreement) effectively integrated Canadian auto and auto part production into a continental market, thus dramatically increasing "productivity in the Canadian assembly and parts industries by creating a larger market for automotive products within which the full benefits of specialization and large scale production could be achieved" (ibid.).

The current crisis besetting the Canadian auto industry and its workers is, however, a shared Canadian-United States crisis—a crisis of Fordism, the mode of industrial production and its underlying regime of capital accumulation. In a sense, the success of Fordist mass production techniques and its accompanying mass consumption forms laid the basis for its breakdown. These tendencies in Fordist auto production and consumption modes included: (1) the promotion of economies of scale through Taylorist division of mass assembly line production into ever more specific and defined tasks; (2) the generation of standardized production systems with a division of labor within the plant "which was inflexible, hierarchical, and characterized by increasing automation, routinization, and mechanization of production tasks" (Holmes, 1988: 39); and (3) a labor-management system typified by hundreds of job categories, seniority rights, and contracts with wage rate increases automatically tied to productivity increases and by an absolute bifurcation of labor issues (e.g., hourly wages and job duties) and managerial prerogatives (e.g., quality standards, product design, and line speed).

With the internationalization of auto production and the introduction of new process technologies by Japan and Newly Industrializing Countries like South Korea to increase productivity, the stage seemed to be set for a possible resolution of the crisis of Fordism and the emergence of a new post-Fordist regime. Characterized by multiskilled workers, flexible production, economies of scope (production of a range of limited batches of different products at the lowest total cost), continuous improvement, and integration and rationalization of assembly and auto parts production, this new mode of regulation of production and consumption promised to overcome the limits of Fordist model and supplant it as a regime of accumulation.

Despite the global nature of the crisis of Fordism, the painful process of industrial restructuring in Canada has underlined the unique benefits and common problems of its auto industry. The increasing globalization of the auto industry has resulted in the sourcing of some parts and subassemblies around the world. This inchoate spatial division of labor around the globe has meant that Canada's energy wealth has encouraged the sourcing to Canada of those auto parts with a high energy content. The historical benefits from a favorable exchange rate with United States and from Canada's national health insurance program have also given Canada a labor cost advantage over its American partner, perhaps assuring Canada of holding on to its share of the more labor-intensive aspects of the auto industry (Holmes, 1988: 42, 43).

At the same time, to the extent that so-called Japanese production methods and other post-Fordist techniques have come to shape and even dominate the current restructuring process, they pose a formidable challenge to the continental auto industry and its workers; and, in a period of enormous over-capacity, they threaten the long-term survival of the existing branch plants of the Big Three in Canada. Compounding this threat are the unfolding consequences of the Free Trade Agreement between the United States and Canada. Touted by the Mulroney government as a method for overcoming Canada's branch plant economy and enabling it to become a player in the global marketplace, this market alternative to a state-centered industrial strategy and to regional/provincial economic development programs, has been a major factor in undercutting the long-standing advantages of the Canadian auto industry. The loss of several hundred thousand manufacturing jobs in Ontario since 1987 and the mass exodus of auto parts suppliers to the United States have rocked the native auto industry and its unionized auto workers (Farnsworth, 1991).

The prospect of a continental trade agreement has also undercut prior economic reluctance of Japanese and South Korean auto corporations to locate assembly plants in Canada. Between 1984 and 1986, Honda, Toyota, Suzuki, and Hyundai in rapid succession announced corporate decisions to build auto transplants or joint ventures in Ontario at Alliston, Cambridge and Ingersoll, and in Quebec at Bromont. Projections of their combined impact upon the Canadian economy indicated that by 1991 total foreign direct investment by these East Asian auto makers in four assembly plants would exceed $1.4 billion, employ nearly 5,000 workers, and produce over 450,000 cars and trucks annually (Holmes, 1991: 162).

The Canadian Auto Workers and Japanese Production Methods

The divergent trends in Canadian and American industrial relations, as analyzed by various Canadian labor scholars (Huxley, Kettler, and Struthers, 1986; Calvert, 1988; and Adams, 1989), illuminate the relative strength and greater political resources of Canadian organized labor in Canadian politics and political economy in comparison with the relative weakness and increasing marginality of American labor unions on the American political scene and the United States economy. These scholars have explained Canadian labor's political and economic advantage in terms of: the more favorable federal and provincial laws supporting union certification; the more militant strategies of organizing and politicking by leading sectors of the labor movement; the success of Quebec's 'Quiet Revolution' in spurring unionization in the public sector; the existence of a social democratic party allied to Canadian labor; and perhaps the red Tory cultural heritage on which the Canadian state was founded. While other students of the Canadian movement (Panitch and Swartz, 1988; Drache and Glassbeek, 1989; and Storey, 1991) have pointed to disturbing counter-trends on the legal, political, and economic fronts, the growing provincial and federal clout of Canadian labor's political vehicle, the New Democratic party, as well as the militant response by key elements of the labor movement, have helped to stem the New Right tide in Canadian politics and recoup some of the losses from the assault on labor's position and status on the Canadian political landscape during the past decade or so.

These divergent trends also help to explain the continued emphasis and relative effectiveness of the more traditional labor-management model within many Canadian plants while American organized labor has moved from the more adversarial model to a more "cooperative" labor-management approach (Wood, 1986). Within the North American auto sector, these differing tendencies and approaches have played themselves out in the different paths taken by the UAW and the CAW in the era of capitalist industrial restructuring from the Arab oil embargo onward. With the rise of double-digit unemployment and inflation, the inroads of Japanese and then South Korean auto firms into the North American and global auto marketplace, the accompanying challenge of "post-Fordist" management and labor relations to Fordist organization, and the ascendancy of a New Right agenda in the United States and, somewhat less so, in Canada, organized labor in the North American auto industry has faced a series of overlapping and mutually supporting challenges to its traditional role and place.

As Sam Gindin (1989) and Charlotte Yates (1990 and 1993) have well argued, the greater success of the Canadian wing of the international auto union in responding to political and corporate incursions on its power and influence lay, in part, in certain internal dynamics within the Canadian wing. While the UAW leadership responded to various developments—like corporate demands for concessions, the union-busting campaign of the Reagan administration, and the packing of the National Labor Relations Board with probusiness appointments—in ways that meant de facto acceptance of a strategic reformulation of the collective bargaining process and the union's power and place within it (Wood, 1986), the Canadian UAW chose to fight these threatening developments in order to preserve the traditional framework of collective bargaining and maintain the vitality of the trade union movement itself (Gindin, 1989: 79–83; and Yates, 1990: 96–100).

By adopting a no-concessions strategy, rekindling the 1930's syndicalist orientation of the auto workers, institutionalizing a 'culture of struggle' through films, music, art, and other political educational materials, fostering internal democracy within the union, and establishing a well-staffed research department to investigate the union's condition and to chart new directions and policy alternatives, the Canadian wing was vaulted into the vanguard position (along with the Canadian Union of Postal Workers) in the Canadian labor movement and found itself on a collision course with its American parent. By 1985, the divisions within the leadership ranks of the international auto union became unbridgeable, forcing the Canadian wing to break away and set an independent course (Scherer, 1988; Gindin, 1989; and Holmes and Rusonik, 1990). The entrance of East Asian auto facilities into the Canadian automobile sector has thrown up the most formidable challenge to the CAW since its split with the international.

The Canadian Auto Workers and CAMI

General Motors, Canada's largest auto maker, and Suzuki Motor Co. Ltd., one of Japan's smallest, announced their decision to locate a $500 million auto assembly plant in Ingersoll, Ontario on August 27, 1986. Christened CAMI (acronym for Canadian-American Manufacturing, Inc. and symbol for a divinity in Shintoism) by GM-Suzuki officers, the plant itself was expected to employ 2,000 workers and produce annually some 200,000 automobiles and sport utility vehicles (SUVs) when it was up to full production, scheduled for 1991.

Neither the size of the incentive package nor the mix of inducements comprising it stirred much commentary. What was most noteworthy about this announcement was that, in addition to the usual cast of characters—i.e., Ontario Premier David Peterson, DRIE Minister Michael Côte, Ontario Minister of Industry Trade and Technology Pat Lavelle, Suzuki President Osamu Suzuki and GM Chairman Roger Smith—Canadian Auto Workers' (CAW) President Bob White was in attendance and a signatory to the agreement (Daw, 1986a). His presence symbolized the decision of the president of Suzuki Motor Co. to avoid a battle over unionization of the plant and to accept from the outset the organization of its workers by Canada's militant auto workers union (Daw, 1988a).

The GM-Suzuki/CAW agreement, took over two years to negotiate (Hunt, 1991; and Pellerin, 1991). The collective agreement materialized out of discussions initiated by President Osamu Suzuki with CAW leader Bob White in Japan in mid-1985. Informal bargaining among the Japanese auto maker and Canadian partner and the union continued through the fall of 1985 and the first half of 1986 and an understanding was finally hammered out in the summer of that year. The formal three-year contract between the two sides was concluded in mid-January 1989 and was ratified by over 80 percent of CAW Local 88's membership on January 21, 1989 (Pellerin, 1991). The flexible labor agreement was a clear departure from traditional auto union contracts and represented a tactical compromise by the CAW to get its foot in the door of an auto plant organized around so-called Japanese production methods (Rinehart, 1991; and Robertson, Rinehart, and Huxley, 1992, 1993).

The CAMI plant's management is divided between GM managers who handle human resources and financing functions and Suzuki management personnel who are responsible for plant design, car models, machinery, and manufacturing, and engineering operations, and sourcing activities (Chappell, 1991b; and Grygorcewicz, 1991). With its modified Japanese style management, CAMI has become an experimental laboratory for training GM executives in the so-called lean production facilities in other parts of Canada and the United States (Chappell, 1991b). For the CAW, it has also been an important testing ground for blending traditional union interests and goals with a management philosophy and production line guided by new assumptions, tasks, techniques, controls, and social relations (Robertson, Rinehart, and Huxley, 1991; and Blount, 1990). In so doing, the CAMI plant and its post-Fordist methods have created a series of problems and dilemmas which the auto union and its leadership have yet to overcome.

In the first place, these new flexible production facilities have instituted new organizational and production methods, including the team concept, quality circles, multiskilling, and a pseudo-egalitarian job classification structure, that are antithetical to traditional labor-management relations and the structure and roles of unions that have unfolded over the twentieth century in the North American labor movement. To this, the CAW response—at least on the surface—has appeared ambivalent and contradictory. On the one hand, on the rhetorical level, the CAW has upheld the virtues of traditional collective bargaining methods and adversarial trade unionism in the face of the post-Fordist threat from East Asia. For instance, in its CAW Statement on the Reorganization of Work (CAW, 1989), the leadership of the Canadian Auto Workers set forth a strong and sweeping eleven-point indictment of workplace restructuring along Japanese Production Method (JPM) lines and rejected virtually all of the major features of Japanese-inspired flexible production. At the same time, the CAW policy statement champions true workplace democracy and supports quality production and technological innovation that does not weaken worker rights, erode workplace conditions, and undercut union independence.

On the other hand, the Canadian auto union made a "tactical compromise" (Rinehart, citing Gindin's characterization, 1991) and entered into negotiations with Suzuki and then with GM and Suzuki that resulted in a union contract at the CAMI plant. In exchange for recognition as the sole bargaining agent for CAMI's production and maintenance employees, the union formally endorsed with only slight modification a flexible production agreement that included the team concept, the *kaizen* (or continuous improvement) process, a highly truncated job classification scheme, and quality circles (CAMI-CAW, 1989).

Since signing the CAMI contract, the union has striven to confront the dilemmas of working in a plant governed by principles and practices inimical to traditional union authority and rights. Indeed, even before gaining union representation at CAMI, the education and research departments in the CAW national office began to work out the problems and dilemmas posed by JPM techniques (Robertson, Rinehart, and Huxley, 1992: 98–100). As CAMI's Local 88 and the CAW national headquarters have come to grips with the day-to-day functioning of the CAMI plant, the value of the 'tactical compromise' has become more apparent. The CAW is confronting a new and evolving set of production methods and industrial relations that, in helping to foment the crisis of Fordism, is severely testing the capacity of unions to adapt to, and to struggle to modify and refashion so-called post-Fordism in the production process and on the shop floor (Wells, 1987; Drache and Glassbeek, 1989; and Robertson, Rinehart, and Huxley, 1992). Because modified flexible production techniques have been appropriated by the Big Three auto makers and instituted in other North American auto plants, and because the rationalizing process of the *keiretsu* structure of Japanese auto producers tends to reshape the production process and labor-management relations of its auto suppliers along similar JPM lines, the only feasible union response is to bring the union struggle to the shop floor and work through and strive to alter the balance of forces shaping the future form and direction of these methods and relations.

While there is no certainty that these efforts will succeed, a survey of CAMI Local 88's monthly newsletters and interviews with CAW local and national representatives (Grygorcewicz, 1991; and Pellerin, 1991) confirm a union locked in a "struggle for the hearts and minds of the workforce" and occupying the strategic space "between a collective agreement that accommodates aspects of team concept and a policy statement of the national union that raises substantial questions about the implications of JPM" (Robertson, Rinehart, and Huxley, 1992: 98). Already, it has become clear that the role and loyalty of the team leaders are pivotal in shaping the outcome of the combat (Robertson, Rinehart, and Huxley, 1992: 97; Grygorcewicz, 1991; and Pelletier, 1991). Whether the production teams become integrated into the corporate philosophy of the company or become vehicles for resistance and reconstruction of the labor process depends crucially on the self-identity of those leaders—i.e., are they appendages of management or representatives of union labor?

Since signing the CAMI contract, the CAW at various levels has undertaken several initiatives to illuminate and support the shop floor struggle. In the negotiations over the CAMI contract, the CAW bargained for the right to monitor the plant's operation. This concession has led to a two-year study by the CAW research team of the dynamics and impact of flexible production methods upon this unionized plant (see Robertson, Rinehart, and Huxley, 1992, 1993). In refusing to take a neo-Luddite position on the integration of new technology into the workplace, the CAW has also investigated in a series of studies the critical issues relating to the impact of technological innovation in industries where it has union representation (Robertson and Wareham, 1987, 1989). The CAW research staff has also turned its attention to an assessment of the union's stakes in the international debate over worker training programs and the incipient policy debate over the same issue among Canadian labor studies and critical political economists.

Meanwhile, Local 88 has begun to participate in an informal communications network of unions in Canada and the United States designed to exchange information and lessons from their shared struggle with flexible production plants. Since January 1991, representatives of CAMI's Local 88 and renegade UAW Local 3000 at Mazda's Flat Rock, Michigan, plant have visited one another, and issued reports on the Mazda local's success in winning concessions from management in its latest contract, and shaped Local 88's new contract with GM-Suzuki in September 1992. Subsequently, these two locals have brought representatives of UAW Local 2488 at the Chrysler-Mitsubishi Diamond-Star plant in Bloomington-Normal, Illinois, into the evolving constellation (Binns, 1991; Fulton, 1991; and Grygorcewicz, 1991).

On the eve of the expiration of the CAMI-CAW contract, Local 88 membership voted overwhelmingly to strike. Although press accounts attributed the triggering of the strike to GM's failure to implement fully and effectively Suzuki's lean or post-Fordist production techniques (Chappell, 1993), Rinehart et al.'s (this volume) examination of worker commitment and labor-management relations at CAMI disputes this interpretation of causes of the five-week strike. Drawing upon the CAW research study of CAMI, the research team traces the rising dissatisfaction of the work force toward lean production, the shifting loyalties of workers from the company and team to the union, and the role of the union in mediating these phenomena. While the CAW continues to look through a glass darkly in confronting some aspects of lean production (e.g., training), the results of the strike demonstrated, as Rinehart et al. argue, that "Local 88 has established itself as a force to be reckoned with by enabling individual workers to translate their discontents into a larger, more effective struggle to protect and promote their rights and interests."

The CAW and Honda, Toyota, and Hyundai Automobile Plants

The CAW chances of winning union certification at the other three plants appeared highest at the Hyundai plant in Bromont. Having worked hard since the seventies to promote union organizing of plants in Quebec, the CAW restructured itself organizationally after its independence to respond to legitimate political and language concerns of its provincial leaders and members, setting up a Quebec regional office and director and establishing a Quebec Council co-equal in status with the Ontario-dominated CAW Council (CAW-Canada Organizing Report, n.d.). In the Spring of 1991, reports began circulating that the auto union effort at Bromont was close to reaching the magic number for union certification—though one field organizer revealed in early August 1991 that its formal request was being deferred (Metic, 1991; Shalom, 1990, 1991; and Daw, 1991). The initial organizing drive centered on job rotation work rules and the sliding-scale pension plan introduced by Hyundai management (Chappell, 1991a).

In mid-March 1993, the CAW applied to the Quebec labor commissioner for union certification of the plant, claiming signatures from a majority of the Bromont/Hyundai production force. The plant management's intransigent opposition to unionization was evidenced in its firing of two Hyundai workers and disciplining five others on the day of the CAW petition (Sinek, 1993). Two months later, the status of the troubled plant was placed in greater doubt when Hyundai-Canada officials announced that it would be shut down in October 1993 and purportedly reopen after retooling in early 1995 to produce Hyundai's next generation Elantra sedan (Chappell and Sinek, 1993). One complicating factor in union organizing had been persistent rumors that Hyundai was considering moving the plant to Mexico (Rose, 1991). Unfortunately, the CAW's strenuous efforts to unionize this East Asian transplant were made moot when the Hyundai management announced that the idled factory would cease automobile production permanently and resume production, if at all, with a new, nonautomotive line at some indefinite point in the future (Rechtin, 1995).

More fundamental problems face the CAW organizing campaigns at two other plants in Ontario. The Cambridge/Toyota and the Alliston/Honda assembly plants have thus far been resistant to unionizing campaigns. As a rule, Canadian plants have tighter security surrounding the facilities and maintain a lower profile in their communities than do those in the United States. Canadians also seem to be less hostile and more willing to grant greater latitude to Big Business in Canada, despite the relative strength of trade unions and social democratic organizations there (Lipset, 1990: 133). So it is not surprising that organizers have been hassled by plant security officers and forced to locate their distributions of leaflets completely off plant grounds (Metic, 1991).

Honda and Toyota, meanwhile, have undertaken a policy of closely screening potential employees for union sympathies (Daw, 1988b) and the Honda management has been accused of finding excuses for firing union supporters in its work force (Metic, 1991). Given Canada's prevailing economic woes and the high wage scales of these plants, the CAW's struggle to unionize these two transplants will face an uphill battle. At the same time, the rising rates of job injuries and incidences of carpal tunnel syndrome and other repetitive stress ailments stemming from assembly line speedup and the *kaizen* process—union organizers believe—will eventually lead to worker restiveness, particularly with the aging of the presently young work force.

Conclusion

As these case studies of two North American auto unions formerly united indicate, the crisis of Fordism posed by the Japanese production methods in the automobile industry, as it has refracted through the politics of workplace restructuring, remains unresolved. While there are, as Harvey (1989) has pointed out, "many . . . signs of continuity rather than rupture with the Fordist era" (171), the "evidence for increased flexibility . . . [in North America and] throughout the capitalist world is simply too overwhelming" (191); thus, it is "dangerous to pretend that nothing has changed, when the facts of deindustrialization and of plant relocation, of more flexible manning practices and labour markets, of automation and product innovation, stare most workers in the face" (ibid.). Contrary to those scholars who have declared that Fordism has been superseded by "post-Fordism" (Kenney and Florida, 1989; and Womack, Jones, and Roos, 1990), Sayer and Walker (1992) forcefully argue that the unfolding tendencies within the global political economy and, by implication, North America suggest that, as against a dualistic framework and binary history of Fordism and post-Fordism, "there are many different routes to flexibility" (200) and what seems to be emerging "are new permutations of each rather than a simple trend towards greater flexibility alone" (199).

The proliferation of these permutations and combinations of Fordism and post-Fordism within the North American automobile industry challenges both the UAW and CAW to rethink their strategies toward workplace reorganization, clarify organized labor's fundamental interests vis-a-vis new forms of post-Fordist or flexible production, and search for wider segments of political support for building a counterhegemonic alliance from the local to the national level addressing the more encompassing ramifications of these developments beyond Fordism.

It is no doubt true that the UAW reveals itself in these contestations over post-Fordism as a far more pluralistic organization than its dominant public image would suggest (Turner, 1991), just as close inspection of the CAW discloses a union caught up in the most difficult dilemmas spawned by post-Fordist tendencies in an era of global restructuring (Wells, 1993). Still, the American auto union has suffered more deeply from the strategic position and persuasive force of leaders like Don Ephlin and Irving Bluestone in presenting an artificial construction of a national executive board and leadership unified behind labor-management cooperation and lean production and the team system. This cooperationist stance has been abetted by the willingness of more traditionalist UAW leaders like Owen Beiber to join in silent alliance with the Ephlin-led faction by allowing it to "be the lightning rod for rank-and-file criticism of labor-management cooperation" (Herzenberg, 1993: 320). Unlike IG Metall and the CAW, the UAW has lacked strategic-minded theoreticians to juxtapose union interests and Japanese production management and to devise strategies and tactics applicable to the interregnum between Fordism and post-Fordism. The outlines of a counterhegemonic strategy for organized labor, sketchily lined throughout this volume, have been only barely fashioned and haltingly instituted in the struggles at Mazda, NUMMI, and CAMI. At best, a negotiated model of plant-level work reorganization has been fashioned—a model and approach which must be eventually surpassed by a counterhegemonic model. Yet, the alternative, an Americanized version of enterprise unionism informing the theoretical vision of the local union leadership core at Saturn, is instructive as a warning of the *reductio ad absurdem* of the worst trends manifest at Spring Hill and at other unionized plants in the process of post-Fordist deformation.

As part of a coordinated and multilevel approach to the crisis of Fordism, any UAW and CAW alternative strategy working at the interstices of Fordism and post-Fordism will, of course, have to evaluate the new risks and new opportunities from the ongoing process of hemispheric and global restructuring in the automobile industry and negotiations between Canada, the United States, and Mexico on the North American Free Trade Agreement (NAFTA). The Pro-Canada Network—a coalition of unions, farmers, environmentalists, women's groups, native people, social justice organizations, peace activists, artists, and church groups which arrayed itself against the Canada-United States free trade agreement—showed the potential and possibilities for organizing diverse segments of Canadian society against assimilation into a continental segmented economy. This coalition and its mobilization strategy provide important lessons for the UAW, despite its failure to defeat NAFTA. The success of Ford and other automakers in building auto and engine assembly plants in Mexico which use lean production methods may, at the same time, provide renewed impetus to the UAW and CAW to develop closer ties with Mexican workers and dissident American auto workers and to reassert the priority for a truly continental labor response (Shaiken and Herzenberg, 1986; and Witt, 1991).

The ascendant power of the New Democratic party in Ontario and Canadian politics raises anew the question of what productive role it may play in the larger Canadian policy debate over industrial strategy, free trade, and industrial restructuring in a more tightly integrated global political economy. Fordism's great material benefits to workers and consumers were derived in large part from organized labor's participation in this mode of production and consumption. While recent developments have been on balance disappointing, Canadian labor's long-term relationship with the NDP may yet net it important benefits at the provincial and national levels. More sobering is the Clinton administration's tepid attitude toward American unions, as well as its overweaning fascination with labor-management cooperation as an instrument for promoting American international competitiveness epitomized by labor secretary Robert Reich's exaltation of the exemplary status of the Saturn model (Nomani and Ingersoll, 1993). Organized labor's role in the old New Deal coalition has steadily eroded since the sixties and revision of the UAW's and other major unions' national political strategies in the national political arena is long overdue.

This tale of two unions in the crisis of Fordism gives concrete expression to the mood Gramsci sought to convey of a similar circumstance when he wrote: "the crisis consists precisely in the fact that the old is dying and the new cannot be born; [and] in the interregnum an assortment of morbid symptoms appear[s]" (Gramsci, 1971: 276). If Fordism is passing, then the return to a purely adversarial model of labor-management relations is impossible. But if post-Fordism is not preordained, the question is: what shall supplant the old industrial relations once the morbid symptoms of jointness and other cooperative labor-managment approaches have passed?

PART
II

THE CRISIS OF FORDISM ON THE SHOP FLOOR
Four Case Studies

The Myth of Egalitarianism: Worker Response to Post-Fordism at Subaru-Isuzu*‡

_____ *Laurie Graham*

The North American automobile industry has become the focus of debate over the nature of the Japanese management model. Some researchers suggest that modern Japanese management provides a new cooperative work force participation-based model (Womack, Jones and Roos, 1990; Cole, 1979; and Dore, 1973), that it provides for greater employee involvement in decision-making (Brown and Reich, 1989) and that it "engages workers' minds with the managerial aspects of their jobs" (Safizadeh, 1991: 61). Other researchers take the 'promise' of work force participation a step farther and suggest that the Japanese model has the potential to expand workers' control at management's expense (Derber and Schwartz, 1988; Kornbluh, 1984; and Edwards, 1979). The Japanese management model is said to produce extraordinary commitment, identification, and loyalty from its employees (Lincoln and Kalleberg, 1985: 738) and claims have been made that "Japanese managers have succeeded in blending technological improvements with good human relations" (Hull and Azumi, 1988: 427). All these claims share the common assumption that the interests of workers and management are fundamentally compatible (Blauner, 1964).

Critics of the Japanese management model challenge this assumption and argue that the Japanese model's participation scheme is a conscious attempt to gain further control over workers by undermining union organization (Parker, 1985; Parker and Slaughter, 1988; and Slaughter, 1983) and defeating future organizational drives (Grenier, 1988).

In their studies of United States-Japanese automobile transplants, Florida and Kenney (1991; 1993) assert that the Japanese model has been successfully transferred to the United States. However, studies of unionized Japanese automotive joint ventures in the United States and Canada (Fucini and Fucini, 1990; Rinehart et al., this volume) document adaptation problems by Mazda's and CAMI's workers. These studies suggest that, even though the intraorganizational structures of Japanese management are present, the manner in which those structures are manipulated by workers does not indicate the direct transference assumed by Florida and Kenney.

Through my hidden participant/observer at Subaru-Isuzu Automotive (SIA), a nonunion Japanese transplant located near Lafayette, Indiana, I examined workers' responses to the Japanese model from the recruitment process through working on the assembly line and focused in particular on the social patterns of behavior among workers and between workers and management. This chapter, based on my experience during selection, training, and working on the line as a team member, challenges the claim that worker control is enhanced by the participatory scheme found in the Japanese model. This finding provides a basis for questioning the conclusion that Japanese management has successfully transferred its intraorganizational environment to the United States in a form that benefits workers and increases their control over decision-making. I will argue that while SIA management attempts to transfer its labor relations model by means of its control over worker selection, orientation, training, and shop floor practices, the contradictions between the company's cooperative labor-management philosophy and worker experiences leads to worker resistance. This resistance begins as individual, covert manipulation of the screening process and evolves into patterns of open, informal collective negotiation on the shop floor.

Background

Subaru-Isuzu Automotive is jointly-owned and operated by two Japanese companies, Fuji Heavy Industries Ltd. and Isuzu Motors Ltd. The Lafayette, Indiana facility opened in 1989 presently employs about 1,900 workers. While total vehicle production was 125,000 in 1992, the plant has the capacity to produce 170,000 vehicles annually. The models assembled at the plant include Subaru Legacy sedans and station wagons, Isuzu pickup trucks, and Isuzu Trooper and Rodeo sport utility vehicles.

In February of 1989 I began my involvement with the selection process. I was intermittently involved in selection until I was hired by the company in July. From July 1989 through January 1990 I worked as a hidden participant/observer in the trim and final department assembling the Subaru Legacy at SIA. This analysis is based on field notes of informal interviews with job applicants, employment specialists in charge of the hiring process, co-workers, teammates, team leaders and management personnel. Through the course of the preemployment selection process and the six months in the plant, I informally interviewed 150 employees. Other data sources include day-to-day observations of co-worker and worker/management interactions and documents distributed by the company. Both management and workers were unaware that they were under observation.[1]

Generally, management systems attempt to increase their control over shop floor production through two avenues: technical and/or social. First, by gaining possession of and thereby controlling the knowledge of how work is done, management attempts to control the technical aspects of work. The implementation of this type of control has been described as Taylorism (Braverman, 1974), despotic (Burawoy, 1985), and direct (Friedman, 1977). Second, some management systems interfere with workers' social behavior and focus on controlling worker's emerging culture of solidarity (as evidenced in the craft ethos of brotherhood) (Montgomery, 1979). Social controls have been described as bureaucratic (Edwards, 1979), giving workers responsible autonomy (Friedman, 1977), and as a system of hegemony (Burawoy, 1985). Japanese management is multidimensional because it seeks to control both the technical and social aspects of production in order to gain a worker's total cooperation in the company's competitive struggle (Graham, 1993). In this regard, the multidimensional approach is most consistent with Burawoy's (1979) concept of hegemonic control with the addition of Thompson's (1989) emphasis on the resistance that is present in workers' adaptations in production (see Yanarella, "Worker Training at Toyota and Saturn," this volume). These two aspects of the Japanese model combine to form a formidable obstacle to workers as they attempt to gain some level of control over their work lives, whether through technical or social means. However, at the same time, this management system of control gives rise to worker resistance. To describe the full range of worker response to the Japanese model, this chapter examines the selection process, orientation and training, and shop floor experiences at SIA.

The Selection Process

Like other so-called post-Fordist transplants in North America (Kenney and Florida, 1993; and Parker, 1985), the first component of SIA's system of control begins before a worker is hired with a pre-employment selection process. To get a job at SIA all prospective employees undergo a battery of tests and observed exercises. The first hurdle in the selection process is a four-hour General Aptitude Test (GAT). Those who score above 85 percent are invited by letter to enter 'Phase I' of a two-phase, pre-employment assessment activity.

During Phase I, a maximum of twenty applicants are processed in a four-hour session. Applicants are divided into four groups, and each group is taken to a separate room where the group participates in team scenarios. During a team scenario, the group is given a problem solving task. One task involved building a circuit board. The group was directed to make decisions concerning the type of board to build and then they were to come up with a method of assembly.

While the applicants performed the scenarios, employment specialists from the state Department of Employment Training (DET) wrote down each applicant's comments. Applicants were told that their comments would be evaluated and scored.

Although applicants were eliminated during all phases of the screening process, Phase I was the most crucial period. During Phase I, the employment specialist told our group that more than 50 percent of all applicants are eliminated in Phase I but that nearly all of those who make it through Phase I are eventually hired. During Phase I, the bulk of the team testing, testing each applicant's ability to be a good team member took place.

After completing Phase I, applicants were sent a letter informing them of their status in the selection process. Successful applicants received a letter of congratulations for having been selected to enter Phase II. In Phase II only 10 applicants participated. It differed from Phase I in that it involved very little teamwork, the testing tended to be individualistic. Applicants were given attitude tests designed to measure their willingness to cooperate with others and adapt to change. They also participated in timed assembly tasks and problem solving exercises.

After successfully completing Phase II, applicants received a phone call scheduling them for a physical exam and drug screening at a local health clinic. If 'drug free,' applicants entered the final step in the hiring process, an interview with three team leaders at the plant. Even though team leaders were hourly employees, they made the ultimate decision as to whether or not an applicant was hired.

I was given two separate interviews. The first was with a woman team leader from body assembly. When she left, two male team leaders, one from body and the other from trim and final, asked me many of the same questions. The team leaders explained that all applicants were given the same set of questions in the interviews. The team leaders wrote down applicants' responses.

Because team leaders read from the same set of questions and wrote down all the responses, one might wonder why they used an interview format. Applicants could have been given a standard questionnaire and could written their responses. Instead of performing its traditional role in the processing of applicants, at SIA, the interview provided the opportunity for a visual assessment. Until the interview, only employees of the state employment office had seen each applicant. Therefore, the interview was necessary for the company to determine if the applicant looked like someone who might fit with the company's image. After I was working in the plant, I asked a team leader if he/she had ever turned down anyone at the interview stage. The reply: "Only one, I turned down a woman who was just too attractive. I was afraid that the men wouldn't be able to keep their minds on their work." Obviously, the woman did not fit that team leader's image of an associate.

One effect of the selection process was to heighten expectations about the nature of work and employment at SIA. Workers developed hope that SIA would be different from other companies. Workers reported coming away from the selection process with the impression that working at SIA would especially benefit them. Several stated that they believed they would be involved in all decisions concerning their work. During selection, an employment specialist told applicants that SIA was committed to involving them in decision-making, that it was a factory where worker safety comes first, and that workers were treated "like family" because they were all part of one big team. Applicants were told that they would be thoroughly trained in all aspects of the job and that "[t]he general welfare of the worker is a high priority, because SIA is searching for people who really want to commit themselves to working there for life."

Many of these promises were repeated in a booklet applicants picked up with their job applications. The booklet directs applicants to ask themselves the following questions before applying at SIA: "Am I committed to the concept of "Quality Consciousness?" Am I willing to share my ideas with others and to constantly strive to improve in all areas? Am I ready to work in a fast-pace work environment? Can I work with others in a team? Does SIA sound right for me?" (*Subaru - Isuzu Automotive: Facts & Information*, 1989: 1)

The booklet stresses the importance of the team at SIA and describes how "SIA is not hiring workers. It is hiring associates . . . who work as a team to accomplish a task." Team leaders are compared to basketball team captains and group leaders to coaches. Team leaders are highly skilled associates, like basketball team captains. They can do all the jobs performed by the members of their team. A group leader is like a coach, responsible for several teams (*Subaru - Isuzu Automotive: Facts and Information*, 1989: 2).

Applicants are told that associates are trusted with responsibility for quality and safety. The booklet is clear: SIA is looking for team players, people who are cooperative and who will strive to make the company a success. In turn, SIA cares about the safety and well-being of its employees and encourages everyone to strive toward achieving their full potential.

Worker Response to Selection

During Phase I, the team oriented part of the selection process, applicants often expressed feelings of resentment, rather than cooperation or support, toward their team members. After Phase I several applicants paused in the parking lot to discuss their experience. Some reported that they were "wiped out" and surprised at the intensity of the day. Other applicants who had not been together as a team tended to talk with each other rather than their teammates. While performing the tasks, it was obvious to them that applicants were in direct competition with team members and if one member dominated the interactions, resentment emerged. The others were afraid of being overshadowed. One applicant complained: "One guy in my team just wouldn't shut up, and the rest of us couldn't get a word in edge-wise."

When I interviewed newly hired workers during the company's orientation and training for new employees, several workers stated that they really were not team players, and that they would rather work alone if given the choice. Some workers said that they knew they had to behave cooperatively with other applicants in order to stay in the selection process, especially during the team scenarios, even though they felt like doing just the opposite. They engaged in a charade in order to get the job. One worker said, "Right from the start, I knew what the company was looking for." Others admitted that they were not always honest in filling out the questionnaire. Workers stated that they wanted the job and that they were not going to "blow their chances" by letting the company know "how they really felt" about management. In fact, workers had the opportunity to know in advance what was expected of them. In addition to the SIA booklet explaining the company's team philosophy, area newspapers had published several articles focusing on the company's "new style" of management based on a team concept that stressed cooperation and quality.

Workers I interviewed on the shop floor expressed the belief that most people had succeeded in being selected because they were smart, not because they were team players. There was general sentiment that SIA used the selection process as a gatekeeper, "to get rid of undesirables," but no agreement as to why they were undesirable. One person thought the process was an effort to screen out anyone who was not willing to be cooperative, because no one could pass the team exercises in Phase I if they were unwilling to cooperate with others. Another said that the GAT test was given in order to cut out anyone who was not fairly intelligent. Another person was fairly certain the whole selection process was aimed at exposing union supporters, because the questionnaire in Phase I would single out "union sympathizers, or at least people who did not believe that what was good for the company was good for them." Moreover, some of the interview questions asked by the team leaders might have indirectly exposed someone leaning in that direction. Another worker said that SIA was trying to get rid of freeloaders, because the timed assembly tasks in Phase II and the film showing what it was like to work in a Japanese assembly plant were both aimed at scaring away "anyone not willing to work."

Other workers had a very positive response to the selection process. This may have reflected the fact that having been successful, we were clearly "better than others." One person I interviewed believed that the selection process was "fantastic." When describing how he felt, he said that, for once, it gave him a chance to be fairly evaluated. Since the process involved much more than simply filling out an application and hoping for an interview, he said, "It gave guys like me, who didn't know the right people, a chance." He felt that SIA had actually "tapped into his potential," that the examiners had "really gotten to know him through the tests." In general, the selection process made workers feel special, part of a chosen few. We were repeatedly told that we had been chosen out of more than 30,000 applicants. While participating in the process, a worker not only discovered what the company would expect of him or her as a worker, but was also drawn into the excitement of selection. Successful applicants felt eager to get the job, as a 'select few' who successfully competed to become an SIA associates, an excitement which they carried with them on to the shop floor.

In conclusion, SIA's rigorous selection process not only gave the company ample time to select its vision of the most 'qualified' workers, but indirectly affect behavior on the shop floor. Since it was not necessary that a true affinity for team participation be part of workers' personalities, the company selected those workers who were willing to adapt to management's efforts to structure worker behavior within the plant. It was essential only for the applicant to understand the rules of the game and to be willing to play by those rules in order to get the job. Whatever motivated the worker to modify his or her behavior to get the job, SIA expected would continue to motivate him or her to behave in a manner to keep it.

Orientation and Training

The second component of SIA's system of control, social control, emerged from the company's orientation and training program. As highlighted in Yanarella's chapter, "Worker Training at Toyota and Saturn," SIA and other transplants depend heavily on this component to exert hegemony over the work force (Allen, 1991; Brauchle and Pendelton, 1992; Cranevale, Gainer, and Metzer, 1990; and Levin, 1993). All newly hired workers entered the company's orientation and training program which consisted of one week of orientation followed by a minimum of two weeks of classroom training.

The information and instruction were clustered into three general categories. The first area included 'nuts and bolts' information on benefits, pay schedules, work rules, uniform fittings, and tours of the plant. Within this area were basic lessons in reading blueprints, using statistical process control, and structuring time studies. The second area involved lessons on the company's history and philosophy, including testimonials from instructors and management, instructions on kaizening, group decision making by consensus, and lectures to demonstrate SIA's egalitarian nature. The third area focused on socializing workers through formal, video-driven behavior training sessions and through the facilitation of informal interactions with other classmates. In sum, the nuts and bolts area of instruction involved practical training while the second and third areas shaped attitudes, values, and behavior.

If the amount of time spent within an area of instruction was an indication of its value to the company, then practical training was not the priority of the orientation and training process. Of 127.5 hours of orientation and training, approximately 56 hours were spent in practical training. The remaining 71.5 hours concentrated on attitudes and behavior.

The orientation and training period served two important functions. First, it provided a bridge between the selection process and the shop floor by facilitating the process of bonding with one's classmates. Second, it structured the worker's initial experience as a company employee before entering the shop floor. The experience was designed to be positive, unique, and worker oriented. It attempted to shape an egalitarian culture that would carry over to the shop floor—a culture that is necessary for a team concept to thrive.

By providing this bridge to new workers, orientation and training succeeded in neutralizing the potentially alienating experience of beginning work in a mass production plant. Workers at SIA often formed stronger bonds with their orientation and training class members than they did with their team members. This bond of friendship was useful in the company's overall attempt to shape a cooperative work force. It laid the groundwork for a smooth transition into the plant which was borne out by my personal experience. As a new worker in a factory environment, I experienced much less alienation and fear than I had when I began previous factory jobs. Orientation and training also created a bond of common experience among all workers in the plant. Like the selection process, it provided a kind of 'universal initiation' for all associates. It was often the first topic of conversation when a new worker joined the team.

In sum, the orientation and training process served as an important bridge. It built upon the initial excitement of selection and introduced the worker to the company philosophy and socialized workers to expected behavior on the shop floor. Overall, workers reported a positive experience. Indeed, this training process resulted in the highest level of enthusiasm workers experienced toward the job. Even those who had been somewhat cynical about the screening process were invigorated by the training experience and hopeful that the team concept would deliver a higher level of job satisfaction than they had previously experienced.

On the Shop Floor

The third component of SIA's system of control also focused on the social aspects of control. It involved an active campaign to create a company-wide team culture premised on the concept of egalitarianism. This was a necessary strategy if the company was to be successful in elevating the responsibilities of team membership and identification to the level of the company. Participation in team culture began with the selection process, continued through orientation and training, and was ultimately played out on the shop floor.

SIA attempted to create an egalitarian culture through specialized symbols, ideology, language, and rituals. The company's organizational structure contained very few levels between top management and workers; managers had no private offices; everyone, from the company president down, wore the same uniforms, parked in the same parking lot, and ate in the same cafeteria. Workers were never referred to as employees or workers; everyone, including management, was an associate. On the shop floor, decisions were to be made by consensus implying the equal involvement of everyone.

The team metaphor was used at all levels of the company. Team leaders were compared to basketball captains and group leaders were coaches. The sport metaphor was further extended to embrace the company's struggle in the marketplace. When SIA defined its corporate character in the Associate Handbook, the second principle was "Together, we must beat the competition." When the company referred to the team, it used the language of team responsibility to create a sense of caring for and an appearance of sensitivity to the needs of its workers, who as associates are players on 'one big' company team: "SIA believes all Associates should be given a chance to develop to their full physical and mental potential. For this reason, all Associate members will be trained in—and will perform—a number of functions. This increases their value to the team and to SIA" (*Facts and Information*, 1989: 2). Company documents and lessons in orientation and training focused on caring terms: safety, quality, trust, pride, and cleanliness. During start-up, workers were directed to make signs to hang in their areas using each of these concepts.

Company rituals included morning exercises, team meetings, department meetings, and company celebrations. These rituals brought workers in contact with management in a relaxed and casual atmosphere. At department meetings the teams sat together in the cafeteria, smoking and drinking soft drinks while the trim and final manager delivered a 'pep talk.' Company celebrations not only included workers, but workers were often the focus of the celebration. At the ceremony commemorating the official start-up of production, state dignitaries, community leaders, and top management from Fuji Heavy Industries and Isuzu were present. The ceremony was laden with images of American nationalism. The marching band from the local university played and baton twirlers performed. At the climax of the celebration, all of the SIA employees marched across the stage through a haze of smoke as the company song "Team Up for Tomorrow" played over the speaker system. An associate from Team 2 told me, "It seems kind of like graduation."

In this nonunion setting, these rituals, promoting egalitarianism and corporate community, were unchallenged by any alternative locus of power. As a result, the forms of worker resistance that inevitably arose from the consequences of management by stress were not institutionalized in ways that can be regularly mobilized for the purposes of dramatically reshaping the work environment.

Worker Response on the Shop Floor

Once production began, contradictions between the company's egalitarian philosophy and the realities of the team concept in a profit making assembly plant rapidly became apparent. Contradictions emerged in two basic areas: SIA's organizational philosophy and its philosophy of work. The first stressed equality and the second was based on individual improvement.

Contradictions in Company Philosophy. Workers found that the company's team philosophy did not benefit the individual worker and that it often would undermine solidarity within individual teams. The responsibility of team membership often forced workers to push themselves to the limit in order to keep up. This pressure existed because of the team structure. When a worker fell behind or made mistakes, the others on the team suffered because they had to correct those errors before the vehicle left their area. Chances were good that if the team member did not solve the problem, he or she would experience resentment from the others. A worker from another team told me that he was training one of his team members on a station and that the team member was very slow. In reference to that worker's slow speed he said, "You know, it kind of makes me mad."

In addition to peer pressure, a form of self-discipline emerged from the team structure. I found that I also internalized the responsibilities of team membership when I found myself going to extreme measures to 'hold up my end of the bargain.' This occurred during a period when management began altering my station. Each change increased the time it took to complete my series of tasks, forcing me to change other areas of the station in order to keep up. At one point, however, it simply became impossible to do the amount of work required, and I kept falling farther and farther behind. Even though I knew the task requirements could not be reasonably completed in the time allotted, I felt guilty and feared that the other team members would resent me for falling behind.

The team structure also gives the company technical flexibility over job assignments. Team members are cross trained to perform each other's jobs; as a result, management can move workers around freely within the team or between similar teams. Although team members were not opposed to cross training and job rotation because it increased safety and cut down on monotony, the flexibility also had negative effects. It allowed the company to hire fewer workers, because other team members could cover for absent or injured workers. When someone was absent, flexibility and cross training also had the effect of job intensification and speed-up.

Another symbol of the company's egalitarian philosophy that was filled with contradictions was its flat organizational structure. This type of structure is designed to bring workers and management closer together by eliminating layers of management and to foster a 'cooperative' work environment through direct worker input. However, at SIA this structure actually intensified management's direct control over the work force. because it relied upon team leaders to constantly monitor workers' behavior. Since team leaders represented the company's interests and served as pseudo supervisors for teams of seven workers on average, team members' actions were under close scrutiny, and if they were inappropriate, a member was pressured to change. At times this meant that the team leader notified the group leader (the first level of management) and that person would receive a 'friendly' visit from the group leader. At other times, inappropriate behavior might attract the attention of the car manager.

Contradictions in Work Philosophy. The second area of contradiction emerged from SIA's philosophy of work: "Always searching for a better way." This was how one vice president described the philosophy of *kaizen* during orientation and training. On the shop floor this meant that workers were expected to continually make their jobs more efficient, striving to work to maximum capacity. Kaizening was directly enforced through periodically decreasing tact time[2] through line speed-up; thereby, forcing workers to shave additional seconds from their tasks. Kaizening was also found to have a 'domino effect'—making one person's job more efficient often meant shifting part of that process to another worker or team, thereby intensifying someone else's job. In sum, the goal of this philosophy of work would require workers to work every second of every minute.[3]

The company's use of consensus in decision-making was also incorporated into its philosophy of work. Ironically, instead of increasing worker input, consensus served to strengthen management's control over outcomes. The unequal relationship between worker and management made it nearly impossible to reach a consensus involving little more than token input from workers. Decisions tended to conform to management's wishes and the topics raised for discussion were controlled and shaped by management.

The Evolution of Shop Floor Resistance

Contradictions between the company's culture of egalitarianism and worker rights became pronounced as line speed steadily increased, injuries emerged (at one point, seven of twelve of the members on my team suffered from hand or wrist injuries), and production quotas loomed. Worker resistance to SIA's system of management took various collective forms. Sabotage emerged as an early and continuing form of collective resistance and often involved workers surreptitiously stopping the assembly line. Collective resistance also took the form of open protest when workers refused to participate in company rituals, in the form of direct confrontation when they refused management

requests, and in the form of organized agitation at team and department meetings. These diffuse forms of resistance ultimately evolved into a more systematic
type of collective negotiation between workers and company. Workers manipulated the company's egalitarian philosophy of fairness and used it to benefit
their own interests. Their strength during negotiations was based on the underlying threat of unionization (Milkman, 1991). Figure 1 represents the evolu-
tionary quality of worker response. Resistance emerged initially as an individual
manipulation of the selection process in the form of a worker charade. On the
shop floor, collective resistance evolved from 1) sabotage as a reaction to work
intensification; 2) open protest in reaction to unfair company policies; 3) direct

Figure 1 Evolution of Worker Resistance

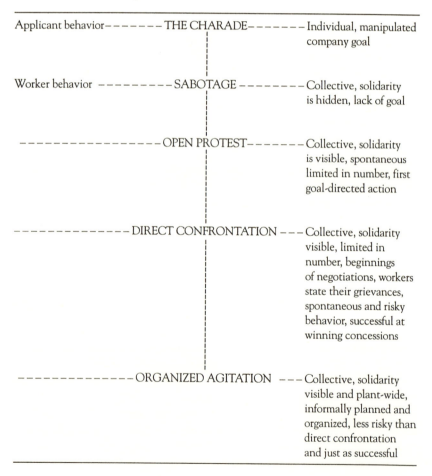

Applicant behavior——————THE CHARADE——————Individual, manipulated
                                                    company goal

Worker behavior —————————SABOTAGE ————————Collective, solidarity
                                                    is hidden, lack of goal

————————————————OPEN PROTEST——————Collective, solidarity
                                                    is visible, spontaneous
                                                    limited in number, first
                                                    goal-directed action

————————————DIRECT CONFRONTATION ———Collective, solidarity
                                                    visible, limited in
                                                    number, beginnings
                                                    of negotiations, workers
                                                    state their grievances,
                                                    spontaneous and risky
                                                    behavior, successful at
                                                    winning concessions

——————————————ORGANIZED AGITATION ———Collective, solidarity
                                                    visible and plant-wide,
                                                    informally planned and
                                                    organized, less risky than
                                                    direct confrontation
                                                    and just as successful

confrontation as a step-up in activity when open protest was unsuccessful; and 4) organized agitation as a form of plant-wide collective resistance.

Sabotage occurred when workers on one trim and final team discovered how to stop the assembly line without management tracing their location. Whenever one of the members of that team fell behind and the 'coast was clear' they would stop the line. This not only allowed workers on their team to catch up, it gave everyone time away from the line. In addition, it provided entertainment for workers as they watched management scramble around trying to find the source of the line stoppage. At one morning team meeting, Team 1's team leader reported that the line had stopped for a total of twenty minutes the previous day and that the company was unable to account for the time. Clearly, that team was taking a chance; but, workers aware of the sabotage never told management. Whether the reason for their solidarity was selfish, because of the appreciated breaks, or was an act of loyalty to other workers, their silence was an act of resistance and evidence of a lack of commitment and failure to cooperate with the company.

Open protest occurred in response to company policies. When management took away a five minute clean-up period at the end of the day, workers responded with defiance. Team members also resisted by refusing to participate in company rituals such as exercises and team meetings in response to what they considered an unfair action by the company.

Direct confrontation with management was the response to unsuccessful open protest. Once the clean-up period was gone, workers refused management's request to work 'after the buzzer' (after the shift ended) to clean-up and put away tools. Even when management directly requested the team's assistance in this matter it was met with resistance at meetings and on the line. The group leader for our area called a special meeting of Team 1 and Team 2 to enlist their help in cleaning up after the buzzer. At the meeting several workers from both teams directly confronted the group leader. A worker from Team 1 said, "This is the kind of bullshit that brings in a union." A second remarked, "This place is getting too Japanese around here, pretty soon you will be asking us to donate our Saturdays." A worker from Team 2 told the group leader: "I'm not a volunteer." Members of both teams explained that clean-up involved more than simply unhooking a tool and putting it away. One worker had nine tools and had to cover all of the brake lines. Others attempted to convince the group leader that they used the five minutes to finish the process on which they were working. Team members argued that they used the time to catch up and get organized for the next day: "So our processes don't get screwed up." An overriding concern was that quality would suffer. As a group, they were adamant that they would not work after the buzzer.

On the following day, the line continued moving until the buzzer sounded. As it happened, I was so far behind on my station, that by the time the line stopped, I did not realize that the buzzer had sounded and I kept working. As two team members walked by they called to me "Laurie, don't do it." As I was leaving, I overheard our team leader ask another team member a question concerning work. He replied, "Look, it's after 3:00, I don't know," and he walked on by. From that day on, whenever the line ran up to quitting time, everyone on the team dropped whatever they were doing and immediately walked out leaving the team leader to lock up the tools and clean the area. At one team meeting the team leader complained that she had stayed almost an hour after work cleaning up and putting away tools. One team member replied, "You are crazy to do it and we aren't going to."

Another example of direct confrontation occurred when two workers from Team 1 turned down unscheduled overtime against management's expressed wishes. The company had posted a policy concerning overtime which stated that scheduled and emergency overtime were mandatory, but unscheduled overtime was not; therefore, team members had the right to refuse. After their refusal, the Human Resources office informed the team leader that those members would get an unexcused absence if they left at 3:00. This action by management caused a third team member and the team leader to threaten to leave in protest. The car manager's first response was to inform the team leader that leaving a moving line was grounds for firing. The four workers immediately seized what they saw as the moral high ground arguing that the new company policy lacked input and was unfairly instituted and that they were being disciplined for following company policy. When it appeared that their show of solidarity would be successful, and that if the four team members left it would shut down the line, management backed down. Later the company let the first two workers leave, without discipline. In return, the other two members agreed to stay.

A final example of collective resistance emerged as organized agitation during team and department meetings when workers banded together in a plant-wide effort to stop the company from instituting mandatory shift rotation. Management handed down the policy stating that it was "Not up for discussion." Everyone would rotate when the second shift was added. Through an informal communication network, workers passed the word around the plant to "keep the pressure on by bringing it up at meetings." Each time there was a department meeting and almost daily at team meetings, workers objected to the policy. Once again, they invoked the company's claim to fairness. Workers argued that rotating would disrupt their lives. Some stated that they wanted to enroll in classes, and this policy would prevent them from furthering their education and increasing their potential. Parents objected that it would be difficult to arrange day care and would interfere with family life. The agitation continued for weeks. Eventually, management changed its ruling and announced that there would be no shift rotation.

Conclusion

At SIA, workers used acts of resistance to 'negotiate' their position with the company. They turned the company's ideology of egalitarianism, its effort to create a culture of cooperation and its claim to be different from United States plants, to their own advantage to resist unfair company rules and policies. Their acts of resistance became righteous acts of indignation as they exposed the company's failure to play by its own rules. The workers' success in preventing mandatory shift rotation, their resistance to working unscheduled overtime, and their refusal to work after the buzzer exemplify how they used resistance to negotiate and cooperate on their own terms.

The emergence of informal, collective negotiations in a nonunion setting has historical precedent. The way in which SIA workers negotiated and turned management's ideology of egalitarianism into their own message is similar to Zahavi's (1983) findings in his historical case study of shoe workers at Endicott Johnson from 1920 to 1940. He describes how that management system consisted of a bond of mutual loyalty for both worker and management. Below the surface, however, workers used the company's policy of mutual loyalty to extract obligations from their employer (Zahavi, 1983). Their exploitation of corporate ideology was used as a means to benefit their own interests. Ultimately, Zahavi describes workers' loyalty was a "negotiated loyalty," whose real meaning was to be found in the behavior of the workers and not necessarily in management's formal proclamations.

At SIA, worker loyalty was expressed through their willingness to cooperate with management's demands. However, it was only through collective action that the balance of power tipped temporarily toward the worker. Ultimately, the acts of solidarity in which workers withheld cooperation, were their most successful means for winning concessions from management. Two forms of collective resistance were found to be particularly successful: direct action and organized agitation. Both were collective means of negotiating worker demands from a position of power.

When workers displayed their ability and willingness to act together, their widespread agitation became most effective. The strength of their position lay in the possibility that they might formalize their solidarity through union organization. A union would institutionalize this phenomenon and stabilize the negotiation process. It potentially provides formal access to worker control on the shop floor. These results raise a specter to management and a promise to workers that, even under participative, post-Fordism schemes, when the interests of workers are challenged, worker solidarity is a naturally occurring phenomenon.

Worker resistance evolved on the basis of collective grievances against management structures, which appeared initially positive, but produced substantially negative outcomes. This supports the contention that the Japanese model represents an extension of management control on the shop floor, rather than an increase in worker participation and autonomy. Based on these findings, the Japanese model heightens while attempting to disguise the exploitation of workers and thus reveals the true nature of post-Fordist production. In the end, the fundamental conflict between the interests of workers and that of management emerge in the Japanese transplant just as it does in the traditional Fordist plant.

The SIA case demonstrates that shop floor realities of post-Fordist production do not square with its more exaggerated claims. In the absence of an alternative locus of power and worker representation, however, new and evolving forms of worker exploitation and resistance will not in themselves lead to significant modification of the structural elements of the Japanese model. Until unionization of the work force takes place, post-Fordism's new and more subtle forms of hegemonic control are likely to reproduce exploitative social relations. The CAMI example shows that a militant union with an independent vision of work reorganization can set in motion a process that alters the balance of power within the factory by combining elements of adversarialism and cooperation in the interests of unionized workers (Rinehart, et al., this volume). In addition, the unionization of the Hyundai plant in Bromont, Canada is evidence that the North American transplants are not impregnable (Yanarella, "The UAW and CAW Under the Shadow of Post-Fordism," this volume).

Notes

* An earlier draft of this chapter appeared as: "Inside a Japanese Transplant: A Critical Perspective," *Work and Occupations* 20 (1993) 147–173.

‡ Comments and criticism by Peter Seybold and Earl Wysong were particularly helpful.

1. Acting as a participant, as well as an observer, involves the researcher in an active role in the research setting and assumes that the researcher's experiences will be similar to others. This study is undertaken with the awareness that one of the difficulties of this methodology is maintaining a balance between depth of involvement as an insider while continuing to observe from the outside.

2. Tact time was the amount of time that a worker is given to complete the job that they perform on each vehicle. It was the same throughout the plant.

3. In a typical American auto plant, workers maintain a 40- to 50-second-a-minute work pace, whereas Japanese auto plants tend to run close to 60 seconds a minute (Fucini and Fucini, 1990: 37).

UAW, Lean Production, and Labor-Management Relations at AutoAlliance*

Steve Babson

Japan's lean production system has been touted as a cure-all for American auto makers. In their best-selling book, _The Machine That Changed the World_, James Womack, Daniel Jones, and Daniel Roos, senior managers at MIT's International Motor Vehicle Project, say that Japanese auto plants are "lean," because management has slashed inventories, pared support staff, and replaced cumbersome factory hierarchies with self-directed work teams. By rotating jobs and sharing responsibilities, multiskilled workers can solve quality problems at their source and boost productivity. More important, these transformations make factory labor more appealing, even liberating, according to Womack, Jones, and Roos. Under lean production, the "freedom to control one's work" supposedly replaces the "mind-numbing stress" of mass production. Armed with "the skills they need to control their environment," workers in a lean production plant have the opportunity "to think actively, indeed _proactively_" to solve workplace problems. This "creative tension" makes work in a lean production factory "humanly fulfilling" (Womack, et al., 1990, 13–14, 99–102).

Freedom, creativity, and fulfillment may sound too good to be true, but nonbelievers will pause before calling these lean production gurus false prophets. The MIT study, funded by $5 million in contributions from the major auto makers and governments of Japan, the United States, and Europe, surveyed ninety assembly plants in seventeen countries. The editors of _Automotive News_ called it a study "of great understanding, and of hope. It shows how to create an industrial world in which workers share the challenges and satisfactions of the business" (_Automotive News_, 1991: 2).

Those who make less extravagant claims about lean production receive less press, but they raise important questions about the lean production's actual operation, particularly its impact on factory labor. What sort of autonomy is possible for workers in the tightly managed factory environment of lean production? Does the system's much-heralded drive for "continuous improvement" create an environment that is "humanly fulfilling," or perpetually stressful? And how variable are the system's characteristics? Above all, can it accommodate, or does it require, an independent union to achieve its emancipative claims (Klein, 1989, 1991; Marsh, 1992; and Parker and Slaughter, 1988)?

AutoAlliance, one of the lean producers cited by Womack, Jones and Roos, provides an opportunity to measure the MIT study against these questions. The results suggest that the emancipative potential of lean production has been misstated in at least two respects. First, in the eyes of American workers at the Mazda assembly plant in Flat Rock, Michigan, where the production system is lean, many see it as mean. Second, union intervention can redefine the meaning of lean production by challenging the system's potential for unilateral management control.[1]

When Mazda announced its plan in 1984 to build an assembly plant in southeastern Michigan, the UAW welcomed the new jobs it would bring to the state. The Flat Rock site twenty miles south of Detroit had previously been the home of the Ford Motor Company's Michigan Casting Center, and when Ford closed the casting plant in the recession year of 1982, the community had lost 5,000 jobs and 64 percent of its tax revenue. Mazda's plan to take over the site and build a modern assembly operation next to the old plant drew generous support from state and local governments, which underwrote the investment with $120 million in tax breaks and subsidies. Nearly 100,000 people applied for jobs when the doors opened in 1986, and while Mazda made no commitment to hire unemployed UAW members, the company did make it clear that it expected the union to represent its employees. The union won an uncontested representation election in 1987, and local officers appointed by the union began negotiating the first contract the following year. In this cooperative environment, with production still well below capacity, the union endorsed Mazda's participative management philosophy and signed a local agreement "based on mutual trust and good faith."[2]

But with the inauguration of two-shift production in 1988, labor relations became increasingly combative, marked by growing conflict between supervisors and workers over job loading and working conditions. Against this background, local-union politics had also become increasingly contentious. An opposition slate promising greater union militancy won the first local election in 1989, but in the fall of 1990, as the collective bargaining agreement's expiration date approached, the new incumbents had reason to wonder if the membership was prepared for a confrontation with management. While the election that spring had returned the militants to office, the contest for local president initially ended in a dead heat. Even the runoff election—won by a margin of only six votes— failed to generate much interest among the 1,000 members who did not bother to vote. At the other end of the spectrum was a militant core, representing roughly one-third of the membership, who favored fundamental change in the bargaining relationship. Yet even their resolve was in doubt as the economy dipped into recession in 1990 and the company made drastic cuts in the scheduled production of Mazda 626s, MX6s, and Ford Probes.

To get a detailed reading of the membership's mood and temper, the union conducted a survey that was unique in two respects. First, it not only gave respondents the opportunity to prioritize their demands for a new contract, as most bargaining surveys do, but also asked them to evaluate their work experience during three years of lean production. Second, instead of mailing the survey or printing it in the local newspaper in the hope some members would respond, it was distributed 'one-on-one' to every worker in the plant by union coordinators, the equivalent of stewards, who made a strong appeal for each member's participation. A one-day training session for coordinators, conducted by Wayne State University's Labor Studies Center, stressed the importance of collecting valid returns; badgering or preaching to respondents was discouraged as inimical to the union's need for a true reading of the members. After collecting 2,380 surveys from a plant population of approximately 2,800, the union had the returns processed by the Survey and Evaluation Service of Wayne State University's Center for Urban Studies.[3]

Discussion of these survey results is supplemented with observations drawn from informal conversations, classroom exchanges, and formal interviews with union officers, committee members, coordinators, and members. Their collective voice should give pause to the managers of MIT's International Motor Vehicle Project.

Words vs. Deeds

As indicated in Table 1, only one out of seven Mazda workers said they could consistently count on their supervisor, a 'Unit Leader,' to implement the company philosophy of participatory management. Of the 72 percent who answered "sometimes" or "rarely," many commented that the supervisor "plays favorites" or adhered to the company philosophy "only when it suits him." These perceptions of favoritism and opportunism could indicate 1) the company's failure to adequately train supervisors, 2) the unreasonable expectations of workers, or 3) the contradictory nature of the company's philosophy. As indicated below, the company's own newsletter acknowledges the first point. The second and third possibilities may both be rooted in the extravagant promises and murky language of the Mazda philosophy. In the employee handbook, the company promises to create a workplace "that promotes warm human relationships and comfortable working conditions"; its consensual decision-making process will achieve "corporate goals through management policies." But these oxymorons about "comfortable factories" and "consensus through management policies" have only disappointed and confused workers (Mazda Motor Manufacturing, 1987: A–3).

Table 1 Perception of Mazda Philosophy

"In terms of considering workers needs and interests, my Unit Leader can be trusted to implement the Mazda Philosophy."

Always: 14%

Sometimes: 44%

Rarely: 28%

Never: 14%

(Valid Cases: 2,186)

The expectation that lean production gives workers 'control' of their jobs has also disappointed Mazda workers, as indicated in Table 2. Each worker in the plant is required to follow a Programmed Work Sheet (PWS) that describes the job cycle in minute detail, including the specific tasks, their sequence, and the seconds allotted for each. The PWS is prominently posted near each work station; most allow a total cycle time of one or two minutes. Contrary to the impression left by the MIT study, these programmed jobs do not permit "the freedom to control one's work"—quite the opposite. The Management Rights clause in the collective bargaining agreement (Article V) establishes the company's exclusive right to "direct and control . . . the methods, processes and means of handling work." In practice, team members cannot alter their Programmed Work Sheets without supervisory approval, and casual deviation from the programmed job sequence is strongly discouraged. "Consistency is all important to quality," as the company newsletter, *New Horizons*, editorialized in a 1990 issue. "If you follow your PWS all the time, every day—regardless of how you feel—quality will follow suit" (*New Horizons*, 1990: 3).

At the same time, however, workers are expected to participate in a process of *kaizen* or "continuous improvement." *Kaizen* does not permit workers or their teams to unilaterally initiate change; rather, changes are the product of a structured process controlled by supervisors and plant engineers who screen proposals from Quality Circles and the suggestion program and then implement those deemed consistent with production goals. Even union militants acknowledge that this management controlled process could produce positive outcomes for workers during the plant's start-up. But once full production was reached in 1988, many began to reappraise the *kaizen* process. Increasingly, changes to the PWS originated with management and were imposed with little or no consultation, particularly the frequent adjustments in line balancing as the volume and model mix of Ford Probes and Mazdas changed. Since such rebalancing is a hallmark of lean production's flexibility, this perception of unilateral management control significantly contradicts the claims made by Womack, et al. (Mazda Motor Manufacturing, 1987: L–3).

Table 2 Program Work Sheet Changes

"My Program Work Sheet has been changed without my consultation."
Never: 20%
Once: 7%
Several times: 38%
Many: 35%
(Valid cases: 2,039)
"The changes made my job . . ."
Easier: 7%
Harder: 67%
No difference: 27%
(Percentages do not equal 100 because of rounding. Valid cases: 1,868)

Eventually, even management had to acknowledge the problem. In an unusually frank article entitled "Kaizen—Friend or Foe," the company newsletter reported the discussions between company President Masahiro Uchida and selected plant employees:

> One participant admitted that these same [management] people who are supposed to support the process are now commonly viewed as 'the enemy.' 'Every time we see someone from the front office, it seems that something negative results.' 'The more kaizen that came from up front, the worse it got. There was no membership participation or buy into the changes' (*New Horizons*, 1990: 3).

These remarks in the company newsletter are consistent with comments from the UAW survey: "No worker input on balancing"; "Changes usually eliminate people"; "Unit Leader pushing for bonus"; "Every time the line is rebalanced, work is added." In response, the company newsletter promised that Unit Leader training in motivational techniques and active listening is "in the works." But the question remains whether these negative appraisals of *kaizen* reflect the breakdown of participatory procedures—in which case supervisor training may have positive outcomes—or whether they reflect the inevitable consequence of a system which is supposed to intensify the workpace.

The second hypothesis is confirmed by Masaaki Imai, President of the Kaizen Institute of America who describes in the Institute's newsletter how Taichi Ohno, Toyota's founding practitioner of kaizen, gave his department managers only 90 percent of the manpower, space, and equipment needed for straight-time production. Each manager was then expected to implement *kaizen* until the department could meet its production targets without overtime. "As soon as a no-overtime equilibrium was met," Imai notes with approval, "Mr. Ohno would come in and would again remove 10 percent of the resources. His way of managing came to be known as the OH! NO! system!" (Imai, 1988–89).

The model articulated here is not one in which workers, as described in the MIT study, "control their environment" or "think actively, indeed proactively" to solve workplace problems. These workers, in contrast, are expected to think reactively to management initiatives. In this sense, their span of responsibility is wider than in a traditional mass production factory, but their span of control has not grown accordingly. *Kaizen* is supposed to decentralize decision-making, but in practice this delegation of authority enhances the power of line supervisors more so than production workers. What remains of worker initiative is tightly bound by 'front office' *kaizen* and by management's process controls, particularly the 'Just-in-Time' inventory system. Where the MIT study sees a "creative tension" that makes work "humanly fulfilling," many workers at Mazda experience tension, pure and simple. Consequently, Mike Parker and Jane Slaughter argue that lean production can actually become "management by stress," with supervisors purposefully pushing the system to its limits—and beyond—to ensure that "wasteful" buffers of inventory and workers are eliminated (Womack, et al. 1990: 99, 101; and Parker and Slaughter, 1988: 16–30).

From a different perspective, Professor Janice Klein of the Harvard Business School observes that *kaizen*'s "attack on waste . . . inevitably means more and more strictures on a worker's time and action." Measured against such regimentation, "our conventional Western notions of worker self-management are often sadly incompatible" (Klein, 1989: 4).

Gatekeepers

In these matters of power and control *The Machine that Changed the World* defers to platitudes. Rather than specify the actual opportunities for worker initiative in day-to-day operations, the authors say simply that lean production gives workers "the skills they need to control their environment," and little else. It is left for the reader to imagine those skills, how workers are trained, and who controls access to jobs and training.

Since job rotation is a hallmark of lean production, we have to assume that cross training of workers is applied across the board. Only then could workers circulate through the complete spectrum of team assignments, including the direct-labor tasks that add value to the product and non value-added duties such as robot servicing, housekeeping, record keeping, inspection, and repair. Cross trained workers, we are told, make lean production an especially flexible system, which permits the rapid redeployment of labor and, given the ability of these multiskilled workers to detect and correct problems at their source, minimizes the need for the specialized repair and support personnel who bloat the overhead costs of mass production. Job rotation also benefits workers, it is argued, by varying the work movements of each team member and reducing the likelihood of repetitive strain injuries.

In a traditional factory environment, management 'gatekeepers' control access to training, job assignments, and transfers, with only a union seniority agreement to regulate the process in organized plants. In the MIT model of lean production, on the other hand, the gatekeeper's role is preempted by the claim that access to training and job rotation is undifferentiated—that there is no room for exercising management discretion if such job training and rotation opportunities are universally available to all workers. Table 3 indicates, however, that nearly half of Mazda workers perceive training and job rotation as less than adequate or universal. Significantly, many who commented on the lack of job rotation explicitly drew attention to the power wielded by their supervisors: some unit leaders reportedly opposed any rotation, others restricted it to a two-job cycle, and others distributed easier jobs to favored employees. Some respondents also commented that the lack of cross training narrowed the range of job rotation and limited opportunities for voluntary overtime.

A common focus for such complaints was the job of robot operator. Access to these jobs is no small matter for workers in a modern auto plant, since robots play a prominent and much heralded role in the production process. At Mazda, some 300 robots are deployed throughout the plant, most of them concentrated in body welding and paint operations. In these departments, robot servicing requires the operator to start the machine and check flow rates, clean spray heads or change weld tips, realign the computer program as necessary,

Table 3 Job Training and Rotation

"Compared to Mazda's promises to train us, the actual training that I have received is . . ."

Excellent: 6%

Fair: 46%

Poor: 43%

None received: 5%

(Valid cases: 2,347)

"In my team, we rotate jobs fairly."

Yes: 52%

No: 48%

(Valid cases: 2,221)

conduct SPC analysis, and make periodic quality inspections. Compared to most direct-labor tasks, the work is less physically demanding, more skill intensive, and less monotonous, and all the more coveted by team members because it offers a considerable amount of voluntary overtime at time-and-a-half wages.

To guarantee all team members access to these favored jobs, the company agreed to a 1988 collective bargaining provision (Article XVI, Section 3 [3]) that all team members "must be trained to be able and capable of performing all jobs within the unit" by January 1, 1989. Soon after signing the agreement, however, the company told the union that this first-of-the-year deadline was "too ambitious a goal" and asked for a six-month extension. For the time being, training in robot servicing was deemed too specialized and too expensive to warrant universal instruction and, as a consequence, access to job rotation and voluntary overtime would be restricted to those few team members who had already received training.

The then-incumbent union leadership accepted the delay, but when the six-month deadline came and went, the company was still well short of its promise to cross train and rotate all team members. Some evidence suggests that training efforts actually got worse rather than better. Survey respondents in late 1990 frequently commented that the initial training during the plant's start-up period had been good, but it had subsequently declined: "New people don't get trained"; "Good at start, poor now"; "It's all OJT" (Walt, 1990).[4]

The outcome is a de facto specialization, 'robot operator,' that concentrates off-line work in a single job category, with management serving as the gatekeeper to these favored jobs. The emergence of this shadow classification has been partially obscured by the policy of training team leaders as robot operators. But where this was not possible, the team's robot operator has been promoted as a second 'team leader,' thereby qualifying the robot operator for the team leader's fifty-cent per hour pay premium. These leaders have no followers, but their added responsibilities as robot operators can only be compensated by this subterfuge in a plant which claims to have no specialized production classifications.

If management is the de facto gatekeeper for robot operator positions, it is the de jure gatekeeper for transfers. Management in a lean production plant may have particularly compelling reasons for limiting movement within the factory. Training costs are significant in a lean production plant precisely because team members are expected to rotate through many, if not all, jobs. Consequently, the cost is greater for retraining workers who transfer from one operation to another. The new team member has to learn not just a new job, but a half-dozen new jobs. Mazda therefore insisted in its 1988 negotiations with Local 3000 that seniority-based transfers be limited to only two per department per month, with all applications above that number left exclusively to management discretion. Since transfer applications between departments can only occur when there are no intradepartmental applicants for an opening, it is very difficult for team members to cross departmental lines by seniority bidding. In almost all cases, the gatekeeper who controls such transfers is a manager.

Restrictions on seniority rights may reduce the company's training costs, but they also restrict the Mazda worker's freedom to seek alternative jobs within the plant. Company rules and publicity releases might persuade the casual observer that lean production provides workers "with the skills they need to control their environment," but the actual practice at Mazda has permitted management gatekeepers to modify these principles with measured doses of specialization.

Work Intensity

According to the MIT study, lean production requires "half the human effort in the factory" compared to traditional mass production. From the managerial perspective of the International Motor Vehicle Project, this appears to be true. After all, the aim of *kaizen* is to eliminate wasted motion and fill idle time, and it should therefore be possible to produce a given output with fewer workers. But from the perspective of the individual Mazda worker, lean production and continuous improvement demand more effort, not less. As indicated in Table 4, three of four survey respondents reported their workload as heavy, and one in four reported difficulty in keeping pace.

Asked if they could sustain the present work intensity, three of four said they would be injured or worn out before they reached retirement. The survey results are internally consistent and leave little doubt that in the somewhat ambiguous phrasing "heavy but acceptable" workload, "heavy" was taken as the dominant adjective, not "acceptable." In Table 5, which cross tabulates the two questions, two-thirds of those who said their job was properly balanced believed they could sustain their work pace to retirement without injury or mishap. In

Table 4 Workload and Health

"My workload is . . ."
Properly balanced: 26%
Heavy but acceptable: 50%
Too heavy, I can hardly keep up: 24%
(Valid cases: 2,185)
"If the present level of work intensity continues . . ."
I can stay healthy and make it to retirement: 27%
I will likely be injured or worn out before I retire: 73%
(Valid cases: 2,186)

Table 5 Health by Workload

Health if Work Level Continues	Workload Properly Balanced	Heavy, but Acceptable	Too Heavy, Can Hardly Keep Up	
Stay Healthy	346 / 63%	202 / 19%	22 / 4%	570 27%
Injured, Worn Out	203 / 37%	852 / 81%	492 / 96%	1,547 73%
	549 26%	1,054 50%	514 24%	2,117 100%

Chi-square = 529.82 DF = 2 Gamma = .795
(Missing cases: 118)

contrast, those who said their workload was "heavy but acceptable" clearly meant the heavy work pace was "acceptable" only in the short run: 81 percent thought they could not sustain their current work intensity to retirement. Statistical measures (i.e., a Gamma of .795) indicate a very strong association between perceptions of a heavy workload and expectations of injury or burn out.

There is corroborating evidence for this widely held belief that Mazda's work pace is unhealthy. According to a detailed study of Michigan's workers compensation records conducted by the *Detroit Free Press*, Mazda's rate of serious injuries, those resulting in loss of limb or function, or requiring at least seven days lost work, was triple the rate for GM and Ford in 1988 (*Detroit Free Press*, 1990: 2).[5] At 4.1 injuries per 100 workers, Mazda's rate was also higher than every size category of the 6,550 supplier plants in Michigan. These comparisons may warrant some qualification. Small suppliers probably underreport injuries, and Mazda's relatively inexperienced workers may have been more prone to accidents in the plant's first year of full production. Still UAW leaders insist that Mazda also underreports injuries, and that the lower average age of those injured, 32 years vs. 41 in the Big Three, should reduce their recovery time. The sheer magnitude of the gulf between injury rates at Mazda and the Big Three also makes it difficult to dismiss the evidence that, compared to mass production, lean production is at least as dangerous to the health and safety of production workers, if not more so.

Whose Team?

These issues of safety, workload, and participation have a direct impact on the relationship between team members and team leaders. The team leaders occupy a strategic border between workers and management in a lean production plant. At Mazda they are nonsupervisory hourly workers, but their responsibilities for record keeping, scheduling, and problem solving straddle the routine tasks of a line foreman. Team leaders monitor quality and have the authority, if serious problems arise, to stop the assembly line by pulling a red cord. They monitor parts inventory and call for resupply. They train new team members in entry level tasks, and are on-call to help if a team member pulls the yellow 'assist' cord near each work station. Since there is no 'utility' work force to cover absenteeism and spot relief, as there is in the traditional mass production plant, the team leader is also expected to fill in for members who are sick or have to leave the line. For all these additional responsibilities they receive a fifty-cent per hour pay premium. The job is stressful, but as one of the few promotion opportunities in the plant, it is prized by many.

The initial agreement between Mazda and the UAW specified a procedure for selecting team leaders that combined seniority with an evaluation process dominated by supervisors (Article XI, Section 6). The company and the union negotiated the criteria, including attendance record, knowledge of team tasks, and participation in quality circles and a point scale for unit leaders to apply to each candidate they interviewed in seniority order with the position going to the first candidate whose rating exceeded a specified minimum point value.

Incumbent team leaders in the supervisor's unit participated in the interview process along with a worker appointed by each applicant. As hourly workers and UAW members, team leaders who participated in this evaluation process could (in theory) serve as guardians of their fellow workers' interests, preventing unit leaders from dominating the proceedings. In practice, they often failed in this role—at least in the eyes of their co-workers. Since incumbent team leaders owed their position to the unit leader's positive assessment of their worth, many apparently deferred to this supervisor when it came time to evaluate team leader applicants. According to union critics of management, when the unit leader did not want a particular candidate to get the job, the applicant inevitably received fewer points than the necessary minimum. Here again, the ultimate gatekeeper controlling access to promotional opportunities was a supervisor.

Consequently, many workers perceived team leaders as junior foremen who served the supervisor, not the team. This impression was reinforced as unit leaders unofficially transferred certain supervisory tasks to trusted team leaders: passing out paychecks, taking attendance, and offering overtime. Team membership resentment of these privileged co-workers was amplified if the team leader was also perceived as a 'screw off'—hogging the easiest jobs, failing to help when problems arose, and leaving the work area. Finally, since many team leaders had first shot at robot training, they also benefited as the 'able and capable' workers who accrued more voluntary overtime.

Table 6 Team Leader Selection

"Team Leaders should be chosen according to . . ."

Present system: 16%

Election: 48%

Rotation: 14%

Seniority: 16%

Other: 7%

(Percentages do not equal 100 because of rounding. Valid cases: 2,244)

For all these reasons, 84 percent of those surveyed (see Table 6) favored alternative team leader selection procedures that removed the unit leader from the process. Significantly, those respondents who reported a heavy workload or a high expectation of injury and burn-out were even more inclined to favor changes in the selection process. Tables 7 and 8 cross tabulate these variables. While only 24 percent of those who indicated their jobs were properly balanced wished to retain the status quo, support for the present system fell to just 9 percent of those who indicated their workload was too heavy. Likewise, while 28 percent of those who expected to stay healthy favored the status quo, support fell to only 11 percent among those who expected to be injured or worn out. This moderate to strong association (.353 and .514) between perceived working conditions and preferred selection process indicates that some members held their team leader at least partially responsible for the intense pace of lean production. They therefore favored a selection process that would make their leaders answerable to the team rather than the supervisor.

Table 7 Workload and Team Leader Satisfaction

Team Leader Selection	Workload Properly Balanced	Heavy, but Acceptable	Too Heavy, Can Hardly Keep Up	
Present System	132 / 24%	147 / 14%	42 / 9%	321 16%
Change System	415 / 76%	888 / 86%	447 / 91%	1,750 85%
	547 26%	1,035 50%	489 24%	2,071 100%

Chi-square = 50.28 DF = 2 Gamma = .353
(Percentages do not equal 100 because of rounding. Missing cases: 309)

Table 8 Expectations of Injury and Team Leader Selection

Team Leader Selection	Expectations of Injury		
	Stay Health	Injured, Worn Out	
Present System	156 / 28%	174 / 11%	330 15%
Change System	405 / 72%	1,406 / 89%	1,811 85%
	561 26%	1,580 74%	2,141 100%

Chi-square = 89.57DF = 1Gamma = .514
(Missing cases: 239)

Most workers also favored strike action as a final means of dispute resolution. Here especially, the gap between stated principles and actual perceptions is glaring. Participatory decision-making, consensus norms, and team dynamics are supposed to reduce the range and intensity of adversarial relations in a lean production plant, and most new hires probably believed such harmony would prevail at Mazda. But after several years' experience, UAW members came to perceive strike action, or the threat of it, as the necessary means for holding management accountable. As indicated in Table 9, nine of ten respondents favored the right to strike over health and safety, work standards, or both. In fact, 21 percent even favored the right to strike over quality issues.

Any doubt that workers took these issues seriously was dispelled in February of 1991 when the members of UAW Local 3000 conducted a strike

Table 9 Strike Support

"To protect our rights during the contract, our members need the right to strike (indicate one or more) . . ."

		Cumulative
On health and safety issues only:	17%	17%
On work standard issues only:	15	32
On both issues:	60	91
Neither:	9	100

(Percentages do not equal 91 because of rounding. Valid cases: 2,220)

authorization vote. To maximize turnout, union officers and coordinators conducted the voting inside the plant. The results were decisive: 2,712 members voted and 94 percent favored strike authorization. Managers who might otherwise have questioned these totals had only to watch the gathering enthusiasm as coordinators distributed blue and yellow stickers with the slogan "Fighting for a Better Contract." Worn on helmets and uniform shirts in violation of the dress code, the stickers gave visual testimony that the membership supported fundamental changes in Mazda's lean production system (UAW Local Union 3000, 1991a; and Lippert, 1991: 1).

A New Agreement

The negotiations that followed were prolonged and acrimonious, but eleventh hour bargaining produced a tentative agreement in March, 1991, and members subsequently ratified the contract by a vote of 2,102 to 433. The media focused on the union's success in achieving parity with Big Three wages and benefits. Equally important, however, were the amendments to Mazda's lean production system. Among these, five deserve special attention in light of the previous discussion (UAW Local Union 3000, 1991b).

First, the new agreement establishes a Temporary Assignment Pool for workers whose jobs are eliminated by *kaizen*, new technology, model changes, production cutbacks, and other events initiated by the company. Where management had been able to reassign such workers without restriction, the new agreement holds them in the TAP pool to cover unscheduled absenteeism as well as to fill the jobs of those workers receiving additional training. Teams will no longer have to 'make do' with reduced labor power when a member is absent, so long as there are workers in the Temporary Assignment Pool. But this last qualification is significant, because any rise in production levels will drain the TAP pool.

Second, the contract mandates additional training to upgrade workers and make them 'able and capable' of performing all the jobs in their unit, including robot servicing. As before, voluntary overtime has to be offered first to the worker with the least accumulated overtime hours; but if the worker isn't able and capable, the company now is contractually obligated to give both the low-hour worker and the truly able and capable worker the overtime assignment with the latter brought in to train the former. Another new provision penalizes the company if the spread between the low-hour worker and the able and capable worker exceeds eighty-four hours, with the liability paid into a newly created Unit Training Fund earmarked for upgrading workers.

Third, the contract doubles the number of monthly transfers per department that management is obligated to fill by seniority. The jump from two to four widens transfer opportunities, but still leaves all transfers above this number to management's discretion.

Fourth, the new contract expands union representation and establishes joint committees on health and safety, training, and equal opportunity. The number of District Committeepersons, or grievance handlers, grows from seven to ten; a health and safety representative is added for the second shift; and a new ergonomics representative is mandated. The contract also establishes a 'Consensus Process' that borrows heavily from language in the UAW-Saturn agreement: "Any one of the parties on the committee may block a potential decision. However, it is understood that the party blocking the decision must search for alternative solutions (Collective Bargaining Agreement Between Mazda Motor Manufacturing (USA) and . . . [UAW] Local 3000, 1991–1994: 87. While establishing veto rights for union representatives, this language applies only to the specific concerns of the joint committees and the Quality Circles, not, as at Saturn, to the wider spectrum of plant issues.

Finally, team leaders will henceforth be subject to recall and election by team members. The new process includes some reasonable restrictions on the democratic process, including minimum criteria for eligible candidates, i.e., good attendance. Incumbents are initially grandfathered into their positions, but every six months they, as well as those elected to subsequent openings, will be subject to recall if two-thirds of the team petitions for their removal. The contract also specifies that team leaders are not to take attendance, offer overtime, or distribute paychecks. In short, rather than serve their supervisor as junior foremen, they are to serve their teams as leaders, trainers, and utility-relief workers. Since those who stray from this definition of their role risk losing the support of their team, the new election-recall process puts significant pressure on wayward team leaders to change their behavior. When the threat fails, the real thing can happen: in the first round of recall petitions in September, 1991, team members gathered the necessary two-thirds support for removing their leader in thirty-three of the plant's 257 teams, 13 percent of the total (UAW Local Union 3000, 1991c).

Worker Commitment

Increased training, transfer rights, and empowerment of team members may enhance employee commitment to efficient operations. If, however these contract improvements are overwhelmed by a further polarization of labor relations, then worker commitment to company goals will prove all the more elusive.

How the company wins worker commitment is no small matter, for in the estimate of Womack, et al., the lean production system does not work without it. In their words, "to make a lean system with no slack—no safety net—work at all, it is essential that every worker try very hard." This dependence on worker commitment is "why lean production is unlikely to prove more oppressive than mass production. Simply put, lean production is *fragile*." A wrong move by management, and "no one takes initiative and responsibility to continually improve the system" (Womack, et al., 1990: 102–103).

But how does lean production actually inspire such commitment? The MIT study says only that management must abide by "reciprocal obligations," including the job security that Japanese companies provide for permanent employees in their main factories. What Womack, et al. ignore is the range of social controls that reward loyal employees and punish uncommitted workers in a Japanese auto plant. In Mazda's Hiroshima and Hofu factories, little more than half of a worker's annual income is paid in the form of seniority-defined base wages: the balance is contingent on the performance of the individual worker, of his (rarely her) work group, and of the company. Group production bonuses, individual capability indexes, semiannual profit sharing, and merit pay all effectively subordinate the worker to company goals, particularly when the foreman's merit rating also determines a worker's access to training, transfers, and promotions. Consequently, Japanese workers who do not 'volunteer' for unpaid time in the Quality Circle or who fail to meet the expected quota of suggestions pay a heavy price for their lack of "commitment." Combined with company-controlled housing and enterprise unions, these social controls make the Japanese system far less vulnerable to a mass withdrawal of commitment than Womack, et al. would suggest. Put bluntly, Japan's lean production system has the potential to be more oppressive than mass production, but still generate *obedience* with a system of performance/merit pay that punishes 'slackers.'⁶

Obedience, it should be stressed, is not the kind of voluntary commitment MIT invokes in its sanitized sketch of lean production. Moreover, the social controls that obligate worker commitment in Japan cannot be transferred to North America. While 'corporate welfare' plans proliferated in the United States before 1929 and even served as a model for Japan's developing industries, contemporary support for such programs is equivocal. Company housing has little appeal in the United States or Canada, and the Japanese variant of enterprise unionism, dominated, as it is, by foremen, violates labor law in both countries. The acceptable range of contingent pay, including bonuses, incentives, and merit is growing in the United States and Canada, but still falls well short of Japanese norms. The 'positive rights' protected by statute (EEOC, ERISA, and OSHA) and popular movements in America further restrict the appeal of untrammeled paternalism.⁷ In a North American variant of lean production, worker commitment must stem from a different constellation of supporting institutions. In the auto industry, two approaches characterize current practice.

Most Japanese transplants pursue a nonunion option. They locate their greenfield operations in semirural economies where labor and civil rights are weakly defended. They staff their expanding operations with young workers who are carefully screened for attitudes compatible with company goals. They pay wages and benefits that, even if less than Big Three standards, still surpass local alternatives. The result is a work force that is largely immune to union organization, at least in the short term. So long as operations are expanding, even the most disgruntled worker has reason to support the system: outside alternatives are bleak, and new jobs within the company give hope for improvement. So long as workers are young, the true costs of healthcare and pension benefits are postponed, and the potential of future burnout is less credible than the current rewards of hard labor (Jackson, 1990: 2; and Chappell, 1989: 3, 49).[8]

Even under these circumstances, however, one-third of the workers at Nissan's Smyrna, Tennessee, plant voted for UAW representation in 1989. Many observers regard that outcome as the definitive rebuke to union aspirations within the growing nonunion transplant sector. But the near-term stability within the nonunion sector cannot be so easily extrapolated into the future. Older workers will demand easier jobs and place a heavier burden on benefit costs; if sales plateau or falter, plant budgets will tighten all the more, and promotion/transfer options will disappear. Viewed from this perspective, the Nissan vote in 1989, rather than ending the matter, will look more like the Ford Motor Company's defeat of the Industrial Workers of the World in 1913. The $5 day was then the 'permanent' solution to labor turnover and union organization; some thirty years later, the UAW had organized Ford.[9]

The union version of lean production could be the mirror image of the nonunion variant: unstable in the near term, but more durable over the long haul. Instability is especially notable at Mazda, where conflict has taken the form of work-to-rules, boycotts of the suggestion program, group grievances, and in-plant demonstrations. Organized protest at other unionized transplants is more muted, but focuses on the same issues of work intensity, burnout, and management control. The outcome of these struggles cannot be easily predicted, but conflict and dialogue could produce negotiated outcomes based on real participation and democracy: joint decision-making rather than pro forma consultation; extension of the 'Consensus Process' to the widest possible array of plant issues; election and recall of team leaders; and negotiation of resources and discretionary buffers controlled by teams.[10]

How Do We Get There?

The emancipative potential of lean production is easy to invoke in the abstract, but difficult to specify in concrete terms. Inevitably, efforts to maximize worker rights collide with efforts to maximize return on investment; compromise can mitigate conflict, but cannot eliminate the irreducible antagonism between these contending positions. Specifying the future of lean production requires, therefore, a detailed indication of how power is distributed and conflict regulated.

MIT's International Motor Vehicle Project has an easier solution: the future of lean production has already been realized in North America, and we need go no further than the Ford Motor Company to measure its bounty. According to Womack, et al., Ford, "the originator of mass production seventy-five years ago," has levels of productivity and quality practically the same as Japanese lean producers in North America. Since lean production generates good results in productivity and quality, and since Ford has these same results, Ford must therefore be a lean producer (Womack, et al., 1990: 86).

This self-serving logic is camouflaged with a thin veil of anecdotal evidence. According to the study's authors, the Ford plants they visited had collective bargaining agreements that:

> had not been changed since 1938, when Ford was finally forced to sign a job control contract with the UAW . . . . Yet, as we walked through plant after plant we observed that teamwork was alive and well. Workers were ignoring the technical details of the contract on a massive scale in order to cooperate and get the job done (Womack, et al., 1990: 99–100).

For a study that heralds its own "rigorous research methods," this is remarkably weak. The historical allusion is not to be believed: the first UAW-Ford agreement was in 1941, not 1938, and with only a few dozen paragraphs of contract language it was far removed from the multivolume 'job control' contract that later evolved. The claim that follows this ahistorical passage is equally hard to accept: MIT's researchers walked through *undesignated* factories and saw *unspecified* workers ignoring *unnamed* technical details to complete *unidentified* jobs. This simply doesn't qualify as legitimate evidence. Nor does it square with the testimony of industry observers who report no 'massive' repudiation of the contract, but instead ascribe Ford's success in the mid-1980s to unusually high levels of capacity utilization, among other factors.[11]

What if MIT's researchers took yet another factory tour, this time through the Mazda plant in Flat Rock? Would they see a lean workplace, worthy of emulation, or would the factory now appear too buffered and contentious to qualify? In either case, the senior managers of the International Motor Vehicle Project face a dilemma. If they believe Mazda is still moving towards lean production in its Flat Rock factory, then they have to acknowledge that adversarial bargaining conducted by a militant union is a possible—and perhaps a necessary—feature of a system that promises workers control and human fulfillment. But if they see a factory moving away from lean production, then they have to acknowledge that it was the workers who decided Mazda was too mean to remain lean.

Notes

* An earlier draft of this chapter appeared as "Lean or Mean: The MIT Model and Lean Production at Mazda," *Labor Studies Journal*, 44 (1993) 3–24.

1. Mazda became a lean producer after the mid-1970s when the Sumitomo group insisted that the troubled company "remake itself in the image of Toyota City" (Womack, et al., 1990: 68, 237). The Flat Rock factory is modeled after Mazda's plant in Hofu near Hiroshima. See Fucini and Fucini, 1990: 20–21.

2. For a summary of the plant's history and contentious labor relations, see Fucini and Fucini, 1990; Hill, et al., 1989; Chappell, 1990; Paterson, 1990; Flint, 1989; and Zellner, 1989.

3. There are seventy coordinators at Mazda, each responsible for roughly forty workers. Given the high rate of survey collections, the returns are treated as a population.

4. For background information on this dispute, particularly as it relates to overtime equalization, see Walt, 1990.

5. Changes in state law make these records unavailable for subsequent years. Mazda reported continued high levels of cumulative trauma injuries in 1989, but claimed its ergonomics program reduced such injuries by 38 percent in 1990 and 14 percent in 1991. Union officials say the drop reflects management efforts to intimidate and punish workers who report their injuries. See Pinto, 1991.

6. My thanks to Professor Shozo Inouye of the University of Hiroshima for sharing his insights on the Mazda pay system. See: Masami, 1985; Koshiro, 1983; Nevins, 1984; and Wilkinson and Oliver, 1989. Inagami, 1985, measures the continuing role of seniority wages in Japan and the growing emphasis since the 1960s on merit evaluations and pay.

7. Florida and Kenney, 1991, focus on the successful transfer of teamwork, job rotation, kaizen, and functional flexibility by Japanese transplants to their American operations, and correctly conclude that these attributes of lean production depend on organizational support rather than culture. While they recognize the absence in the United States transplants of performance/merit pay systems, they ignore the parallel absence of enterprise unions, company housing, and other features of Japanese corporate paternalism. On the role of United States corporate welfare plans as a model for Japanese industry in the 1920s, see Garon, 1987: 170–171.

8. For a generally sympathetic account of the Honda, Nissan, and Toyota transplants, see Gelsanliter, 1990. For a contrary opinion, see Junkerman, 1988.

9. For a participant-observer's account of worker resistance inside the nonunion Subaru-Isuzu plant in Lafayette, Indiana, see Graham, this volume.

10. For a review of worker concerns expressed in longitudinal survey-interviews conducted at the GM-Suzuki plant in Ontario, see Rinehart, Robertson, and Huxley, this volume. For suggestive accounts of what negotiated outcomes might look like and what impact they might have on economic competitiveness, see Cooke, 1990; and Turner, 1992.

11. Research by Daniel Luria, Program Manager at Michigan's Industrial Technology Institute, indicates that the largest identifiable determinant of superior plant productivity as measured by labor hours per car in the 1980s was capacity utilization. In analyzing twenty selected North American assembly plants, both Big Three and Japanese transplants, where labor hours per car varied from nineteen to sixty, and holding constant differences in model size and complexity, differences in capacity utilization accounted for 41 percent of the variance while traditional vs. modern work organization

accounted for 23 percent. At the time of the MIT study, 'modern operating agreements' had been negotiated at only a handful of Ford plants, including the body assembly operation at the Wayne Escort plant which ranked fifth in the ITI productivity rating, but not the Dearborn/Mustang plant which ranked third (Luria, 1990). What was common across all Ford plants in these years was extremely high capacity utilization reaching 120 percent in 1988. See Versical, 1988.

CAW, Worker Commitment, and Labor Management Relations Under Lean Production at CAMI*

James Rinehart, David Robertson, Christopher Huxley, and _____ the CAW Research Team on CAMI

Cooperative labor-management relations have become a hallmark of con-temporary Japanese industrial relations and are often cited as a key factor under-lying the remarkable performance of that country's economy, and especially its automobile companies. Cooperation is reflected by the low incidence of strikes, and by data on the diligence of workers showing that the Japanese labor force logs substantially more hours of work per year than workers in other industrial-ized nations. There is less agreement on the reasons for these cooperative labor-management relations.

Supporters view worker commitment and cooperation as voluntary, an attitude nurtured by the special character of Japanese organizational structures and management practices.[1] This corporate environment supposedly features employment guarantees, housing and welfare programs, worker participation, multiskilling, and the reunification of the conceptualization and execution of work (Kenney and Florida, 1988; Lincoln and Kalleberg, 1990; and Womack, Roos, and Jones, 1990).

The critics attribute Japan's peaceful industrial climate to an organization-al milieu that has created compliance rather than voluntary cooperation among workers. Individualized wage payment systems enable management to reward cooperative workers and penalize uncooperative ones, including those who refuse overtime and involvement in Quality Control (QC) circles. More impor-tant, enterprise unionism leaves workers without an effective collective force to challenge management prerogatives and demands (Clarke, 1990; Dohse, Jurgens, and Malsch, 1985; Kamata, 1982; Okayama, 1987; and Turnbull, 1988).[2]

Despite weaker or nonexistent employment guarantees in Japan and the absence of individualized remuneration, Japanese auto transplants and joint ventures in North America have been notably strike free. While it is true that most transplants operate without unions, the aura of high trust that surrounds transplants has been reinforced by reports on the New United Motor Manufacturing (NUMMI) plant, a unionized joint venture of General Motors (GM) and Toyota in Fremont, California. NUMMI, whose production and management systems are patterned after Toyota, has been praised for turning a trouble-plagued car plant into a model of efficient production and conflict free labor-management relations (Adler, 1993; Brown and Reich, 1989; and Shimada and MacDuffie, 1987).

Florida and Kenney's (1991) research on transplants makes the more far reaching claim that with few modifications, the system of Japanese production management (JPM), along with enlightened personnel policies, has been successfully diffused to transplants, unionized and nonunionized alike.[3] The media, especially influential trade journals like *Automotive News*, have applauded the efficiency and consensual labor relations of Japanese companies and their North American offspring. Dissident views, like Parker and Slaughter's (1988) critical analysis of the team concept, are sometimes noted, but JPM, or in the words of Womack, Roos, and Jones (1990), lean production, is consistently portrayed not only as a worthwhile but a necessary model for restoring industrial competitiveness.

In light of these generally benign images of transplants, the five week strike in the Fall of 1992 at CAMI, a unionized Suzuki-GM auto assembly plant in Ingersoll, Ontario, is of particular interest.[4] This action by members of Local 88 of the Canadian Auto Workers (CAW) union assumed historic significance since it was the first time a transplant or joint venture in North America had experienced a work stoppage. The strike attracted considerable media interest not only because it was undertaken in the midst of Canada's deepest recession since the 1930s, but also because it raised questions about an emerging form of workplace organization whose immunity to overt conflict had been taken for granted.

This chapter examines CAMI's efforts to construct a workplace characterized by worker commitment and cooperative labor-management relations and offers an explanation of why these efforts failed. The discussion then focuses on the question of CAMI exceptionalism. Why, of all the North American transplants, did CAMI experience labor-management conflict? Is CAMI an aberration?

The CAW Research Group on CAMI

The findings and arguments presented here are part of a broader project initiated by the Research Department of the CAW. The CAW Research Group on CAMI brought together two union research staffers, two academics, and three union committee persons to monitor, over time, a production and management system with which the union had little direct experience but many concerns.[5]

In contrast to previous studies, such as the those sponsored by the Massachusetts Institute of Technology (MIT) based International Motor Vehicle Research Program (Womack, Roos, and Jones, 1990), the research focused on the organization of work and social relations on the shop floor. The Research Group explicitly set out to address a set of worker-relevant questions whose answers had been largely assumed in research undertaken by the MIT group. For example, what price, if any, do workers pay for whatever competitive advantages are enjoyed by lean production firms? And what is the role of an independent union under a lean production system?

To answer these questions, the CAW national leadership and CAMI management agreement granted the CAW Research Group access to the plant and the work force during working hours.[6] The researchers spent one full week at the plant at four regular intervals over a two year period in 1990 and 1991. At each visit the researchers conducted forty-five minute interviews with a randomly drawn sample of 100 workers. For various reasons (turnover, injuries, promotions to team leader) some of the original members of the worker sample had to be replaced. Consequently, comparisons across time drew upon the responses of persons who were interviewed in all four rounds, as well as the responses of those who were interviewed only in the final three rounds. The interview schedules consisted of fixed-choice and open-ended questions.

The CAW researchers also conducted open-ended, taped interviews with team leaders, the skilled tradespersons, union representatives, and managers from all levels of the organization. While the same workers were interviewed each time (with the exception of drop-outs and replacements), the other interviewees were not always the same persons. All interviews were done on company premises and most on company time.

Finally, the research group tracked changes in the labor process over a two year period by carrying out repeated observations of selected work stations on the shop floor. Technology, job content, line speed, work loads were recorded, and researchers talked to team leaders and workers on the job. In sum, this was the first study of a Japanese or joint venture plant in North America to draw systematic information from a randomly selected sample of workers and to have had such unrestricted access to the shop floor.

Constructing Consent

The initial agreement between CAMI and Local 88 of the CAW was prefaced by the assurance that it was "negotiated and will be administered in the spirit of mutual trust and in support of CAMI's values." CAMI went to considerable lengths to construct a high trust workplace. The protracted recruitment process was highly selective (about 2,300 people were hired from some 43,000 applicants).[7] The orientation training, referred to as *nagare*, given during the newly recruited workers' first week at the plant, was heavily loaded with ideological content.[8] Workers were taught that their ideas would be valued, that they would have the chance to develop their abilities and that they would receive fair and respectful treatment. They also learned about CAMI's values— empowerment, *kaizen*, open communications, and team spirit. Each of these values was related to the goal of developing a loyal and diligent work force.

CAMI is a team concept plant. At the most general level, team concept refers to a collaborative partnership between management and workers. In CAMI's view everyone from the company president to the worker on the line is part of one big team, partners pulling together to beat the competition. This image is reinforced by the absence of time clocks, reserved parking spaces, and executive cafeterias. All workers wear similar uniforms with first name labels above the pocket. There is no category of employees called workers. Hourly paid personnel who work on the shop floor are known as production associates, team leaders, or maintenance associates. All are members of the same bargaining unit.

All workers are organized into teams under the coordination of team leaders. On an everyday basis teams are the medium in which workers' attitudes and activities are shaped. Each team has a space for meetings and breaks. Team members are encouraged to adopt team names, to do *taiso* (preshift calisthenics), to pass on their improvement (*kaizen*) ideas to team leaders and submit *teians* (suggestions) and to form QC circles that issue proposals for reducing costs. Ideally teams are repositories of CAMI culture, but even if workers are not committed to company values, peer pressure within the team can operate to boost attendance, job performance, and *kaizen* activities.

Teams at CAMI have various production-related functions. Teams provide a vehicle for training and job rotation and absorb indirect duties (housekeeping, some material handling, minor maintenance, and inspection) performed in traditional auto plants by special categories of workers. Nevertheless, it is socio-cultural rather than technical considerations—the objective of manufacturing compliance and consent—that lie behind the corporate construction of work teams. Work at CAMI is not, for the most part, a team based production system but a system of teams superimposed on a traditional assembly line operation in which output is based on the individual efforts of each worker carrying out standardized jobs. The team can support and reinforce individual effort, but for most jobs at CAMI the individual has not been supplanted by the team as the operative unit of production. Teams at CAMI are more an expression of social engineering than of a fundamentally new system of production.

The Elusiveness of Consent: Survey Responses

How successful has CAMI been in selecting and developing a work force dedicated to the company and its values? Survey respondents were asked a series of questions to ascertain their evaluation of and commitment to policies and practices associated with key company values that purportedly distinguish CAMI from traditional workplaces and establish the framework for cooperative labor-management relations.

Open-ended responses revealed that the broad definition of the team concept—CAMI as one big team—had little meaning to most workers on the shop floor. Team concept meant neither equality of all employees nor partnership with management, and the CAMI value of team spirit increasingly was regarded as little more than an empty slogan. For most workers team concept had a concrete referent that signified where, and with whom, they worked day after day. That workers did not subscribe to the company's idea of partnership also was indicated by their distrust of management. When asked, "Do you think management at CAMI would 'put one over' on workers if they had the chance," 80 percent of respondents in round one and 98 percent in the final round answered "yes." And when the sample initially was asked if a union was needed at CAMI, "because no matter how cooperative the relationship there will always be differences between workers and management," 57 percent "strongly agreed" and 41 percent "agreed." With each round a growing proportion of workers "strongly agreed" that a union was needed, and by round two and thereafter no one disagreed about the need for a union. In the final round 81 percent "strongly agreed" and 19 percent "agreed" that a union was necessary.

Figures 1 through 4 show the changes in worker attitudes about CAMI and its values. These figures reveal two salient points. First, a substantial minority, and in some cases a majority, of respondents exhibited skepticism about CAMI's values and practices. Second, with each subsequent interview this skepticism was expressed by a growing proportion of workers. By the final round at the end of 1991, nearly 90 percent of the sample viewed CAMI as no different from other companies; over 90 percent felt common cafeterias, uniforms, and parking areas were smoke screens that masked differences in power; almost three-quarters regarded CAMI as undemocratic; and over 80 percent viewed it as competitive and stressful.

To provide an overall picture of how successful CAMI has been in transmitting its philosophy and developing a loyal work force, a commitment index was constructed based on respondents' answers to seven questions.[9] From these responses three categories of workers were distinguished. Those who scored high on the index believed in CAMI values and were dedicated to the company and its objectives. Respondents who scored in the middle range held both positive and negative opinions of the company. Those who scored low on the index

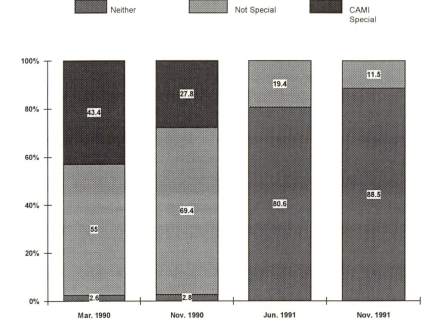

Legend: Neither | Not Special | CAMI Special

Mar. 1990: 2.6, 55, 43.4
Nov. 1990: 2.8, 69.4, 27.8
Jun. 1991: 80.6, 19.4
Nov. 1991: 88.5, 11.5

Question and Response
Categories:

Which of the following statements comes
closest to your feelings about CAMI?

- CAMI is a special kind of experiment,
designed to change the way people work
in Canada. I am enthusiastic and excited
about it.

- There is really nothing special about
working at CAMI, and, in fact, all things
considered, CAMI really isn't any different
than other corporations.

Figure 1 Percentages of respondents who viewed CAMI as special or
no different from other companies.

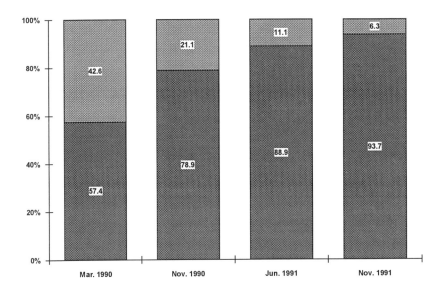

Legend: Smoke screen | Good Thing

Chart values:
- Mar. 1990: 57.4 (Smoke screen), 42.6 (Good Thing)
- Nov. 1990: 78.9 (Smoke screen), 21.1 (Good Thing)
- Jun. 1991: 88.9 (Smoke screen), 11.1 (Good Thing)
- Nov. 1991: 93.7 (Smoke screen), 6.3 (Good Thing)

Question and Response Categories:

Which of the following comes closest to your feelings about common cafeterias, dress codes and parking areas?

- It's a good thing, it's starting to make managers and workers more equal

- It's nothing but a smoke screen. The reality is that management still has all the power.

Figure 2 Percentages of respondents who viewed cafeterias, dress codes, and parking areas as a good thing or a smoke screen.

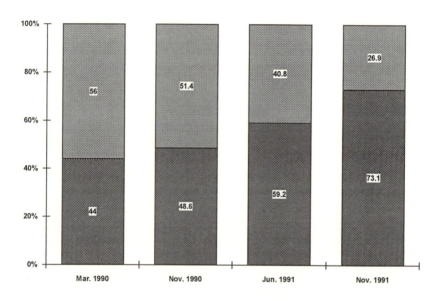

Undemocratic   Democratic

Question and Response   Which best describes the atmosphere
Categories: in CAMI?

                               - Democratic

                               - Undemocratic.

Figure 3 Percentages of respondents who viewed CAMI as
democratic or undemocratic.

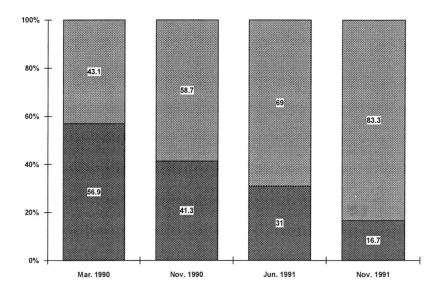

| Competitive and Stressful | Cooperative and Helpful |

Question and Response
Categories:

Which best describes the atmosphere
in CAMI?

- Competitive and stressful

- Cooperative and helpful

Figure 4 Percentages of respondents who viewed CAMI as
competitive and stressful or cooperative and helpful.

questions viewed CAMI as just another factory and indicated no attachment to the company and its values.

As Figure 5 indicates, the proportion of high and moderately committed respondents declined through each of the four interview periods. By the final round 19 percent fell into the middle category, while only one percent indicated high commitment. From another viewpoint, the percentage of respondents who were uncommitted to CAMI steadily grew from 41 in round one, to 56 in round two, to 70 in round three and to 80 in the final round. Despite a highly selective recruitment process, the ideals taught in *nagare* training and the company's emphasis on developing high trust relations and a participatory environment, workers' disenchantment with CAMI grew. This trend was dramatic, as the number of workers who indicated no commitment to CAMI virtually doubled over the two year research period.

Empty Promises

While CAMI was in the start-up mode, labor-management relations were relatively harmonious and the working environment relaxed. With the onset of

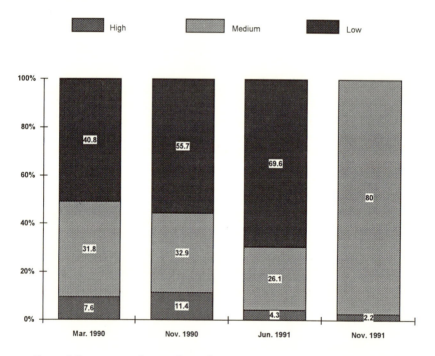

Figure 5 Percentages of respondents whose answers to seven questions indicated high, medium, or low commitment to CAMI.

full production all this changed, and the meaning of 'lean' became clearer. Workers learned how it felt to perform highly standardized jobs with short—one and one half to three minute—time cycles, day after day. They learned that the lean production version of job enlargement—responsibility for in-line inspection, stocking small parts, reporting faulty equipment and housekeeping—requires no special training, and that heavy workloads left them little or no time to handle these indirect tasks anyway. Workers discovered that job rotation within teams, which although regularly practiced, was not equivalent to skill development and multiskilling but rather to multitasking—a different phenomenon altogether.

This recognition was paralleled by growing dissatisfaction with CAMI's training effort. Workers found out that their participation in the continuous improvement of operations (*kaizen*) was circumscribed by the goals of cost-reduction and work intensification rather than the construction of safer, easier, or more interesting jobs. This would have come as no surprise to those workers who had noticed the section in the CAMI training manual that read "*kaizen* must always be tied to concrete cost reductions." The manual shows a group of workers waving good-bye to a co-worker following what was described as a successful team effort at *kaizen*. In time the word *kaizen* came to be used on the shop floor as a shorthand expression for job elimination.[10]

Staffing levels and workloads were among the most prevalent and contentious issues to arise over the course of the two year study. A manager interviewed during the final visit described staffing as "one of the biggest issues for me since I've been here." Staff levels were determined by a combination of work standards imported from Japan and a computer program of standard times to establish, theoretically, the number of people needed to meet production quotas. No allowance was made for unscheduled absences, turnover, maternity leaves, injuries, a more difficult model mix, or other unexpected developments. Because there was no relief crew, team members were expected to cover for their injured or absent co-workers by working harder.

The ramifications of CAMI's policy of operating with a lean, bare-bones work force became obvious with production in full swing. A team leader summed up the problem: "The staffing problems were that they had on the lines exactly what we needed, so if we had a person off or a person hurt or something we were scraping. We were working twice as hard as we should be. We weren't getting the help we needed to run the line."

Another team leader observed that his team has no time to spend on the kinds of indirect labor tasks mapped out in training sessions:

> We generally work quite a bit of overtime in our area and [an area leader] wanted us to work till four in the morning. All the lines would be done at two, and this particular area leader thought it was

insulting that we wouldn't stay till four o'clock in the morning to help clean the plant up, so when the manager got there in the morning it would be nice and clean. Who are you trying to bullshit? Let him walk through and see how this place looks. Give us some more people and we'll clean the place up. Put some more people on the line and we won't be so busy in this area. And that is generally the bottom line. There is not enough people on the line to do the work.

This team leader looked back wistfully to a more relaxed period when workers had time to do their jobs and to pitch in voluntarily to deal with housecleaning and other indirect duties. "When I started here guys would go out of their way to repair something that was broken. Now they say, 'the hell with it,' and I can't blame them. They just don't have the time to do it."

Staff shortages developed to the point where some managers started siding with the union's demands for extra staffing. A union representative said: "Believe it or not, sometimes the area leaders come to us and say, 'we need more manpower and we've tried everything.' It's like, 'will you do anything for us?'" Another union rep commented:

We'll talk to the area leaders and we'll talk to the managers and they'll agree with us, but then they have to process the manning requirements through the Japanese management and that seems to be where the stumbling block is. They put it on hold. Their favorite line is, 'Well, we don't do it this way in Japan.' But our line is, 'This isn't Japan.'

Lean staffing was exacerbated by CAMI's penchant for continuous improvement. Roving *kaizen* teams comprised of management personnel pared away staff. Floaters were routinely removed from teams to fill shortages elsewhere in the plant. *Kaizen* dictated the continuous increase in line speed without adding workers. Historically, such speed ups in Big Three plants have been vigorously resisted, leading to compromises whereby faster line speed and increased staffing have become inseparable. Things are different at CAMI, as explained by a manager:

We have figured out what the manpower should be, there is no question about that, but then as far as increasing, you may at a point increase the line speed without adding people. And that's sort of foreign, because in GM, like I say, whenever you increase the line they figure you're going to add manpower. The two things go hand in hand [at GM but not at CAMI].

The dictates of lean production led to an alarming ("explosive" in the words of one manager) increase in repetitive strain injuries (RSIs), which exacerbated staffing problems and interrupted job rotation schedules, which further intensified RSIs. Overwork was blamed on injured workers, causing dissension within teams. As production intensified, the control apparatus tightened up. An assembly team was told by the area leader that they needed written permission to go to the washroom; a worker was unable to get away from the line to take his insulin; overtime was scheduled arbitrarily; and there were frequent complaints about interteam transfers, the strict absenteeism policy, and the difficulty of getting an authorized day off. Workers were critical of management's refusal to replace absent workers or those off on RSI, to allow workers to listen to radios and read newspapers, or to wear shorts in the hot summer months. During the final research visit a union representative said: "We're getting guys written up for the most moronic things, like they think we're in high school or something."

Several managers offered candid assessments of the source of shop floor problems. One remarked:

> It's easy to get this thing started . . . it was like a honeymoon for us. We were only building a hundred, hundred and fifty five trucks a day . . . . We were hardly building any cars too, because we were in start-up . . . . It was a lot of fun when you had time. The line would go down at two in the afternoon because you met the day's production. You cleaned, you TPMed [total production maintenance], you worked on problems. And guess what? Now the line runs from seven until three-thirty . . . here's two hours overtime.

Another manager gave the following explanation for CAMI's failure to realize its professed values:

> I personally think that because of our push for vehicles, our push for quantity, our push for numbers, because of the overtime we've had to work, because of their schedules, that our use of the values has suffered . . . . I'm not saying that it's worse than other plants, and in fact it may be better than other plants, but to me it's a bit of a disappointment.

Team leaders, local union representatives, and managers described a growing disparity between the ideals of CAMI and their application and the consequent disillusionment among the work force. A team leader observed: "When I first came here I thought it was going to be the greatest place on earth . . . . *Nagare* really pumps you up really good, they know how to do that. But once you get out on the floor and start working for a while it's a lot different." Another team leader described the drift away from the ideals of CAMI philosophy: "We . . . were getting awards and getting this and getting that. And it's gone downhill, seems that we're going the way that every other factory goes. That is a letdown. That's why I came here . . . . I thought it would be different, everybody'd have a good time."

Recognition of the disparity between ideals and reality was not restricted to production associates and team leaders. A manager stated: "One of the concerns that we had heard—this is already over a year ago—is that what's being taught at the training sessions is not necessarily the same as what's practiced on the floor. So we've tried to tone down some of the segments of the (training) program." In an early round, an area leader felt CAMI was living up to its ideals as much as could be expected in an environment where, after all "production . . . is the backbone of what we're doing." During our final interview, however, she did admit that CAMI values were being ignored: "As far as . . . the environment, I think it's getting more traditional as the days go on. You don't want that to happen."

CAMI's failure to deliver its package of promises had become so apparent that management initiated a "back to the values" campaign. Admitting that CAMI values were not being practiced, one manager said:

> I'm not naïve enough to say that every area leader or manager practices the same way, but one of the objectives that we have for this organization for this year [1991] is to again get clearly focused on the values; to not drift from the way we tried to set up the organization . . . . I think it's important to keep working at it, especially as we get more into this routine of building vehicles. It's not the same as what it was when we started out . . . when there was more time.

A union representative was less enthusiastic about the company's attempt to reaffirm its values: "They came out with a piece of paper, and that's about it . . . said they wanted to get back to the basics, you know . . . just like something right out of *Nagare*. The guys are down there building cars. The last thing they want to hear about is open communication, *kaizen*, empowerment, especially when the management doesn't practice it themselves."

Sources of Workers' Discontent

Florida and Kenney (1991) maintain American workers have had little difficulty in adapting to lean production. Where problems have surfaced, as at Mazda's plant in Michigan, they attribute them not to lean production itself but to its partial or inadequate implementation. They quote several workers to the effect that American managers are too inflexible or threatened by the new, more consultative system to make it work properly. "American middle managers, especially those recruited from U.S. auto corporations, have experienced great difficulty adapting to Japanese production organization and management" (1991:389).

When workers struck CAMI, *Automotive News* (September 21, 1992) cited local union spokespersons who attributed the strike to the actions of traditional tough minded managers brought in from the GM system. The article concluded: "Angry workers at the transplant are blaming GM for their unhappiness, not the Japanese management philosophy GM is trying to follow here."

This explanation of problems inside transplants is perhaps the most misleading of all misconceptions of Japanese production management. The partial implementation explanation allows lean production enthusiasts to explain away operational or labor relations problems. In effect, it insulates lean production from criticism. As a result, assertions of the superiority of labor-management relations under lean production can never be empirically disputed.

It is all too easy to attribute shop floor problems that have arisen at CAMI to the arrival of hard-nosed GM bosses who have circumvented the prescribed lean production management. In contrast, the research at CAMI suggests it is the system of lean production that produces shop floor problems and hard-nosed management. In other words, it is not the partial but the complete implementation of a production system single-mindedly devoted to maximum output with minimal labor input that is the source of problems experienced by workers.

Lean production is a system that strives to operate with minimal labor inputs. It is a system whose objectives are to take time out of labor and labor out of production. It is a system that aspires to the elimination of all production buffers save one—workers who will toil harder and longer whenever required. Thus the ideals taught to new workers in *nagare* training at CAMI—team spirit, partnership and win-win outcomes—have little chance of survival once the lean production system is in place. At the end of the two year period of study far fewer CAMI workers would have disagreed with the team leader who said: "People are certain to come to the realization that regardless of how highly they talk of this place or make it sound, that basically it's just another auto plant."

Worker Resistance and the Role of the Union

Workers regularly contested the dictates of lean production at CAMI over the course of the study. Interest and participation in QC circle and suggestion (*teian*) programs declined. By the end of the two year study fewer workers did *taiso* (preshift calisthenics). Attendance at preshift team meetings dropped off. Workers often no longer knew their teams' names or even if their teams ever had names. Grievances increased.[11] There were instances of work slow downs, and work refusals became more common. Teams acted in solidarity to obtain relief workers; to resist losing a team member; to regain an off-line sub-assembly position; to demand more frequent job rotation; and to protest unsafe working conditions and the company's stringent dress code. Shackled by a weak first contract but strengthened by the policies and advice of the national CAW, the local union increasingly supported or led these struggles. Even a partial list of union actions gives a sense of the kinds of issues taken up and their outcomes.

The union assured workers that refusals to do preshift exercises, to hand in *teians*, or to participate in QC circles would not lead to grief or punishment. The local supported a collective campaign to pull the andon cords to protest understaffing on the door line that brought two extra workers to the area.[12] The local unsuccessfully pushed for the right to listen to radios and won the right to have reading material other than that distributed by the company in team areas. The local's support of workers' demand to wear poppies on Remembrance Day or shorts in the summer led the company to relax its strict dress code. CAMI would not respond to the union's demand to remove workers from disciplinary tribunals, but the company gave some ground on the union's demand to grieve discharges of probationary workers. The local successfully spearheaded a struggle against CAMI's policy of arbitrarily determining cross training moves between teams in different departments.

Several actions of the local merit special consideration. In the start-up phase to full production workers complained of some team leaders who were acting like bosses and who identified with the company rather than the union and the team. In early 1990, 400 workers attended Local 88's meeting to discuss the role of team leader. By way of response the local produced a set of guidelines for team leaders. The guidelines stress that the team leader is a unionized pro-duction worker who is a "technical advisor, not a personnel manager." The dis-tinction between team leaders and managers is summed up by the statement that the function of the team leader "is to support production," while that of the area leader "is to manage people."

The union also played a leadership role in the struggle over health and safety. The collective agreement originally stipulated that the union members of the Joint Health and Safety Committee (JHSC) would come from the ranks of elected committeepersons. Given the busy schedules of committeepersons, the union felt this important committee should also be staffed by those who could devote more of their time to health and safety. After much debate, the company agreed to allow the union to designate two full-time JHSC members from out-side the shop committee.

The company was reluctant to recognize the right of workers to refuse unsafe work under Section 23 of the Ontario Health and Safety Act. Workers were sometimes threatened with discipline for exercising this right. At other times, managers pressured workers to cut corners in various ways, like ignoring the locking-out of machines in order to minimize down-time. In response to mounting concerns throughout the plant, the union safety representatives called in the Ministry of Labor. Subsequently, the Ministry issued twenty-eight orders and forced the company to recognize the right of workers to refuse unsafe work. Interestingly, CAMI responded to these events by trying unsuccessfully to rescind its agreement to allow the two extra health and safety representatives.

The refusal to perform unsafe work became an important weapon for workers, who began to use Section 23 to protest the threat of injury posed by the rapid pace of work and inadequate staffing. The June 1991 issue of Local 88's newsletter, *Off the Line*, contained a half-page picture of a team that collectively invoked their right to refuse unsafe work due to a lack of relief and rotation and a failure to replace workers placed on restricted work because of RSIs. The title of the page on which the photograph appeared was "Changing the Definition of 'Teamwork'." The words under the picture read, "What does teamwork mean to you? To the members of Final 4 YOE Assembly it means solidarity."

The action of this assembly team was only one of a number of similar collective protests taken in the plant. In resisting the company's subordination of workers' physical well-being to production and cost reduction, the union fostered the genuine empowerment of workers to use the Health and Safety Act as a weapon to defend their rights and their bodies. Activities like these constituted the building blocks for a strong local union. Local 88's involvement in and direction of workers' struggles not only led to important victories but also promoted the self-confidence, cohesion and collective power of workers. The local has given workers a distinct point of reference, one that stands in sharp contrast with and provides a challenge to the philosophy of the company. Local 88 established itself as a force to be reckoned with by enabling individual workers to translate their discontents into a larger, more effective struggle to protect and promote their rights and interests.[13]

The Strike

With the first contract on the verge of expiration, Local 88 received an almost unanimous (98 percent) strike mandate from the membership. There was nothing unusual about the issues that prompted the strike. Wages and benefits, which were below Big Three levels were important considerations, as were conditions inside the plant. However, in-plant conditions—RSIs, workloads, team leader selection procedures, lack of relief workers, strict absenteeism policy, and arbitrary management decisions—assumed a special significance in light of the package of ideals and values professed but not delivered by the company. At the plant entrance, for example, strikers sported a large banner with CAMI's 'old values'—"open communication, empowerment, *kaizen*, and team spirit" crossed out and replaced by the 'new values' of "dignity, respect, fairness, and solidarity." Throughout the five week strike around the clock pickets were maintained, as were the morale and solidarity of the workers, many of whom walked a picket line for the first time.

The new three year contract narrowed the wage and benefit gap between CAMI and the Big Three. These gains were important in their own right but they also constituted a defeat of CAMI's goal of breaking away from pattern bargaining and tailoring remuneration to the economic performance of the individual enterprise. In-plant gains included a one year 'experiment' with elected team leaders, limitations in job standards and line speeds, beefed-up union involvement in health and safety matters, and the establishment of product support groups to provide pools of relief workers.

Is CAMI the Exception?

Commentators often characterize labor-management relations in the auto assembly transplants as remarkably stable, citing the failure of some high profile union organizing drives and the absence of strikes. Such indications should not, however, be taken as sufficient evidence of markedly superior working conditions or labor-management harmony. Claims for the liberated environment of lean production so forcefully advanced by Womack, Roos, and Jones (1990) need to be critically reappraised.

The CAW Research Group's findings on CAMI presented here do not stand alone. A small number of transplant studies undertaken from the vantage point of the shop floor have challenged the popular notion that working conditions under Japanese production management are superior to those that have prevailed in traditional North American plants. According to Berggren (1992, 1993:5), the content of work in auto transplants is much the same as it was at the height of the so-called Fordist regime of the post-World War II period. "If anything," he observes, "the rhythm and pace of work on the assembly line is more inexorable under the Japanese management system than it ever was before." While touring transplants in Canada and the United States, Berggren and his associates were struck by the heavy overtime demands on workers. They concluded that: "From a biological and medical perspective they [the transplants] are simply understaffed" (Berggren, Bjorkman, and Hollander, 1991:7).

Fucini and Fucini (1990:199) reached a similar conclusion in their study of Mazda's new assembly plant in Flat Rock, Michigan, where the Japanese company was keeping "a thinly stretched work force in perpetual motion." Babson (1992, this volume) concurs in his study of the reality of lean production at Mazda, which like CAMI was unionized. Even proponents of lean production admit that work under this system is fast-paced and stressful (Adler, 1993;

Kenney and Florida, 1993; and MacDuffie, 1988). Strict attendance policies, dress codes, and rules of conduct also characterize transplant operations (Babson, 1992, this volume; Graham, 1993, this volume; Junkerman, 1982, 1987; and Kendall, 1987). If past experience in North American industrial relations is any indication, these are not the kinds of conditions out of which long term industrial harmony is fashioned. Transplant stability as measured by the absence of strikes and a low level of unionization can be attributed not to the supposed consensus-producing features of lean production but to a number of other factors including prevailing economic and political conditions. Workers in all North American plants in recent years may have been relatively immune to unionization and shown a reluctance to strike. Also relevant are the massive employment losses in the auto industry and in manufacturing in general, declining union density and political influence, and the threat of plant closures and relocations. It is no coincidence that transplants have tended to locate in rural or exurban areas with no union history where wages are low and jobs are scarce. Moreover, transplants wholly-owned by the Japanese have actively resisted unionization through outright intimidation of prounion workers and other blatant forms of antiunionism (Yanarella and Green, 1993; Kenney and Florida, 1993; and Parker and Slaughter, 1988).

Evidence suggests that social relations inside the nonunion transplants are also less than ideal. Graham's (1993, this volume) participant-observation study revealed considerable conflict and worker resistance at the nonunion Subaru-Isuzu (SIA) plant in Indiana. There is no way of knowing if SIA is typical of nonunion transplants, since other similar operations have not been subjected to independent shop floor research. However, Graham's study does suggest that a nonunion environment cannot be equated with harmonious labor-management relations.

In the United States the unionized transplants' concerted efforts to nurture worker consensus and transform local unions into partners have been facilitated by the national United Automobile Workers' (UAW) disavowal of adversarial tactics and support for labor-management cooperation. As Berggren (1992, 1993:181) observes, "The labor-management collaboration and teamwork at NUMMI [Fremont, California] was heralded by Solidarity House as the future, and an embodiment of central union aspirations." The CAW national office, in contrast, agreed to some major modifications of standard work rules and practices as a quid pro quo for unionization at CAMI, but subsequently went on record as opposed to the specifics of lean production (e.g., teams and kaizen) if they degraded working conditions and eroded union independence. The CAW recommended cooperation only when workers had something to gain from it, and affirmed its dedication to representing the independent interests of workers (Canadian Auto Workers, 1990). In this context, the CAW encouraged the CAMI local to forge an identity independent of the company and to defend and promote workers' interests.

Despite the UAW's endorsement of cooperation, labor-management relations at the local level in all United States auto plants, including the transplants, are decidedly uneven (Turner, 1991). Little has been written about the Diamond-Star plant in Normal, Illinois, although Berggren (1993:181) was told by the local union president that workers' attitudes had shifted from trust to distrust of management. At Mazda in Michigan, working conditions and shop floor relations have paralleled in many respects those at CAMI. The initial group of appointed, procooperation local union leaders at Mazda were replaced through elections by a more militant slate. There have been recurrent in-plant demonstrations, work stoppages, work-to-rule actions, and boycotts of the suggestion program. In 1991 the membership gave a 94 percent strike mandate. The strike was averted just before expiration of the deadline (Babson, 1992, this volume; and Fucini and Fucini, 1990). Substantial gains were achieved, including relief workers, improved training, a more liberal policy on transfers and the right to elect team leaders. These developments suggest that philosophical differences between the CAW and the UAW are important but not necessarily decisive. An hour or two more of deadlocked negotiations and Mazda, not CAMI, would have become the exception.

This leaves NUMMI as the ostensible model of harmony in a unionized transplant. While there has been no systematic investigation of shop floor relations at NUMMI, labor-management relations on the shop floor do not appear to reflect the same degree of acrimony as do those at Mazda or CAMI, nor have NUMMI workers come close to striking. While lean production adherents' explanations of this state of affairs seize upon internal conditions, such as union cooperation, management's emphasis on building high-trust relations and worker participation, contingent conditions are not discounted. Both advocates and critics of lean production give some explanatory weight to the severe trauma experienced by NUMMI workers, many of whom were thrown out of work for several years by the closure of the GM plant that is now NUMMI (Adler, 1993; Parker and Slaughter, 1988; and Turner, 1991). It is not unreasonable to assume that these workers are still haunted by the fear of job loss and that this influences their actions. Moreover, the low level of conflict at NUMMI is relative in the sense that workers, particularly those in assembly, have evinced modes of resistance that suggest deep discontents with working conditions and management. These include a petition signed in 1988 by 1,000 workers protesting understaffing and the strict absenteeism policy and the election in 1991 and 1994 of many candidates of the opposition People's Caucus. Among the issues in these elections were heavy workloads and speed-up, the high rate of RSIs, and management favoritism. It is telling that in 1994 the Administration Caucus campaigned on a platform of fear, warning that a victory for the People's Caucus would result in the closure of the plant. Despite this tactic, the opposition took about one-half of the union positions, including chair of the bargaining committee.

Proponents of lean production are likely to define CAMI as an aberration by invoking the partial implementation thesis or stressing the militancy of the CAW. In one respect only are they right. The strike does distinguish CAMI as exceptional, at least until there are similar manifestations of industrial conflict in other transplants. However, the conditions that produced the strike appear in unionized as well as nonunionized transplants. In this sense CAMI is not unique.

The role of the national union remains to be addressed. Major philosophical and policy differences between the CAW and UAW are important, but they do not decisively shape local union politics. Certainly, the CAW's rejection of labor-management cooperation and its critique of lean production have influenced Local 88 leaders and members. But apart from the strike itself, developments at CAMI are quite similar to those at Mazda. If anything, Mazda workers have manifested greater shop floor militancy than CAMI workers. Perhaps NUMMI is the most distinctive unionized transplant. While NUMMI may lie at the 'harmonious' end of a continuum of unionized transplant labor-management relations, the distance between it and its polar opposites—CAMI and Mazda—is not all that great. At the end of the day, local militancy or quiescence cannot be imposed from the top by union leadership. It is in the complex interaction of external economic conditions, national union policies, shop floor social relations among workers and between workers and managers, and the character of local union leadership to which we must look to understand local union philosophies and actions.

Notes

* An earlier draft of this chapter appeared as "Worker Commitment and Labour Management Relations Under Lean Production at CAMI," *Relations Industrielles/Industrial Relations*, 49 (1994) 750+.

1. Early explanations of the Japanese miracle emphasized the peculiarities of Japanese culture and personality (Vogel, 1979). Current interpretations give little weight to culture, stressing instead the character of Japanese organizational, production and management structures.

2. Recent developments in the heartland of lean production indicate that labor-management ties are wearing thin. Workers and unions have come to recognize the price they have paid for working under this system, and they are raising questions about the human costs of their companies successes. In what *Automotive News* (February 17, 1992: 82) described as a landmark report, the Confederation of Japan Auto Workers Unions (1992: 23) lamented declining worker morale and asked: "For whom is the company making progress?" The report complained about long hours of work, excessive overtime demands, work force reductions, the use of temporary workers, and inadequate wages. To achieve these goals (especially the reduction of yearly work hours from an average of 2,300 to 1,800) the Confederation recommended extended model change cycles, a

reduced number of models, and variation-parts for each model. Faced with these demands and an unprecedented decline in sales and profits, Japanese auto companies are restructuring their operations. Nissan which announced in 1993 plans to close its massive Zama assembly plant has built and Toyota plans to build new plants with amenities and a labor process that reportedly is less strenuous than in extant facilities. The auto makers also are in the process of prolonging production runs of some models, reducing variations in models, cutting back overtime and adding several paid holidays. See Mary Ann Maskery, "Japanese Auto Union Demands a Better Life," *Automotive News*, February, 1992.

3. Womack, Roos, and Jones (1991) are characteristically cautious about worker commitment in transplant operations, arguing that it is contingent on employment security.

4. CAMI opened in 1989 and is now operating two shifts with about 2,300 shop floor workers, about 20 percent of whom are women, and whose average age is under thirty.

5. This project is partially funded by Labour Canada. The views expressed in this chapter are those of the Research Group and not those of Labour Canada. In addition to the authors listed, the members of the CAW Research Groups on CAMI are: Steve Benedict (CAW Local 112), Alan McGough (CAW Local 27), Herman Rosenfeld (CAW Local 303), and Jeff Wareham (CAW Research Department). The two university-based members of the research group had planned on initiating their own study of CAMI, but on learning about the CAW research plans, accepted the union's invitation to join the research group. As in the case of previous work, this chapter reflects the collaborative contribution of all members of the Research Group.

For a half-time report on the Research Group's findings, see Robertson, Rinehart, and Huxley (1992). For a more comprehensive summary of the final results, which were distributed to CAMI workers, see Robertson, et al. (1993).

6. The only formal requirement demanded by CAMI management was that they had the right to comment on the results of the investigation, and that any such comments would form part of the final report. See "Comments by CAMI," in Robertson, et al., 1993, pp. 53–61.

7. There is no evidence that CAMI tried to screen out workers with previous union experience. In round one over one-half of the workers in our sample had union backgrounds.

8. A training manager explained that the term *nagare* is borrowed from the lexicon of the Suzuki production system. The word in Japanese is associated with movement that is both swift and smooth.

9. The seven questions were: 1) "If you find a way to do your job that is easier or faster than the specified way, what do you do? Keep it to yourself, share it with a few co-workers, tell the team leader, or submit a suggestion?" 2) "Some people say that when the team concept has been tried at other plants the teams work more for the good of the company than for the good of the workers. Based on your experience at CAMI would you agree or disagree?" 3) "Which of the following best characterizes the atmosphere at CAMI—democratic or undemocratic?" 4) "Do you think everyone should participate in the suggestion system?" 5) Which of the following statements comes closest to your feelings about CAMI? (a) CAMI is a special experiment designed to change the way people

work in Canada. I'm enthusiastic and excited about it; or (b) There is really nothing special about working at CAMI, and in fact, all things considered, CAMI really isn't different than other corporations." 6) "Do you think managers at CAMI would 'put one over' on workers if they had the chance?" 7) "Many observers have commented that managers at CAMI and other team concept plants have gotten rid of many of the things that made them seem superior to workers. They point out that managers no longer have separate parking areas, cafeterias, and dress codes. Considering this issue, which of the following statements comes closest to your feelings about common cafeterias, dress codes, and parking areas? (a) It's a good thing, it's starting to make managers and workers more equal. (b) It's nothing but a smoke screen. The reality is that management still has all the power."

10. So far job elimination at CAMI has meant not lay-offs or job loss, but reduced team size. From the workers' point of view, *kaizen* or job elimination translates into doing the same amount of work with fewer people. When we asked respondents in round four, "Which best describes CAMI's efforts at reducing waste and increasing efficiency," 92 percent chose "reducing jobs" over "increasing jobs" (8 percent); 61 percent chose "working harder" over "working smarter" (39 percent); and 90 percent chose "a more demanding workplace" over "a more comfortable workplace" (10 per cent). On occasion, however, workers have used the *kaizen* process to achieve outcomes that are in workers' interests, such as their creation of off-line subassembly areas to allow workers periodically to rotate off the more physically demanding main line. For a discussion of CAMI's *kaizen* process and the participatory programs associated with it, see Rinehart, Robertson, Huxley (1993).

11. Participation in QC circles dropped from 56 percent in round one to 38 percent in round four. The corresponding figures for participation in the suggestion program were 82 percent and 45 percent. Nearly all respondents (98 percent) reported having done *taiso* at some time, but by the final round only one percent said they were still doing it. In round one 85 percent of respondents said they always attended team meetings; 46 percent reported doing so in round four. Only four grievances were filed in 1989, but by October, 1991 the grievance load had reached 150. In September 1992, just before the strike, the number of unresolved grievances had ballooned to over 400.

12. Hanging above each work station are yellow and red andon cords, and at regular intervals in the aisles there are overhead andon boards. If a yellow cord is pulled, the andon board alerts the team leader, and area leaders, which work station is having trouble. The line remains in motion, and annoying electronic tunes continue until the problem is resolved. The red andon stops the line.

13. Union leaders of Local 88 and Local 3000 of the Mazda plant have established an ongoing relationship to discuss and address their common problems. The first meeting of the two locals from different national unions and different countries was held in January 1991.

Worker Training at Toyota and Saturn: Hegemony Begins in the Training Center Classroom

_____ Ernest J. Yanarella_

Worker training has become the new buzzword of the nineties in corporate board rooms and policy making circles in the United States and Canada. Among policy makers struggling to fashion industrial policy by another name, worker training proposals have been touted as one of a set of quick fixes for curing what ails America's political economy. The Office of Technology Assessment's major report, *Worker Training: Competing in the New International Economy* (OTA, 1990), gives ample testimony to the concept's political currency. With a change-over in presidential administrations in early 1993, the key roles of three leading worker training advocates, Robert Reich, Ira Magaziner, and Hillary Rodham Clinton, in the new Clinton White House have only heightened interest and lent greater legitimacy to such proposals (Reich, 1991, 1993; Kondracke, 1992; and Magaziner and Clinton, 1992).

Where corporate cues point and federal dollars tempt, academic entrepreneurs surely follow. Spurred by the publication of such books as Tom Peters' *In Search of Excellence* (1982) and Alexander Hiam's *Closing the Quality Gap* (1992) and by the proliferation of corporate leadership and human resources institutes inspired by the new corporate ideology and its supportive training ethic, scholars from diverse, and until recently conflicting, disciplines have discovered the virtues of worker training in the emergent era of lean production and joint-management or consensual decision-making (Ferman, Hoyman, and Cutcher-Gershenfeld, 1991; Schurman, Hugentobler, and Stack, 1991; Tomasko and Dickinson, 1991; and Tannenbaum and Yukl, 1992). On the other hand, critical policy theorists drawing upon the experience of organized labor in Germany with codetermination have articulated a view of worker training as a collective good and suggested important lessons for worker unions in giving shape and substance to a democratic corporatist model of worker training (Streeck, 1985, 1989, 1993).

125

Nowhere has this trend in the corporate, policy, and academic worlds been more self-evident than in the troubled North American automobile industry. In the midst of the influx of Japanese transplants into the North American auto marketplace, the accompanying overcapacity caused a tremendous glut in that market, and the painful processes of continental and global economic restructuring undercut the past market share and economic hegemony of the Detroit Big Three there and world-wide. Management practices associated with Toyota and other Japanese automobile corporations have been increasingly institutionalized in American and Canadian (and increasingly Mexican) auto assembly plants as a means to promote higher quality and greater productivity with a smaller work force and to better compete in a more tightly integrated and far-flung international political economy (Katz, 1985; Kochan, Katz, and McKersie, 1986; Shaiken, Herzenberg, and Kuhn, 1986; Womack, Jones, and Roos, 1990; Drache and Gertler, 1991; Molot, 1993; and Kenney and Florida, 1993). Variously known as Japanese Production Management (JPM), lean production, and post-Fordism, this new management strategy or model has given worker training a revered place in its administrative pantheon.

This chapter is concerned with examining the reality and myth of worker training in so-called lean production facilities in the auto industry. It will analyze the role, extent, and functions of worker training at two assembly plants shaped by JPM and its training ethic: the Georgetown/Toyota plant and the Spring Hill/Saturn plant. Ultimately, these worker training programs will be evaluated in terms of their implications for a political strategy for organized labor inhabiting the changing, confusing, and kaleidoscopic world between Fordism and post-Fordism.

Critical to understanding the heightened role of worker training in the new work environment of the eighties and nineties and its consequences for any evolving labor strategy to shape and direct its outcomes toward advancing worker interests is an appreciation of the general contours and thrust of Antonio Gramsci's theory of hegemony. The thesis of this chapter is that if in the emergent era of Fordism whose outlines Gramsci so presciently anticipated "hegemony is born in the factory" then in the interstices of Fordism and post-Fordism, the ideological struggle for the hearts and minds of workers is increasingly being relocated. That is, corporations have more and more turned to a new weapon and a medium for extending and giving new form to their hegemonic power to a point where hegemony is borne in the training center classroom.

Gramscian Perspectives on Ideological Hegemony and Fordism

Gramsci's problematic of ideological or cultural hegemony owes its origins to the general condition of industrial capitalism in Western Europe after 1919, including the failure of the Second International, as well as in the special circumstances of Italian history, society, and economy. In large part Gramsci's revisionist turn was triggered by the proletariat's embrace of the world view of the ruling class and by the resultant failure of class-consciousness to develop within its ranks. Through his comparative historical and philosophical investigations as well as his studies of popular culture, Gramsci came to realize that "the system's real strength does not lie in the violence of the ruling class or the coercive power of its state apparatus, but in the acceptance by the ruled of a 'conception of the world' which belongs to the rulers" (Fiori, 1970: 238). The theoretical task was to discover how the ruling class was able to exercise what he came to call its hegemony over the working class and then to fashion a counterhegemonic strategy for undermining this everyday resource of the ruling class and establishing a new working class hegemony over society in the interests of all humankind.

In recent years, the meaning of Gramsci's notion of hegemony has been subject to considerable theoretical debate and ideological contestation. One oft-quoted preliminary formulation is offered by Gwyn Williams, who sees it as: "an order in which a certain way of life and thought is dominant, in which one conception of reality is diffused throughout all its institutional and private manifestations, informing with its spirit all taste, morality, customs, religious and political principles, and all social relations, particularly in their intellectual connotations" (Williams, 1975: 587). Seen in this way, Gramsci's notion of cultural hegemony takes ideology out of the minds of individuals (as in the positivist rendering of ideology qua belief system) and into its total economic-political-cultural context, while redefining the nature of power of modern capitalist societies in such a way as to incorporate the whole matrix and various levels of institutions through which power relations are mediated (and masked) in society.

Gramsci's recognition of the radical implications of the role of ideological hegemony in the twentieth century led him to ruminate over the concept of the state in its historical evolution and the place of its instruments of violence and coercion. It is important, in this respect, to realize that Gramsci rejects a simple identification of hegemony with ideological consent and the state with coercion. Instead he speaks in various places of hegemony as involving a balance of "coercion + consent" and describes the state in terms of "political society + civil society, in other words hegemony protected by the armour of coercion" (Gramsci, 1971: 263). That is, this Italian radical theorist was striving to go beyond dualistic categories and broaden the notion of the state and intertwine instruments of consent and coercion in order to revise the terms of debate among Marxists concerning the role of the state and its coercive mechanisms in advanced capitalist society. From this perspective, the state's instrumentalities of violence and coercion are seen as a necessary, though not controlling, aspect of state power and the hegemonic force of the ideological and cultural ideas saturating the various "private organizations of civil society" (including religious institutions, unions, schools, cultural and civic groups) is recognized as the daily bulwark of state rule and class domination.

In many ways, Gramsci's enduring contribution to revolutionary thought in the twentieth century was to offer a more fruitful strategic and political alternative to the sterile options of parliamentary or representative forms of participation or militarized forms of insurrectionary activity within the context of formally democratic, capitalist polities. In his view, one of the special advantages of twentieth-century capitalist societies lay in the fact that the state was fortified by a powerful and protective system of "trenches" and "fortresses" in civil society that at once shielded the center of power from direct attack and acted as a mighty reservoir of public support even during periods of economic crisis or foreign assault. Strategically, this advantage did not mean that a strategy for fundamental change should be fought *only* on the superstructural or cultural front. Hegemony for Gramsci incorporated both elements of coercion and consent and therefore involved the reciprocal interplay of base and superstructure, of economy and culture, that militated against any strategy of frontal attacks on established power. Given the reinforced armor of the state provided by the institutions of civil society, Gramsci instead advocated as a tactical priority what he called a "war of position" conducted primarily on the cultural front, rather than a "war of maneuver" involving overt military actions. Until the ideological supports to the ruling class's authority in all of their manifestations are assaulted and undermined, the hegemonic force of the ruling class will prevail in any struggle, even during moments of catastrophic crises or internal transformations.

Because Gramsci believed that any counterhegemonic strategy had to be based upon a subtle and sophisticated grasp of the new and evolving patterns of hegemonic power and incipient forms of economic organization in modern day capitalism, he turned his attention to signs and hints evidenced by the emergence of mass production in America—what he called "Fordism"—indicating the dawning of a new phase or epoch in Western capitalism.

The touchstone of the extensive theoretical work on Fordism and its putative successor, post-Fordism, is Gramsci's essay, "Americanism and Fordism" (Gramsci, 1971: 277–318). For Gramsci, the central issue was whether the changes set in motion in the United States by the development of assembly-line production by Henry Ford and techniques of scientific management by Frederick Winslow Taylor amounted to signs of a dawning historical epoch or were a conjuncture of events signifying nothing (277). Already anticipating the regulationist's idea of Fordism as a new regime of accumulation (and accompanying mode of production *and* consumption), Gramsci answered this question by characterizing these American developments as "the biggest collective effort to date to create, with unprecedented speed, and with a consciousness of purpose unmatched in history, a new type of worker and of man" (302).

Writing in the transition from craft production to mass production, Gramsci struggled to come to terms with the implications of this new form of work organization and hegemonic system for the working class in the United States and Western Europe. In a political economy like America's, spared the dead weight of feudalism, Gramsci believed that the rationalization of production and labor triggered by Ford and Taylor would "succeed in making the whole life of the nation revolve around production," such that "hegemony here is born in the factory and requires for its exercise only a minute quantity of professional political and ideological intermediaries" (285).

The comparatively high wages paid to this new worker would necessitate producing a new and rationalized worker-consumer of puritanical temperament and new habits who would preserve, "outside of work, a certain psycho-physical equilibrium which [would prevent] the physiological collapse of the worker, exhausted by the new method of production" (303). On the consumption side, this new, more highly paid worker would be called upon through Ford's puritanical initiatives manifested in the Five Dollar Day experiment to assume a new level of self-regulation by spending his extra money wisely and rationally and by adopting a frugal, morally upstanding, and healthy lifestyle (Meyer, 1981). As Emily Martin (1992: 121) has speculated, the triumph of Fordist mass production *a la* Gramsci would constitute not only a new production process and a new worker, but rely on "new constructions of sexuality, reproduction, family life, moral ideals, masculinity, and femininity" to produce a new Fordist body.

Puritanical habits were necessitated, according to Gramsci, by the physically grueling nature of mass production techniques. Along the way, a brutal process of selection would occur where "a part of the old working class will be pitilessly eliminated from the world of labour, and perhaps from the world *tout court*" (Gramsci, 1971: 303). Moreover, not only did Gramsci recognize the coercive side of Ford's use of the company's sociology department in investigating the private family life of the worker to determine if he was living up to its high standards, he also speculated on the possible role of the social movements in the United States like prohibition becoming "a function of the state if the private initiative of the industrialists prove[d] insufficient" (ibid.). In so doing, his subtle analysis of Fordism as an inchoate hegemonic system point to the mutual implication of coercion and consent.

Gramsci's hope in the working class's ability to overcome this emergent epoch and new hegemonic system was grounded in a number of sources. Ironically, one of those sources lay in the limits of this new form of economic organization in rationalizing work and reifying consciousness. That is, although Fordism and Taylorism relentlessly reduced work to its repetitive, automatic, and mechanical aspects, Gramsci believed that in the process only the body, not the brain, was mechanized. While the worker's body was being subjugated to a new and more brutal work rhythm and regimen, the brain becomes completely free and worker consciousness develops a revolutionary potential. This is why, Gramsci acknowledges, Ford undertook a series of educational initiatives to inculcate the largely immigrant work force into the patriotic values of Americanism (310).

Yet, inhabiting the margins of this Gramscian text and tempering his speculations on the emerging system's vulnerabilities was his quiet recognition that "the revolutionary working-class movement was in a phase of retrenchment and defeat throughout the capitalist world" (278). Absent its renewal and regeneration as a collective movement, any changes or modifications taking place within this new and unfolding regime of accumulation would take the form of a 'passive revolution,' where changes, reforms, even new contradictions within the continuing crisis of capitalism would occur, but without the likelihood of any overcoming of those deeper splits and contradictions or any ultimate resolution of that crisis beyond capitalism.

Worker Training in the Era of State Industrial Recruitment

The implications of Gramsci's work for an assessment of worker training must be seen in the context of the crisis of the Fordist regime of industrial production and capital accumulation rooted in part in the restructuring of the global political economy and the ascendancy and dissemination of Japanese production techniques into the North American automobile industry.

Beginning in the early 1980s, leading Japanese automobile companies built ten auto transplants or joint ventures with American auto makers in the United States and Canada. With rare exceptions, a significant part of the politics of state or provincial recruitment of these new, so-called 'post-Fordist' assembly plants was the incorporation into government incentive packages of funds for worker training (see Table 1). Indeed, as the popular business, and academic literature shows, training and development have become a significant element of the production systems and assembly operations of the Japanese transplants, Japanese-American and Korean-Canadian joint ventures, and Saturn (Allen, 1991, 1992; Armstrong, 1991; Brauchle and Pendleton, 1992; Carnevale, Gainer, and Meltzer, 1990; Geber, 1992; Heltman and Furuta in U.S. Department of Labor, 1990; Levin, 1993; and Partridge-Ullrich and Heeter, 1988).

In the following discussion, worker training at the Georgetown/Toyota plant will be examined against the backdrop of the possible internal transformation of Fordism's accumulation paradigm and hegemonic system into a neo-Fordist paradigm and hegemonic system that Dohse et al. call Toyotism and into what Burawoy has called a factory regime characterized as "hegemonic despotism."

Table 1 Training Funds in State Incentive Packages

Plant	Location	Total Government Investment in millions of dollars	Training Funds in millions of dollars	%
United States				
Nissan	Smyrna, Tenn.	33	11	33.3
Mazda	Flat Rock, Mich.	48.5	19	39
Diamond-Star	Bloomington, Normal Indiana	83.3	40	48
Toyota	Georgetown, Ky.	125	55	44
Honda	Marysville, Ohio	20	.74	3.7
Subaru-Isuzu	Lafayette, Ind.	86	21	24.4
Saturn	Spring Hill, Tenn.	80	30	39
Canada				
Honda	Alliston, Ont.	11	—	0
Toyota	Cambridge, Ont.	81	15	18.5
CAMI	Ingersoll, Ont.	112	40	36
Hyundai	Bromont, Que.	18 (+ 110 million interest paid on loan)	7.3	40.5

Sources: Mair et al. (1988); Milward and Newman (1990); Green (1990); Yanarella and Green (1993); Kenney and Florida (1993)

Team Toyota and Worker Training in Georgetown, Kentucky

On December 5, 1985, Governor Martha Layne Collins announced the decision of the Toyota Motor Corporation to locate an $800 million auto assembly plant in Georgetown, Kentucky, Within a few short weeks, news reports disclosed that Toyota's choice of the Scott County location was heavily influenced by a $125 million package of economic incentives offered by the state administration. Despite mounting opposition from area environmentalists, organized labor, and small business owners (Yanarella, 1990), the host of environmental, contractual, and constitutional questions was ultimately resolved, the over 100,000 job applications were ultimately whittled down by a multi-stage and highly selective employee screening and recruitment process to some 3000 workers, and the Toyota Motor Manufacturing (TMM) plant was built on time and began production in December 1988.

Table 2
Breakdown of TMM training funds expended from Kentucky state inducements

Area	Federal Funds	General Funds	Total
Assessment Activities	$4,553,311		$4,553,311
Pre-Hire Training Stipends	46,353	64,014	110,367
On the Job Training	2,139,208	29,469,516	31,608,724
Japanese Instructors		7,094,516	7,094,516
Training Developed by Toyota		7,043,522	7,043,552
Non-Manager Training in Japan		1,951,225	1,951,225
Manager Training in Japan		883,571	883,571
Maintenance Skills Training		724,553	724,553
Facility Operations		611,958	611,958
Interpreters		418,253	418,253
	$6,738,872	$48,261,128	$55,000,000

Source: Commonwealth of Kentucky, Cabinet for Human Resources, Department of Employment Services (1993)

As part of the $125 million inducement package presented to Toyota by the Commonwealth of Kentucky, $7.2 million was budgeted for the training or skills development center and $33 million to the general category of training. In addition to the payment or reimbursement for all building and personnel costs relating to the training facility, these funds were to be paid over a five-year period—as Table 2 reveals—to cover a wide range of training and training related activities. When federal funds for assessment, pre-hire training, and on the job training are included, total support for Toyota's worker and manager training program, exclusive of costs related to the training center itself, grew to $55 million.

Origins and Background. The origins of the significant commitment to employee training by Toyota can be traced to the human resource management program generated out of the post-war struggle and success of Japanese auto makers in crushing militant unionism in Japan (Halberstam, 1986: 170–184; Gordon, 1985; and Kenney and Florida, 1993). Through class struggle and labor turmoil, the Japanese production model—including labor-management relations and human resource development—was negotiated. Although the bitter post-war struggle between Japanese capital and labor led to the crushing of militant unionism there, a complicated vector of political forces best understood in a Gramscian framework gave birth to a production system which epitomized contradictory elements like enterprise unionism and lifetime employment, new forms of managerial control and human resource development, greater work rationalization, and increased worker prerogative to the social control impetus underlying its admittedly innovative work organization.

As the new Fordist regime was being sedimented into the automobile sector of America's political economy, Antonio Gramsci speculated on the possible emergence of a new psycho-physical equilibrium coming into existence that would prevent physiological collapse of the Fordist worker. This psycho-physical equilibrium would be manifested by the manufacture of new forms of consent that, though originally instituted as "something purely external and mechanical," could "become internalized if proposed by the worker himself, and not [seen as] imposed from the outside, if it is proposed by a new form of society, with appropriate and original methods" (Gramsci, 1971: 303). In developing an updated theory of Japanese corporate hegemony to support their post-Fordism thesis regarding the Japanese movement beyond Fordist mass production and the organizational transfer of Japanese production methods to America through Japanese auto transplants, Kenney and Florida have identified the distinguishing feature of post-Fordism as the success of this new regime and model in harnessing of workers' intelligence to the production process and in generating a new basis of consent to that process (Kenney and Florida, 1993: 39–40).

Dohse et al. (1985), Burawoy (1979, 1985), and Garrahan and Stewart (1992) have each offered alternative theoretical readings of the Japanese production system. In following the trajectory from Fordism to Toyotism, Dohse and his collaborators embrace a neo- or hyper-fordist interpretation of Toyotism (their shorthand for Japanese production model), seeing the modifications and advances in the Toyota production system—the most mature or purest form of this new production and organization model—as essentially an extension or more elaborated and more exploitative manifestation of Fordism achieved, in their words, "under conditions in which management prerogatives are largely unlimited" (Dohse, et al., 1985: 141). Likewise, Burawoy takes note of parallels between earlier versions of market-based despotic factory regimes and the Japanese model of production, and is moved to characterize the latter factory system as a form of "hegemonic despotism" (Burawoy, 1979: 200; 1985: 143–145 and 154n38). His rationale for this typification lies in his view that this new factory regime simultaneously fosters work intensification and discipline *and* worker dependency and submissiveness through the company's ability to ensnare the worker in an encompassing hegemonic system of values and relationships imposed on and off the job.

More recently, Garrahan and Stewart's analysis of Nissan's experience of locating and organizing the plant and surrounding community in Sunderland, England, sees the Japanese production system as instituting a "new regime of subordination." On their view, the driving spirit of the company, the so-called 'Nissan Way,' constitutes a set of relations of subordination and process of legitimation on the shop floor which transform Nissan's 'tripod of success' built upon the values of quality, flexibility, and teamwork into a new regime of subordination grounded in control, exploitation, and surveillance (Garrahan and Stewart, 1992: 111).

The common failings of these views are threefold. Each exhibits a ten-dency to reduce different variations on the Japanese production model into a series of dualistic/either-or categories, suggesting that JPM yields quality or con-trol, flexibility or exploitation, teamwork or surveillance, worker empowerment or managerial control, but not both. This leads to the elimination of the political play between these and other polar categories, which is the ground for labor strategy and political action. (This point will be discussed further in the conclu-sion.) Because there is such a strong tendency on the part of JPM critics to pose the model in almost one-dimensional terms and to invest its corporate hegemo-ny with virtually totalitarian power, even where hegemonic practices are appealed to in order to explain the system's power, theorists tend to revert to the language of adaptation and accommodation in explaining forms of resistance. Burawoy is a good illustration of this proclivity, given his use of the politically oxymoronic term, hegemonic despotism, to describe the Japanese factory regime and his preferred use of adaptation over resistance in characterizing all worker responses under capitalist hegemony (1985: 111 and 76 n.61, respectively).

While Kenney and Florida may have rushed to judgment on the issue of the supercession of Fordism by post-Fordism, they are in my opinion correct in underlining the centrality and cardinal importance to be found in JPM's ability to pump more surplus out of workers, not so much through line speed-up and other forms of worker exploitation, but through the incorporation and strapping of the intellectual capabilities, as well as physical labor, of workers to the pro-duction process. In explaining this new facet of so-called post-Fordist produc-tion, we are clearly moving into the political and conceptual terrain of hege-monic power where cultural resistance and political action on the shop floor assume new and critical importance.

In Gramscian terms, worker training in these changed circumstances takes on the characteristics of a fulcrum for generating new forms of system legitimation and ideological consent and shaping new forms of worker skills development and deskilling. Regarding the form, corporate training programs are not themselves exhaustive of the hegemonic system inscribing the Japanese model of production; rather, the elements constitutive of that model in their ideological expressions contribute to the system as a whole. On the other hand, as the Toyota and Saturn training programs demonstrate, ideological hegemony does indeed begin in a nontrivial sense in the training classroom.

Georgetown/Toyota's Worker Training Program. Even prior to the construc-tion of the Georgetown/Toyota plant, the groundwork for the corporate training and development program at the facility was being laid. The foundations of the program were built upon the over two-decade experience of Japan's preeminent automobile corporation in developing and incorporating training practices into its production process. Inspired by its company axiom that "quality begins with training and ends with training" ("Training—A Top Priority," 1988), the original training personnel worked to adapt and integrate the rigid and standardized Toyota training program, including its manuals and other educational materials (Toyota Motor Corporation 1984, 1987, n.d.), into the new greenfield site located on the border between this small central Kentucky town and its countryside (Allen, 1993; and Hinton, 1993).

The TMM training facility is located on the grounds of the Toyota assembly-engine complex as a separate two-story, 46,000-square foot building containing office space for training personnel, eight training areas and six classrooms for general and specialized training, and three laboratories for skills development using assembly robots and machinery ("Training—a Top Priority," 1988; Allen, 1993; and Hinton, 1993). In addition to training Toyota plant employees at the Georgetown center, Toyota's service training facility in Lexington, Kentucky provides supplier training as part of the overall training program (Chappell, 1992: 8).

Substantively, Georgetown TMM's training program, driven by the company's overriding corporate values and goals, sought to translate Toyota's mission statement, "enrich society through the making of automobiles," into a systematic and continuously improving approach for the development, planning, implementation, and assessment of a training regimen driven by the company's overriding corporate values and goals and interwoven into every operation of the auto assembly plant (cited in Allen, 1992: 41). According to the plant's former manager of training and development, the Toyota program is organized around the shape of a triangle. The first component, on the job training, is by far the most important training element, according to Toyota's production philosophy. Given its commitment to a highly regimented and standardized work process, the Toyota production model has challenged the training process to: (1) identify the specific skills or competencies necessary for each worker to master his or her job task(s) on the assembly line, (2) break down these competencies into specific components, and (3) formulate step-by-step instructional programs to hone these competencies. More than skill, the operative term employed in Toyota's training and development practices is the term, 'competency,' understood as a measure of success within a standardized work process.

Off the job training is the second key element of the TMM training program. If on the job training is predominantly intended to develop the production worker's 'hard' or technical skills in performing the standardized worker operations comprising auto assembly production, off the job or classroom instruction is associated with those organizational or 'soft' skills for promoting organizational knowledge, problem solving, and team and interpersonal skills. These soft skills contribute to: (1) the worker's understanding and loyalty to the goals and values of the corporation and its production process; (2) his or her ability to work together with others to smooth production when a problem or trouble spot develops on the line; and (3) his or her willingness to apply personal intelligence and creativity to improve the quality of the product and the efficiency in producing that product (Allen, 1991, 1992, and 1993; and Toyota Motor Corporation, 1985: 8–11).

Voluntary training activities comprise the third component of Toyota's training regimen. This volitional dimension to training may be broken down into two areas: activities like quality circles, interest groups, and organizational clubs, where soft skills like interpersonal, team, and leadership skills are developed through professional facilitators from the training department; and promotional activities, where workers make the personal decision to seek advancement to another higher classification such as team leader or group leader. Subsequent to applying for promotion, a worker must undergo the requirements of a three-month, prepromotional program composed of two hours a day of training before or after his or her work shift over two months followed by daily off-hours battery of tests and assessments over a one month span (Hinton, 1993).

TMM's training program annually targets as its goal delivering at least fifty hours per year of training to each team member. It is, moreover, divided into four areas or levels which are directed or available to wider or narrower target groups among its employees (Heltman and Furuta in U.S. Department of Labor, 1990: 29). The first area, significantly and symbolically called orientation and assimilation, inculcates newly hired workers into the operational principles of the Toyota manufacturing and organizational philosophies and provides an introduction to the various soft skills, like problem solving, interpersonal, listening, and team skills (Thompson, 1991: 32, 33–34; and Toyota Motor Corporation, n.d.). This orientation and assimilation session, originally a week in length and now two and a half days, is required of all employees (Hinton, 1993). The second training level delivered to each employee by the training center involves a more in-depth instruction into the Toyota Production System—including problem solving, quality circles, standardized work, productivity, and waste reduction—to which some ninety-one hours of training are devoted during the first year (Toyota Motor Corporation, n.d.). Management and employee development is the third training area. Its clientele is management, supervisory, and administrative personnel. This area comprises some 154 training hours with the purpose of enhancing soft skills like social, communications, and leadership skills (Heltman and Furuta in U.S. Department of Labor, 1990).

The fourth and final training level, skilled trades, is specifically targeted to maintenance and tool and die workers. In important respects the most structured, detailed, and arduous of training levels, skilled trades members in the plant are continually trained toward 'certification' in each of 25,000 specific tasks identified by Toyota's Japanese industrial engineers as comprising the responsibilities of skilled tradespeople in the Toyota production process. Divided between some 1,680 hours of scheduled classroom time and on the job training combining self-paced training from manuals and standardized training from team leaders, this area of specialized training is estimated to take seven years or more to complete (Allen, 1993; and Heltman and Furuta in U.S. Department of Labor, 1990; but compare Robertson, 1992b: 37–38).

Important differences mark the training programs at Toyota's Japanese assembly plants like Tokaoka, its joint venture with General Motors at Freemont, California (NUMMI) and its transplants at Georgetown, Kentucky (TMM) and in Cambridge, Ontario (TMMC). At its North American assembly operations, intensive training into Toyota's production system and corporate ideology is provided to American and Canadian team members to culturally integrate these employees into a corporate world view and work orientation assimilated more naturally through Japanese culture and secondary education. Moreover, as indicated above, all TMM employees go through the first two levels of corporate training and education to imbue them with the guiding values, beliefs, and objectives of Toyota's corporate culture (Heltman and Furuta in U.S. Department of Labor, 1990). Whereas Japanese assembly plants rigidly restrict the recruitment pool for promotions, TMM has until recently allowed any interested TMM member on his or her own initiative to enter the prepromotion process. But in the last two years, according to Hinton [1993], enrollment size in prepromotion training courses have been capped. This concession to American values of individualism and personal mobility has, as we shall see, significant implications.

One notable difference exists between delivery of corporate training at TMM and at NUMMI. Because of its unionized character and the legacy of past labor-management practices, NUMMI's training program retains vestiges of the UAW apprenticeship approach to worker training while TMM's program, due to its nonunion status, is thoroughly permeated by a human resource development approach (Allen, 1993; OTA, 1991: 188; and U.S. Department of Labor, 1987).

Finally, most of the training materials were directly translated from the Japanese language, but two departures from Japanese practice have been made. Manuals have been rewritten to make reference to female workers and examples have been Americanized. Classroom pedagogy has also been changed to foster a more interactive teaching and learning environment for American workers (Hinton, 1993).

The Dialectic of Company and Community Hegemony at TMM

By virtually all quantitative and most qualitative measures, the Georgetown/Toyota plant is a highly successful and harmonious manufacturing operation. Its Camry model has won numerous awards from J.D. Power and other industry overseers. Its work force and production levels have continued to climb with each new expansion of the facility. Its assembly line workers, according to

Toyota-sponsored surveys taken twice a year, are highly satisfied with the company and closely identify with its success and thus far seem impervious to union blandishments. Despite early opposition from labor, small business, and environmentalist quarters (Yanarella, 1990), community sentiment for TMM and the economic growth that has accompanied it remain high—though an undertow of apprehension and uncertainty has been detected among some Scott County citizens (O'Boyle, 1992: 1).

This pervasive plant and community support for the Georgetown/Toyota auto complex is best understood in relation to TMM's double-pronged mobilization strategy aimed at exerting its hegemony over both the company's employees and the area's citizenry in a more encompassing hegemonic process. At Toyota, company hegemony begins in the training center classroom through the extensive attitudinal training and cultural integration that are part of the first-year training and development programs run by TMM's training professionals. As a dynamic, constantly changing, hegemonic form of managerial control, company hegemony involves, as Kenney and Florida (1993: 271–272) argue, socialization, daily routines, discipline, and resistance. Cultural and attitudinal training socializes workers into the TMM's corporate culture—including those norms, beliefs, rules, values, and behavior deemed appropriate. Such socialization, while it starts in the training classroom, is continuously strengthened through a set of reinforcing mechanisms and processes—quality circles, voluntary activities, recognition and awards dinners—that are sedimented into the pattern of the worker's daily routines.

Discipline—the third element Kenney and Florida see as comprising what they call company control—takes softer, less formalized and overtly punitive forms in so-called lean production facilities like Toyota (see Sakolsky, 1992). Because the authority structure is less hierarchical and more apparently egalitarian at TMM, the disciplinary power of post-Fordist management is occluded through careful recruitment and selection of modal workers, heavy cultural indoctrination, a highly articulated production system combining highly standardized work and mechanisms for continuous improvement, and forms of almost therapeutic counseling to change inappropriate behavior. The highest measure of its success occurs when workers take it upon themselves to discipline themselves and other workers and in effect become managers unto themselves and their own ranks. The TMM's ideal of a plant run by self-directed teams, which former training manager John Allen (1993) acknowledged was still years away from realization, takes on a different meaning when interpreted in this light. Still, the coercive core of hegemony (qua force + consent) always stands in the background and can be brought into play by the fear or threat of termination flowing from TMM's managerial prerogative (Yanarella, 1993).

Finally, company hegemony at TMM and other Japanese plants is constituted in the shifting play of forces between management and labor and through an ongoing challenge-and-response pattern flowing from managerial initiatives and worker demands, the evolving state of political struggle, and competing forms of worker acquiescence and resistance on the shop floor.

TMM's company hegemony is only one part of the larger hegemonic patterns and processes characterizing its mobilization strategy. Modeled after the Toyota City experience in Japan, the Georgetown/Toyota plant has witnessed the elaboration of series of hegemonic patterns in the Scott County area that function to organize and shape a form of community hegemony. Far more than any other Japanese transplants, TMM has attempted to incorporate hegemonic design into the community life of Georgetown and Scott County citizens through the replication of some of the elements of its hegemonic integration of corporate and community, and economic and social spheres of Toyota City.

Through a steady stream of corporate giving, a complex web of company-community institutions, including political, industrial, educational, and cultural ties, and a vigilant staff of public relations employees working to polish or defend its corporate image, Toyota's management has sought to reshape the local community into a supportive environment for Toyota's larger plans and a showcase for a mass-mediated national audience in the United States. Its training strategy, for example, has become a model for joint educational reform programs in the Scott County school system and the country at large (Kenney and Florida, 1993: 293; and Wilson and Schmoker, 1992). Moreover, in building on American shores a somewhat nativized *keiretsu* structure integrating secondary and tertiary suppliers into its production complex (Mid-America Project, 1992), Toyota Motor Manufacturing, Inc. has used its training organization as a means for educating and disciplining wider elements of its production network into the Toyota production system. Finally, as part of their voluntary activities, TMM workers are actively encouraged to participate in community organization to further Toyota's community image—thus serving as a vital link between the processes of company and community hegemony. Like other levels of its hegemonic processes, these too have been subject to criticism and challenge, necessitating corporate adaptation in a continuing and ceaseless effort to rebalance and augment the ongoing and dynamic hegemonic equilibrium.

The Saturn Project and Worker Training in Spring Hill, Tennessee

The Saturn Project, according to auto industry folklore, began in the early eighties as a dream of Roger Smith, General Motors' chairman (Keller, 1989: 93–96). This new experiment was to be GM's bold bid to compete head to head with the Japanese auto makers in the subcompact car market—a market hitherto ceded by GM to its domestic and then foreign competitors due to its low profit margin. Backed by the commitment and clout of GM's chairman and designed by the Committee of 99 drawn from management and organized labor, Saturn was intended to leapfrog the competition and build subcompact cars in a revolutionary way using a whole new production system and a unique labor-management contract (Jordan, 1988: 13–14; and Alpert, 1988: 239–248).

Although many of the Roger Smith's hopes for a highly automated, 'paperless' factory of the future ran aground of technological and organizational realities, many others reached fulfillment when GM formally announced its decision in early January 1985 to form the Saturn Corporation as a subsidiary of the parent auto maker and to solicit bids from states and localities for a new production facility (Milward and Newman, 1990: 41–43; and Fox and Neel, 1987: 7–16). In the six month bidding war for this prized plant site, some thirty-eight states offered a variety of incentive packages to lure the Saturn investment to their boundaries. When the industrial recruitment process ended in July 1985, Tennessee's $80 million bid ($50 in road improvement and $30 million for worker training) was declared the winner and its Spring Hill green-field site, located approximately thirty miles south of Nashville, was selected (Hilman and Pratt, 1985: 1; and Milward and Newman, 1990: 35). (For a breakdown of Saturn training funds expended, see Table 3.)

Despite Saturn's location in a right-to-work state, GM agreed from the outset of the project to negotiate a union contract with the United Auto Workers union. A radical departure from traditional union-management contract, the Saturn compact between union and management established an alternative model for union-management relations in the auto industry. While some proponents of the Saturn experiment like Bluestone and Bluestone applaud it as an approximation of an innovative enterprise compact of the future (Bluestone and Bluestone, 1992: 191–201), others see 'Saturnization' as a labor-management paradigm that will undercut traditional collective bargaining and transform the UAW into a completely decentralized organization populated with locals modeled after company unions of the American past and the Japanese present (Russo, 1986).

Table 3

Breakdown of Saturn training funds expended from Tennessee state inducements

Area	Total Federal and State Funds
Coordination	$4,066,000
Development and delivery of pre-employment training	5,698,000
Development and delivery of job-related training	12,036,000
Total	$21,800,000

Source: State of Tennessee, Department of Economic and Community Development, Office of Director of Industrial Training (1993)

Among its key provisions is its commitment to jointness or worker-management cooperation at every level of the plant's operation. This extension of formal worker participation in management, planning, and operation involves the creation of jointly represented committees grounded in consensus decision-making and problem solving from the shop floor to the strategic planning council. The contract also reduces the number of job classifications from over one hundred to one for unskilled workers and three to five for skilled workers. Other trappings of Japanese production management—including use of the team concept, extensive training for all workers, protection against layoffs except for catastrophic events or severe economic conditions, reduction or elimination of status differences between labor and management—are also included in the contract or structured into plant operations and worker-management relations. The last noteworthy provision involves a pay formula that would eventually put up to 20 percent of union worker pay 'at risk' annually to performance, quality, training, and profit objectives or expectations (Saturn Labor Agreement [text], 1986).

Saturn's Worker Training Program. Recently, Florida and Kenney (1993: 119) prematurely characterized this experiment as little more than "group fordism." Yet Saturn's comprehensive and thoroughgoing training ethic standing at the center of its guiding managerial philosophy and organizational practice demonstrates that Saturn is the closest approximation to a 'pure' post-Fordist model in any unionized American auto plant today and a formidable challenge to an international auto union in decline to fashion a counterhegemonic strategy for turning the post-Fordist rhetoric of workplace democracy and continuous learning into reality.

Fashioned by the 99 Committee from diverse Japanese and American training models and approaches and housed in a $10 million, two story facility on a hill above the automobile assembly and engine plants, the Saturn training and skills development program is in many respects the linchpin of the new labor-management compact and the centerpiece in GM's overall management strategy to restore General Motors to its former place of glory in the global automobile marketplace. With a staff of thirty personnel and an operating budget of around $9 million, the program annually logs more than 800,000 hours of training for over 650 courses and meets the labor-management target of delivering an average of ninety-one hours per year for each worker (High, 1993). Besides plant employees, the training center annually conducts regular training courses for retail franchise personnel—from salespeople, franchise managers, and auto mechanics to receptionists—as part of the company-union partnership, Saturn Training and Education Partnership (STEP), which includes Maritz Communications Company as its design partner (Cottrell, et al., 1992).

Echoing Saturn's corporate mission statement commitment to meeting the global competition in the auto industry by marketing American automobiles that "are world leaders in quality, cost and customer satisfaction through the integration of people, technology and business systems" (Saturn Mission, n.d.), the Saturn training mission expresses the goals of creating and maintaining a "training structure that enables Saturn team members to build a world class product" and of developing the "knowledge, skills and attitudes needed to perform at a level of excellence in both the technical and human environment" through the program's "needs driven, competency based and cost effective training" (Saturn Corporation Training Mission, n.d.).

Prior to the plant's start-up operations, Saturn's team members were receiving between 300 and 700 hours of training ("Building the 1992 Saturn," 1992). Owing in part to the pressures of full production, the car's growing sales volume in the marketplace, and the addition of a second and third crew, this level of training has been reduced to a commitment to 175 hours of instruction in the first year and then 92 hours per employee annually—or about 5 percent of total work hours (Moskal, 1989; Woodruff, 1993; Geber, 1992; and High, 1993). Like Toyota's first year training regimen, Saturn initiates its newly hired employees through a one week orientation training that includes eight hours each of classroom instruction in conflict management, listening and assertion, consensus decision-making, and creative thinking, plus a four hour overview of Saturn management and production philosophy (High, 1993). During the succeeding eight to twelve weeks, new team members will alternate their training activities between formal classroom and structured on the job training spending half the time learning soft skills and the other half being schooled in technical skills. There, some fifteen hours will be devoted to further instruction in the Saturn production system and another fifteen hours allocated to team building through the center's Excel course involving outdoor or wilderness activities (High, 1993; Saturn Education Tracking System, 1993; and Wagner, et al., 1991).

In comparison with TMM's and other transplant and Big Three corporate training programs, two distinctive features of Saturn's training operations stand out: its individualized training programs (ITPs) and its train the trainer (T3) process. Each year, every employee participates in a process that generates an ITP that is entered into the company's computerized educational tracking system. Over the course of the year, it is expected that each employee will complete his or her ITP through that person's designated team training champion, who is responsible for helping to determine each team member's needs and for deciding when each team member can be spared to register for and take the relevant courses (Geber, 1991: 32; and High, 1993). These courses range from short courses on ergonomics awareness (one hour) and blueprint reading (four hours) to lengthier and more advanced skills training courses on autocad (forty hours) or robotic electronic maintenance (forty hours). More specialized skills development or troubleshooting training takes place in the training facility's Workplace Development Center, where team members taken off the production line can work out design, equipment or other problems with Saturn industrial engineers on a simulated assembly line (guided tour of development center by High, 1993). Through an elaborate and routinized performance evaluation process, employee ITPs are carefully tracked and 'certification' of skills level achievement is recorded.

Adopting a training idea originated by training developers almost twenty years ago, Saturn human resource managers have fully incorporated the train the trainer or T3 approach (Saturn Corporation, 1992) into its education and development regime for a variety of reasons. First, given its joint management structure, which builds in equal representation between management and union, and a consensus approach to decision-making, which requires that no decision can be made without every committee or council member feeling 70 percent comfortable with the proposed resolution, company hegemony at Saturn takes the form of a cooptation strategy geared to assimilating the unionized work force into company's world view, institutional structures, values, interests, and goals. At Saturn, the T3 program coopts union workers into a training and assessment program that draws upon cutting edge ideas in human resource management grounded in a personal development/individualistic framework. The T3 approach also allows the training center to field the enormous number of courses and to fulfill the (now) nearly one million hours of training time scheduled annually as part of Saturn's training mission commitment.

Saturn's Hegemonic Strategy of Cooptation: Problems, Challenges, Prospects. The result of this cooptative hegemonic strategy begun in the training classroom on each side of the instructor's desk or lectern is the enmeshing of union workers into the web of corporate values, beliefs, and interests—in sum, a world view in the Gramscian sense—underpinning the Saturn experiment that blurs the distinction between capital and labor and promotes belief in the identity of interests between management and union.

To elaborate, exceptional to the Saturn contract has been the elimination of a cornerstone of GM-UAW contracts since the thirties, the so-called management rights clause of Paragraph 8, and its substitution by vaguely worded Sections 10 and 11 provisions on structure, decision-making, and consensus calling for "full participation by the Union" and "use of a consensus decision-making process" involving "free flow of information and clear definition of the decision-making process" (Saturn Agreement [text], 1986: E–2). This has meant that in the everyday operation of the Saturn complex the terms and locus of corporate hegemony have shifted from the conventional hierarchical arrangements epitomized in the contractual managerial rights provision at the strategic level to the more formally participative and pseudo-egalitarian relations underpinned by more veiled forms of ideological hegemony worked out within joint committees and in training sessions at the ideological level.

To illustrate, an important part of Saturn's operations involves the multiplicity of joint committees from top to bottom that implicate representatives of rank and file union workers and management in consensus decision-making on long-term strategic and more immediate day to day issues, including training. The daily jointness or worker cooperation process at Saturn has tended then to serve as a socialization process for union representatives and to a degree assimilate the unionized work force generally into the corporate ideology, values, and priorities infusing the Saturn mission statement and guiding philosophy.

Evidence of the blurring of the sense of separate identity and conflicting interests includes the oft-cited observation by visitors that it is impossible to distinguish the formal presentations of salaried employees (management) from those of nonsalaried employees (union) at the plant or the training center. Within the training domain, the sharing of instruction between union and management representatives is so thorough that, not only do salaried and nonsalaried employees exchange assignments of visitor presentations on the Saturn philosophy, but union and nonunion representatives alternate the teaching of the sixteen hour GM/UAW History course (CRS # 4347)!

The scrapping of formal managerial rights for the appearance of greater democracy and equal labor-management influence points to the critical role of training at Saturn. Unquestionably, the Saturn training program is one of the most extensive and innovative among American and Japanese auto assembly plants in the United States. As institutionalized, it has furthered the program of corporate hegemony for which it was partially designed by management. Yet it could not have been so remarkably successful as an instrument of managerial control without the active concurrence and support of the UAW national and local union leadership.

The UAW national headquarters has straddled the fence on issues of worker participation versus worker power. That is, as the UAW international has suffered a veritable hemorrhage in membership, plummeting from 1.53 million members in 1979 to 862,000 in 1991 and representing less than 68 percent of American auto workers in 1991 from 86 percent in 1978 (Slaughter, 1992b), it has sent mixed cues to union locals about post-Fordist or lean production-type practices, triggering a diverse set of responses from plant to plant spanning outright resistance to virtual total accommodation. More alarming is the key function played by the local union leadership headed by Local 1853 president Michael Bennett in manufacturing consent and enforcing corporate policies cloaked as common interests among the rank and file membership.

Throughout the brief life of the Saturn Corporation the union local president has been a consistent and unflagging supporter of its corporate mission and training philosophy. Indeed, his role in sedimenting the new labor-management relations at Saturn and forging its new enterprise compact is so great that Saturn's top training manager stated that "Saturn would not be what it is today without Mike Bennett" (High, 1993). Since coming to Saturn, Bennett has assumed a position of authority within the Saturn Corporation that has directly involved him in the implementation of the jointness program. Buying into the corporate outlook on globalization of the auto marketplace, he has departed from the national union's negotiating stances on a number of issues, including his belief that the UAW national "can't continue to remove wages from competition in the international economy" (Editorial, 1992: 8). He has also envisaged the future of labor unions in the era of global restructuring "at the local level" where such organizations can help firms "explore opportunities to compete, be more flexible, less costly . . . and to provide the stockholder with a return on investment without lowering the [workers'] standard of living" (ibid.). His only major rift with Saturn management has been over the reduction of first-year training hours from 700 to 175 (Woodruff, 1993).

One of the ironies of the permeation of participative processes in Saturn has been that the internal transformation of Local 1853's leadership hierarchy into an agent of corporate hegemony has been accompanied by the ebbing of local union democracy and the progressive breakdown of local union leadership solidarity with other locals in the auto international (Slaughter, 1992a; and Yanarella and Green, 1994). For example, the local president has buffered himself from the rank and file by two layers of appointed union officials totaling 350–400 holding positions as work unit module advisors and business unit coordinators (Hinkle, 1993a). In the March 1993 campaign for local president, Bennett was criticized by his opponents for his authoritarian, heavy-handed rule over the local (Hinkle, 1993b).

On the training front, the influx of new production line workers from other plants and the eruption of rank and file restiveness have in part precipitated a crisis of corporate identity at Saturn that Bennett and his corporate partner have sought to overcome through required participation by all Saturn employees in a twenty hour training module entitled, "Saturn: Yesterday/ Today/Tomorrow," as part of their training program (High, 1993). Scheduled from March 15 to June 28, 1993, this corporate mission renewal module was offered 112 times to accommodate the entire Saturn work force and administrative personnel and office staff and totaled 2,240 hours of training time, effectively accounting for nearly 22 percent of each employee's 1993 ITP (Saturn Corporation, 1993). Thus, the stresses and strains caused by a compliant and rigid local union leadership and new union hires from plants not imbued with the philosophy of jointness and Saturn's corporate world view have meant that company hegemony has had to be more aggressively produced and reproduced on the shop floor and in the training classroom to stem the effects of the legacy of adversarialism and the persisting rank and file doubts about the convergence or commonality of management and labor interests.

Saturnization and the New Americanism. Unlike TMM, Saturn has eschewed seeking to extend its corporate hegemony into community life surrounding Spring Hill and Maury County. Despite relatively modest expressions of corporate goodwill to the community and some involvement by local public institutions in vocational education programs, the Saturn Corporation has made no move to incorporate Maury County, Spring Hill, and Columbia (the next closest larger city) into any larger hegemonic design. Although Spring Hill's new town center provides a skeletal outline of such a planning design, the secrecy and security surrounding Saturn, as well as tensions precipitated by the corporation's commitment to hiring only union workers, have created considerable suspicion and disappointment among the public.

As a subsidiary of GM imbued with Roger Smith's ambitions and dreams of turning the Saturn experiment into a catalyst for reversing GM's declining fortunes and for bringing the auto giant into the twenty-first century, Saturn has catapulted its hegemonic initiatives and impulses onto a national arena in the form of shaping the public image of the car and the corporation through mass advertising. Saturn has also employed its training program as a model for innovative public education and into an instrument for instructing its retail force in its marketing philosophy and its mechanics in the principles of its training and production system. In the process, it has elaborated a new Americanism—albeit, a much weaker and shallower version of patriotism than the one Gramsci saw linked to Fordism—that it is attempting to sell to the American citizenry through its television commercials and other types of advertising.

Since its development by the Committee of 99, the Saturn philosophy, as distilled in its corporate mission statement, has taken the shape of a distinctly American management ideology combining highly individualistic ideas and assumptions from human resource management with equally American notions of the promises of advanced technology. With the American automobile industry, its corporate management, and union labor under challenge, Hal Riney and Partners, Inc. have turned the Saturn production philosophy's commitment to labor-management jointness and heavy emphasis on high technology production into award-winning advertisements touting Saturn as a different kind of car and a different kind of company with a different kind of unionized work force (Serafin, 1992). The subliminal message is that Saturn is not only the wave of the future, but also the car and manufacturer to restore GM and, by implication, America's leadership position vis-a-vis foreign competitors in the global economy through its supposed 'win-win' approach to production and sales.

The Saturn training and development model, like Toyota's, has become an exemplar for innovations in public education in Minnesota and Florida. In St. Paul, Minnesota, Saturn's methods and inspiration have spawned the Saturn School of Tomorrow, a learner-centered school program blending individualized personal growth plans devised by students who are responsible for their own learning and the most powerful and practical emerging educational and computer technologies (Bennett and King, 1991; and Hopkins, 1991).

Ironically, Saturn's mass advertising campaign and its educational clones suppress or leave unstated both the highly competitive nature of the North American marketplace in a era of enormous production overcapacity and the increasingly zero-sum nature of the American economy for new graduates, leaving the mistaken inference that the sad state of American education and the American auto industry will be overcome and the common good achieved by each person and each company pursuing its particular goods with goodwill and a cooperative team spirit. Teamwork and collective action are not however easily deducible from individualistic behavior and market assumptions.

Worker Training at TMM and Saturn Compared: A Union Labor Perspective

The Gramscian problematic of ideological hegemony suggests that the meaning and substance of worker training is subject to multiple renderings, depending upon the prevailing vector of political forces and the state of the hegemonic struggle. Training may be articulated in a certain way and pulled in a direction that dilutes worker skills, reduces potential worker mobility or promotes close identity with the prevailing corporate world view or it may be redirected to genuinely empower workers, deepen and improve their skills and their portability to other jobs and other firms, and strengthen worker solidarity and identification with labor interests. In a general sense, the value of worker training is not in dispute. It is the hegemonic corporate culture that twists and reshapes the substance and agenda of worker training in a manner inimical to worker identities, interests, and group loyalties. As Tony Bennett has so well put it, "such [hegemonic] processes neither erase the cultures of subordinate groups, nor do they rob 'the people' of their 'true culture'; what they do do is shuffle those cultures on to an ideological and cultural terrain in which they can be disconnected from whatever radical impulses which may (but need not) have fueled them and be connected to more conservative or often downright reactionary cultural and ideological tendencies" (Bennett, 1986: 19).

Toyota Motor Manufacturing, Inc. at Georgetown, Kentucky, and Saturn Corporation at Spring Hill, Tennessee, present two fascinating and, in some ways, convergent training models and hegemonic processes. Table 4 summarizes the similarities and differences between these two cases. For organized labor, a number of critical observations must be underlined. First, TMM's work organization and training program illuminate one of the deeper ironies of post-Fordist production processes. For all the stress placed on teamwork and the pursuit of collective goals in the social organization of auto production, the Toyota case shows the extent to which JPM and its transplant variants generate at the point of production highly fragmentizing and individualizing tendencies within the work force. At TMM in Georgetown, the concessions to American culture have precipitated an organizational model of production and training process that has generated social stratification through the expansion of the job classification structure from three to five and now to ten job categories, incorporates a prepromotion training process that fosters the pursuit of individual career mobility within the plant, and has spawned a pay system that has instituted a structure of wage differentials that divides the work force and fosters the individualist game of internal careerism at the expense of collective interests and goods. As Beaumont (1991) notes in his study of union policies and responses to employer initiated human resource management (HRM) developments in Canada, Britain, and the United States, HRM should be seen by more militant trade union organizations as "a set of policies, practices, and arrangements designed essentially to 'individualize' and weaken individual membership commitment and loyalty to the union" (305). This insight is affirmed in Garrahan and Stewart's study of the unionized Nissan/Sunderland plant in northeast England in their treatment of the way training and teamworking generate a synergy in the fulfillment of individual and corporate goals. For them, the key to this synergy lies in the unstated principle that "employees must act as individual market competitors" (1992: 54).

By contrast, the Saturn agreement, crafted for a unionized plant built on codetermination principles, meets a set of formal criteria for promoting greater

Table 4
Comparison of Toyota and Saturn training programs—a summary

	Toyota	Saturn
training level:	extensive—650,000 hours	extensive—1,000,000
model:	Japanese/HRM	Japanaese/HRM
hours of training per worker annually:	50	91
structure:	top-down/professional	jointed/professional
workforce:	nonunion	union
hegemonic strategy:	company/community	co-optation/mass-mediated national
hegemonic strength:	high	moderate high, subject to erosion
counterhegemonic possibilities:	slight, highly contingent on major reversals	moderate, depending on local and national factors

economic justice and collective interests that, for Clark (1989) and perhaps Turner (1991), may be the key to the future for the American labor movement. "The Saturn Project," Clark (1989: 190) states, "implies a form of corporatism . . . [and] quite different political values: group interests as opposed to individual interests, codetermination as opposed to economic warfare, and a culture of collective action as opposed to American individualism." Yet, much of the evolution of this model depends upon the relative balance of hegemonic and counterhegemonic forces operating at the local, national, and continental levels. The unfulfilled promise of the Saturn experiment is that the union leadership has refused to take up the gauntlet thrown down by the catchwords of management's post-Fordist world view and work organization and to strive to redefine and rearticulate them in a truly democratic direction and in a manner convergent with the values and interests of organized labor and the mass of nonunion labor.

Where a sense of collective worker interests and identity has been radically individualized, on the one hand, or falsely and wholly identified with corporate goods, on the other, it is small wonder that the nonunion work force at Toyota shows such support for Toyotism and its training program. In biannual survey polls financed by TMM management to assay worker attitudes, team members' support and identification with the company (measured by the question whether they would be better off if the company is economically better off) have been close to 95 percent (Allen, 1993). The hegemonic processes of this preeminent Japanese auto firm have worked their magic over concepts like teamwork, worker empowerment, and up- and reskilling, in a hegemonic articulation that speaks to the deeper needs of workers who have experienced their opposites in work life at other plants, jobs, or occupations. Who will condemn workers' yearning for satisfying work, personal dignity, democratic voice, and job security in a world in flux and a national, regional, and global political economy undergoing dramatic restructuring?

In sum, both point to the critical need for organized labor to treat the political struggle taking place at the point of production and in the training classroom with the utmost seriousness and to formulate a strategy of counterhegemonic action based on the originating impulses and interests that fueled the labor movement. Lowell Turner (1991) has been among a handful of students of organized labor who has taken the challenge of the work reorganization and the new industrial relations as a political problem to be confronted and puzzled out by American unions. Recognizing the strategic importance of the training component of a union-led work reorganization program, he has issued a clarion call to the American union leadership to carve out an independent vision and suggested the merits of a corporatist model and apprenticeship training program developed in concert with the works councils by IG Metall, Germany's auto industry union and leading organization in the German labor movement (ibid., 160–162). Emanating from IG Metall's post-war experience in leading the German movement for work reorganization based on a union concern for work humanization and the pursuit of 'rationalization protection,' skills upgrading through societywide apprenticeship programs, and solidaristic wages, Turner sees a set of criteria, principles, and interests constituting the German auto union's autonomous vista on new work organization and the role and content of worker training within that restructured workplace.

Using these standards, Turner has offered a very sobering assessment of the Toyota-led NUMMI model of workplace restructuring and employee training (Table 5). Yet, as Turner (1991), Streeck (1989, 1993), and others demonstrate, the capacity of Germany's IG Metall to implement this union-led program has been based in no small measure on a set of legal-constitutional and political con-

Table 5 Comparison of workplace reorganization and training strategies by IG Metall in German auto factories and by the UAW at NUMMI

IG Metall Principles of Group Work	NUMMI
1. Broad assignment of varying tasks for the group; long cycle time	Teams either skilled or unskilled (production); narrow range of tasks for most teams; short cycle time (around one minute)
2. Broad group decision-making competence	Job rotation and division of work, with approval; otherwise limited to "input"
3. Decentralization of plant decision-making structure	Somewhat, for teams, team and group leaders (who oversee several teams)
4. Decentralized technology and production concepts; trained "semiskilled" systems monitors to oversee advanced technology	Traditional technology in most of plant
5. Equal pay for group members	Yes, with extra pay for team leaders
6. Special training for disabled and socially disadvantaged (solidarity as basis for group work)	No
7. Personal and occupational development	Limited, except for team leaders and apprentices hired from within
8. Group meetings, at least one hour per week	One half-hour every two weeks
9. Representation of group interests within system of interest representation	Limited and informal; union represents individual not teams
10. Voluntary participation	Mandatory participation
11. Pilot projects before broad implementation	No
12. Joint steering committee to oversee group activities	No

Source: Turner (1991: 161)

ditions not easily duplicated in the American context by a labor movement in numerical decline and strategic retreat in the face of a continuing corporate offensive. The likelihood of legislation in the United States instituting tripartite, corporatist bargaining at a period when the national labor movement is in disarray and where organized labor's allies are few and weak politically is tantamount to nil. Worse still, many of union labor's putative supporters in the academic realm have apparently succumbed to the lure of new labor-management models that radically bifurcate the formal elements of worker participation from the underlying substantive elements of union power.

Perhaps a better, more proximate strategy for UAW political action may be found in the efforts of Canadian unions, particularly the Canadian Auto Workers (CAW), to fashion a new vision and a counterhegemonic strategy for workplace reorganization (Table 6). The literature on the Canadian labor experience in confronting the challenge of JPM and global restructuring is large and continues to grow (CAW, 1989; Robertson and Wareham, 1987; Robertson, Rinehart, and Huxley, 1992; and Yanarella and Green, 1993, 1994). Within this sizable and burgeoning literature, scholars, union activists, and organizers have begun to participate in larger theoretical-strategic debates on worker training triggered by the proliferation of so-called post-Fordist or JPM approaches to large-scale manufacturing (e.g., Muszynski and Wolfe, 1989; Robertson, 1992a, b, and c; Mahon, 1990; and Jackson, 1992).

Table 6 Comparative auto union responses to post-Fordist work reorganization

I. American Model of Conflict and Accommodation
  A. **Labor movement:** fragmented and decentralized, where the national labor federation (AFL-CIO) is highly splintered organizationally and has little leverage in governmental policymaking
  B. **Auto union:** United Auto Workers—a fairly centralized national union with historically active, democratic unions with a long tradition of an adversarial, arms-length relationship between labor and management
  C. **Union strength and membership:** declining numbers and influence in the industry which encourages a capitalist-managerial offensive against unionization
  D. **Bargaining:** model of pattern bargaining giving way to local plant bargaining; growing problem of whipsawing by management
  E. **Union-management relations:** a mixture of adversarialism and cooperation with balance varying from plant to plant and local union to local union
  F. **Orientation to work reorganization:** lack of an independent vision for alternative work reorganization and a consistent strategy for responding to managerial initiatives ("management acts, union reacts")

II. Canadian Model of Conflict and Struggle
  A. **Labor movement:** fragmented and decentralized with a national labor federation (Canadian Labour Council) which is moderately cohesive and has variable access to government policymaking depending upon strength and involvement of the NDP

Table 6 *continued*

B. **Auto union:** Canadian Auto Workers—a highly centralized national union with exceptionally active, democratic unions characterized by strong national and local leadership, a militant, syndicalist tradition, and a system of adversarial industrial relations

C. **Union strength and membership:** significant strength within the industry and high and steady membership numbers, despite corporate assault and economic restructuring

D. **Bargaining:** persistence of model of pattern bargaining despite Big Three pressures and location of East Asian auto transplants in Canada

E. **Union-management relations:** predominance of adversarialism in traditional plant settings and negotiated involvement in nontraditional, post-Fordist settings

F. **Orientation toward work reorganization:** formal opposition to post-Fordist work reorganization and labor-management cooperation combined with an evolving autonomous union vision that involves negotiating union participation in lean production and struggling to take a proactive stance toward redefining its egalitarian facade and reshaping the balance of power at all levels of union-management relations

III. The German Model of Democratic Corporatism

A. **Labor movement:** cohesive, but decentralized with a national labor federation (*Deutscher Gewerkschaftsbund* or DGB) that is formally decentralized with one dominant union (IG Metall) and a dual system of works councils mandated by law that is dominated by members of DGB union and increasingly a vehicle for the expression of union interests

B. **Auto union:** IG Metall—the major union within the German labor movement with democratic unions, significant influence at the plant level through domination of works councils, and strongly-backed views on workplace organization, worker security, and production processes that shape the direction of productivity coalitions at the firm level toward successful economic adjustment strategies that protect worker interests

C. **Union strength and membership:** high and stable union strength and membership

D. **Bargaining:** corporatist bargaining among peak and subpeak organizations occurring in a variety of forums and at a number of levels—from nationally coordinated, regional collective bargaining to political processes that result in social and labor market policies, to the tripartite institutions that govern Germany's vocational education system

E. **Union-management relations:** a dual system of sixteen unions nationally and legally independent works councils locally characterized by close union-works council relations and regional collective bargaining that is nationally coordinated by centralized unions and employer unions in a democratic corporatist fashion

F. **Orientation toward work reorganization:** the formal integration of unions and works councils into managerial decision-making at every level is highly

Table 6 *continued*

constrained by an independent vision of work reorganization (organized around the theme of work humanization) and other substantive issues (e.g., use of new technology and design of new jobs) and imposed external labor market rigidities (no layoffs) and high wages in exchange for a system of internal labor market flexibility—leading to training and retraining of the existing work force by the firm and development of a strategy of upmarket diversified high-quality production in which market success offsets high manpower costs

Source: The German model is adapted in part from Turner's (1991) analysis of IG Metall and the German labor movement.

Chief among these recent contributions to the training debate from the Canadian labor movement is Robertson's proposed labor agenda (see Table 7). While these criteria are general enough to serve as guidelines for the American labor movement, a key point should be emphasized: that they grow out of the framework of a more militant, syndicalist Canadian labor tradition and continue to carry the marks of a history of political struggle, an approach to labor-management relations, and a series of decisions and actions affecting the power balance between capital and labor that influence the possibility of future rank and file mobilization. Thus, this labor agenda on training for Canadian (and

Table 7 Robertson's training agenda for Canadian labor

1. Training is a basic working right and an integral part of the job.
2. Training objectives and goals have to be developed in specific and measurable terms, such as hours per worker, and all workers guaranteed that training.
3. Training should be conducted during working hours and without production pressures.
4. The goals, content, and delivery of training programs should be codetermined and should be based on principles of adult education.
5. Training should be developmental. The programs should teach skills that go beyond a particular job or work area.
6. Training programs should be open to all workers, not just the youngest or the fittest, and special efforts should be made to use training as a vehicle for social equity.
7. Training should be geared to raising the level of skill of the entire work force, not just selected occupations or selected areas.
8. Training should support and develop a worker-centered definition of skill and not be restricted to job performance or academic factors.
9. Training should support the development of good job design and technologies which respect the skills of the worker.

Source: Robertson (1992a)

American) unions must be put squarely into the context of the orientation of leading sectors of the Canadian labor movement toward work reorganization—specifically, their formal opposition to post-Fordist work reorganization and labor-management cooperation combined with the development of an unfolding autonomous union vision that involves negotiating union participation in lean production plants and struggling to take a proactive stance toward redefining its egalitarian facade and reshaping the balance of power at all levels of union-management relations.

These two alternate models—the Canadian model of conflict and struggle and the German model of democratic corporatism—open up for the UAW union a new strategic vista on work reorganization and worker training and new political ground for labor-management contestation. Obviously, the only place to begin is with the present state of strategic thinking and political struggle. Although the UAW response to JPM and lean production is more pluralistic than the Saturn case would suggest, its upper leadership and research ranks have far to go in assimilating the insights and lessons from our friendly neighbor and Europe's superpower.

The first priority of the UAW and American labor generally would seem to be rebuilding of union membership and increasing union strength through national labor law reform and renewal of organization drives at the grassroots or plant level. The advantages of Canadian labor law are at least one reason why its labor movement has been able to weather the corporate onslaught of the eighties without the precipitate decline of union numbers and political clout experienced in the United States. Though it must be admitted that the decentralized nature of Canadian labor, including the CAW, has put pressure on union locals to buy into JPM and other employee involvement programs, the hard-won victories and advances by militant Canadian unions to organize hitherto nonunionized sectors of the labor force and even, in the case of the CAW, to promote union campaigns at the transplants (e.g., the Hyundai plant in Bromont, Quebec) demonstrate that organizing *is* a viable alternative to collaboration or inaction.

Second, the German and Canadian examples in the auto sector point to the need for the research and strategic arms of the American auto union to fashion their own independent stance toward worker training and other elements of work reorganization. In the United States, the formulation of elements of that vision will likely involve resuscitating and revitalizing past practices. For example, the long-term tradition in the United States auto industry of apprenticeship programs sponsored and directed by the UAW has in the past implicated the union not only in a process that conferred formal skill certification of its members successfully completing the program. It also institutionalized the collective and distinctly worker interest in workplace skills development that is recognized across industries and can be taken with workers changing jobs within or across industrial sectors. For all the training hours invested in skills development at Toyota and Saturn, neither program confers the kinds of certificates past UAW apprenticeship programs have and in some cases still do. Indeed, the TMM goal of training workers in multiple skills that develop only half of what certified electricians, plumbers, and other skilled tradespeople learn to qualify for certification demonstrates that the ideal of a multiskilled workers in Toyota's management philosophy is a misnomer and points to the greater accuracy of the term, multifunctioned worker (Robertson, 1992b: 37–38). Much of the skills development falling into the category of technical training is company-specific skills training that reduces the worker's future or potential mobility because those skills are not transferable to other plants.

Critics of corporate training programs like Toyota's and Saturn's also point out (Robertson and Wareham, 1987; and Robertson, 1992a) that upwards of 70 percent of GM training programs fall in the category of cultural or attitudinal training (i.e., indoctrination into the reigning corporate ideology). If the UAW cedes to corporate management this vital terrain of corporate hegemony, it will have already lost the initiative in defining the stakes, content, and objectives of skills development and work reorganization.

Sadly, the critical importance of the American apprenticeship model for the UAW has been all but forgotten. At NUMMI, where residues of the apprenticeship heritage can still be found in the GM-Toyota plant's training program, certification earned by workers there does not carry sufficient weight to confer upon them true journeyman status in specific skills (OTA, 1990: 188). Even worse, the national UAW research department seems oblivious to the role and potential of apprenticeships in protecting and advancing worker values, goals, and interests. An illustration of this blindness, Turner (1991: 162n4) has noted, was a presentation by a member of the UAW Research Department that unfavorably compared the group work model in Germany grounded in a societywide and union-directed apprenticeship program with the supposed virtues of the Japanese teamwork model!

The experiences of leading unions in the German and Canadian labor movements highlight a third imperative: the need for American trade unions to press for solidaristic approaches to wages, training, and teamwork. In the auto industry, wage structures and joint union-management programs for team organization and training are still manifest as part of the Fordist legacy of a "continuing separation between skilled and unskilled or semiskilled workers" (Turner, 1991: 160). Yet, as Robertson's labor-directed training agenda and Streeck's cogent and compelling analyses of the German model indicate, training should be recognized as a human right and a collective good. As the Toyota case study has shown, where training is individualized and becomes one basis for a highly differentiated wage system, it pits worker against worker and obstructs the advance toward collective identities. By contrast, Rianne Mahon follows the

spirit of Robertson and Streeck by arguing for an alternative of "diversified quality production" for Canada, spearheaded by a strong union movement united by
progressive technology and wages policies on the model of the German labor
movement (Mahon, 1987, 1991).

A fourth element of a galvanized labor strategy for America involves the
concrete political struggle to realize the democratic potential of pseudo-demo-
cratic practices comprising post-Fordism's new forms of managerial and hegemonic control. Operating within a distinctly Gramscian framework of politics,
power, and maneuver, this strategic option emphasizes the critical role of
organized labor, in coalition with other subaltern groups and movements
(Brecher and Costello, 1990; and Laclau and Mouffe, 1985), in working with
the prevailing vector of political forces to deflect and remold tendencies toward
authoritarian forms of post-Fordism in a counterhegemonic direction to realize
the democratic promise of worker involvement, teamwork, multiskilled training, and other presently illusory claims of flexible production on the shop floor
(e.g., Carroll, 1990; Harp, 1991; Wells, 1987; and Robertson, Rinehart, and
Huxley, 1991). Because organized labor in the United States is so weak and
Marxist class analysis so poorly reflects the complicated nature of power in late
capitalist America, national unions and changed-oriented groups promoting
social justice, public health, and peace with nature must strive to fashion what
Gramsci called a new historic bloc in the counterhegemonic struggle.

Fifth and finally, labor scholars as knowers and actors must renew their
commitment to the eminently political importance of their intellectually mediated practice, motivated by that 'pessimism of intellect, optimism of will' shaping
Gramsci's own political activities. The training debate and the more encompassing Fordist/post-Fordist controversy demonstrate anew that the areas of academic
discourse and policy debate are key hegemonic sites on which are being fought
theoretical and political contests shaping in large and small ways the hegemonic
practices in the larger dynamic and contradictory social whole implicating work,
power, and language.

Approaching those intellectual labors with militant hope, intellectual
clarity, political patience, and personal responsibility, students of labor studies
acting in dialectical fealty with the labor movement's animating and sometimes
forgotten goals and values will refuse to succumb to intellectual self-loathing or
to any sense of political impotence toward the theorizing enterprise—an activity
understood not as some abstract exercise, but as a passionate engagement in the
task of objectivating the larger framework of social life, intellectual-material
work, and interpersonal communication in all its contradictoriness and possibilities. This is the truly singular contribution of those social theorists and intellectuals in the academy living, as Gramsci (1971: 9, 323) argued, in the company
of fellow human beings who, because they too are symbol-makers and engage in
"critical-practical" activity, are in a general sense intellectuals too. Far from

being an abstract dispute among academic specialists, then, the post-Fordist debate affects all of us and calls for the contributions of all intellectuals because, in a fundamental sense, it is over who shall harness the generalized intellectual-ized labor, how it shall be done, for what purposes, and at what cost.

PART
III

BEYOND THE CRISIS OF FORDISM
The Role of Organized Labor

The Transformation of the NLRA Paradigm: The Future of Labor-Management Relations in Post-Fordist Auto Plants*

_____ _William C. Green_

The North American auto marketplace witnessed a major restructuring during the 1980s. Seven Asian automobile assembly plants along with four Japanese-Big Three joint ventures—AutoAlliance, CAMI, Diamond-Star, and NUMMI—and GM's Saturn were built across the industrial heartland of the United States and Canada.[1] This common experience, accompanied by a transformation in industrial production methods and the reorganization of work defined in terms of Japanese lean production techniques and cooperative labor relations, created a crisis for the Fordist regime of industrial production, its system of labor-management relations, and organized labor. As of 1995, these developments have fragmented and weakened the labor movement. The United Auto Workers (UAW) and Canadian Auto Workers (CAW) still have contracts with the Big Three auto makers, but they have not yet organized the Asian lean production transplants.[2] The UAW and CAW do, however, represent workers at the joint ventures and Saturn, but these collective agreements clearly reflect the impact of lean production principles which cede greater control to management. Lean production's impact on North American labor relations has also created a crisis for the National Labor Relations Act (NLRA) paradigm, the legal foundation for United States and Canadian labor-management relations, which carves out a limited right for labor to organize, to negotiate with management over wages, hours, and working conditions, and to take concerted action, but which otherwise gives labor and management a wide berth to privately determine the substance of their collectively bargained contracts.

In this chapter, I will argue that the NLRA paradigm's crisis is, in fact, a dual one. The paradigm's public law dimension, based on United States and

Canadian labor statutes, is threatened by Asian transplants which have traded upon its narrow statutory confines to avoid unionization and suppress union organizing efforts by using lean production-based plant location criteria, worker recruitment and training methods, and team concept production practices. At the same time, the paradigm's private law dimension, based on collectively bargained agreements, is being altered by the Big Three-Japanese joint ventures and Saturn which have used the NLRA's freedom of contract to abandon the highly formalized and detailed contracts produced by adversarial labor-management relations and to negotiate lean production high-trust cooperative labor agreements with the UAW and CAW. In addition, the Saturn Labor Agreement has employed codetermination principles to extend labor participation beyond joint shop floor governance to strategic decision-making. Yet these agreements, along with the Asian transplants' antiunion strategy, have been quite correctly perceived as management efforts to use lean production and codetermination principles to extend and enhance managerial power at labor's expense. As a consequence, the NLRA paradigm has become contested terrain. Labor and management's arguments and actions have already begun to redefine the paradigm's adversarial character and set the parameters and establish the agenda for the current debate over United States labor law reform.

To explore this argument, the first part of this chapter will provide a crossnational framework to analyze the NLRA paradigm's dual crisis and the prospects for United States labor law reform. The second part will define NLRA paradigm and outline the nature of the challenge it confronts from lean production labor relations. Then the chapter will explore the consequences of lean production's recruitment methods, cooperative labor-management programs, and team concept workplace practices for the NLRA paradigm, first at the nonunion Asian transplants and then at their joint ventures with the Big Three auto makers and at Saturn. Finally, the last part of the chapter will draw upon these experiences to assess the prospects for United States labor law reform.

The Structure of Labor-Management Relations

The North American automobile industry has become the setting for a struggle over competing visions of labor-management relations in a post-Fordist world. A management vision, defined by Japanese lean production, is most ably extolled by James Womack, Daniel Jones and Daniel Roos (1990) and by Martin Kenney and Richard Florida (1993). A competing labor vision, more sensitive to the cruel reality of the shop floor and the need for a more humane workplace, has been has been expounded by Knuth Dohse et al. (1985), Rianne Mahon (1987), Mike Parker and Jane Slaughter (1988), Alain Lipietz (1991), and Barry Bluestone and Irving Bluestone (1992). Together these visions define the issues and interests involved and reveal the tensions among contending labor systems built upon Fordist adversarialism, Japanese cooperation, and German codetermination; but both are faulted by their failure to appreciate the political and legal foundations for labor-management relations and the limitations these realities impose upon any vision for a new industrial order.

One way to understand this struggle over competing visions, assess their political and legal dimensions, and explore their impact on organized labor's current predicament and the prospects for its survival and prosperity in the years ahead is to employ a crossnational perspective offered by Lowell Turner (1991) who argues that labor-management relations are structured by two variables: "first, the extent to which unions are integrated into the process of managerial decision-making, especially concerning work reorganization; and second, the existence of laws or corporatist bargaining arrangements" (Turner, 1991: 12). These two variables are the defining elements for four labor relations systems summarized in Figure 1 and briefly described below.

Model 1 describes the German labor-management relations system in which labor unions are integrated into the process of managerial decision-making through the medium of union-dominated works councils. This integration occurs from a base which is independent of management, because it is supported by the Works Constitution Act of 1952, and by a corporatist bargaining structure in which a nationally cohesive labor union movement, coordinated by one cohesive labor federation (the DGB or *Deutscher Gewerkschaftsbund*) and enjoying Social Democratic Party support, is engaged in regional collective bargaining with centralized employer associations.

Model 2 describes a labor-management relations system which Turner does not explicitly discuss. His analysis suggests Model 2 would exist in countries where adversarial labor-management relations prevail, national labor law is

Figure 1 Labor-management relations system

Integration Into Managerial Process

		Yes	No
Laws or Corporatist Bargaining Arrangements	Yes	1 Germany	2
	No	3 Japan	4 United States

supportive of arms-length negotiations, and corporatist bargaining structures are strong. In Model 2 countries, these three elements would be rooted in a nationally cohesive labor union movement coordinated by a peak labor federation which engages in collective bargaining with centralized employer associations, enjoys popular support, and plays a critical role in the life of a nationally prominent political party.

Model 3 describes the Japanese lean production labor-management relations system which prevails, not only in Japan, but also in Japan's North American nonunion transplants. In this model, workers and their enterprise unions are integrated into the process of managerial decision-making in a "decidedly subordinate way" (Turner, 1991: 14). Integration is defined on management's terms and corporatist bargaining arrangements do not exist, because workers and their unions are not supported by national laws which provide them with an independent legal basis for participation and because labor unions are fragmented and enjoy little popular and political support.

Model 4 describes the United States and Canadian labor-management relations systems dominated by adversarial arms-length bargaining. Unions are not integrated into managerial decision-making because the National Labor Relations Act and Canadian labor laws do not provide the legal basis for independent participation in managerial decision-making, although integration does occur on a single firm or plant basis at management's initiative. Finally, corporatist bargaining structures are weak. In both countries, organized labor's peak associations—the AFL-CIO in the United States and the Canadian Labor Congress (CLC) and the Canadian Federation of Labor (CFL), among others, in Canada—are fragmented, but organized labor in Canada, unlike the United States, enjoys popular and political party support sufficient to allow it to have a meaningful impact on labor law reform.

These four labor relations systems are not equally favorable to the interests of organized labor. Turner argues that if labor unions are to survive and prosper they must abandon adversarial arms-length bargaining strategies and become integrated into a firm's managerial decision-making. For him, managerial integration involves "substantial participation with management regarding plans to reorganize work before actual decisions are made on the shape of the new organization and the pace of implementation" (Turner, 1991: 16). This will be a dangerous move, he argues, unless union participation is supported by national legislation which creates a legal framework for labor's independent status in managerial decision-making. Union participation also requires a corporatist bargaining structure, the dynamic element of which, he says, is "a cohesive labor movement . . . one that includes a relatively small number of national unions and is effectively, if not formally, centralized, either through a dominant central labor federation or through the centralizing influence of one dominant union" (Turner, 1991: 17). Unless unions become integrated on these terms, Turner argues, they will be subordinated to management and continue to decline (Turner, 1991: 15). In sum, his analysis suggests that change is necessary. If organized labor keeps to its present path (Model 4) or accepts a lean production-based labor-management relations system (Model 3), its future will be bleak. To survive and prosper, unions will need to move towards the German codetermination system (Model 1), but in doing so, they will have to confront a formidable dual task: building a cohesive labor movement and altering the current labor law paradigm.

The Legal Foundations of North American Labor-Management Relations

Legal paradigms are models which structure and direct human behavior. These paradigms draw upon a nation's history and traditions and are reflected in its public law—its constitution, statutes, administrative law, and judicial decisions—and in private agreements. The four labor-management relations systems described in the first part of the chapter are each based on a labor law paradigm. These paradigms, depending upon the particular nation's labor history and practices, may be grounded in constitutional principles regarding employment and work and by legislation establishing the general structure for labor-management relations and the respective roles of labor, management, and government as they may be refined by administrative and judicial decisions and by labor and management's collectively bargained agreements and grievance arbitration decisions. Labor law paradigms, thereby, express the existing labor-management consensus; and in times of paradigm change, they also structure the strategies of the participants, establish the parameters for their interaction, and define the prospects for legal change. In North America, labor relations are governed by the National Labor Relations Act (NLRA) paradigm and its Canadian variant.

The NLRA Paradigm

The United States labor-management relations system is structured by the National Labor Relations Act (Wagner Act) of 1935. Since its passage, the NLRA has been amended most notably by the Labor Management Relations Act (Taft-Hartley Act) of 1947 and its meanings have been elaborated by the National Labor Relations Board (NLRB) and the federal courts (Klare, 1989; and Hogler and Grenier, 1992: Ch. 3). This legislation and its administrative and judicial case law constitute the NLRA paradigm's public law component to which must be added the substantial body of private law contained in labor and management's collectively bargained agreements and grievance arbitration awards.

The NLRA paradigm carves out a limited role for government regulation of labor-management relations. The National Labor Relations Act was passed for the express purpose of promoting industrial peace by granting workers the legal right to freely choose a union, bargain collectively with management, and take concerted action to advance their organizing and bargaining rights (NLRA, Sec. 7; and Rainsberger, 1989: 94). The NLRA paradigm was narrowed further by the NLRA's Taft-Hartley Act amendments which placed substantial curbs on union power by creating six labor unfair labor practices, and by authorizing state governments in Section 14(b) to enact 'Right to Work' statutes which prohibit union membership as a condition of employment (Moore and Newman, 1985). With these changes, Taft-Hartley abandoned the Wagner Act's encouragement of organizing and collective bargaining and substituted a policy which provided that the NLRA would be "'a neutral guarantor of equal rights or, at least, reasonably balanced rights'" (Adams, 1989: 55). As a consequence, the Taft-Hartley Act represents an "institutionalization of the perception of unions as a third force" in the work place (Rainsberger, 1989: 98).

The NLRA provides for labor's right to organize by establishing procedures for workers to select a union (NLRA, Sec. 9) which include an NLRB-supervised election campaign (NLRA, Sec. 3), a secret ballot, and if the union wins, NLRB certification of the union as the bargaining unit. The NLRA also imposes on employers and employees the duty to bargain in good faith over wages, hours, and terms or conditions of employment including grievance rights and procedures, but the statute does not explicitly limit the subjects of good faith bargaining. Instead, it is the Supreme Court's decision in *NLRB v. Borg-Warner* (1959)[3] which restricts bargaining to mandatory subjects—wages, hours, and terms or conditions of employment—and leaves all other bargainable subjects to management's discretion (Note, 1959; Harper, 1982). As a consequence, the Supreme Court, by recognizing a broad category of permissive bargaining subjects, most often alluded to in management rights clauses of collective contracts, preserved management's exclusive right to make strategic decisions and, subject to collective contractual provisions, to govern the workplace. To protect labor's legal right to organize and unionized labor's collective bargaining rights, the NLRA prohibits unfair labor practices (NLRA, Sec. 8) and authorizes the NLRB to hear and, subject to judicial review, to decide unfair labor practice claims.

This public law component created the structure for labor's organizing and contracting behavior and allowed labor and management the freedom to complete the paradigm by creating a body of private law contained in their collectively bargained agreements including provisions for grievance settlement. As Thomas Kochan, Harry Katz, and Robert McKersie have observed: "[t]he NLRA did not dictate the terms or conditions of employment, but endorsed a process by which the parties could shape their own substantive contract terms" (1986: 24). The UAW has used this limited regulatory framework to organize the nation's auto workers and, in its often adversarial relationship with the Big

Three auto makers, to negotiate highly formalized and detailed collective bargaining agreements. The 1948 GM-UAW collective agreement has defined the three major elements of the NLRA paradigm's private law component: first, a three year wage and fringe benefit structure negotiated by the UAW's national office; second, a job control-focused work rule structure whose "general principles and rules governing seniority, job classifications, production conditions, and mechanisms for resolving grievances" are negotiated by the UAW's national office and whose detailed job descriptions are negotiated by each local for the plants it represents (Holmes, 1989: 101); and third, a contract administered by the local union under the supervision of the national office.[4]

Canadian Labor Law Paradigm

The Canadian labor-management relations system is based on federal and provincial legislation, dating from 1948, which bears the imprint of the National Labor Relations Act (Wagner Act) of 1935 and which bestows upon provincial governments primary responsibility for private sector labor relations (Adams, 1989). This Canadian legislation also creates a limited regulatory labor-management relations system to promote industrial peace by granting workers the limited legal right to freely choose a union, bargain collectively with management, and take concerted action. To implement these rights, federal and provincial labor relations boards, subject to judicial review, are responsible for "union certification, unfair labor practices, and in some cases, industrial conflict and the regulation of internal agency affairs" (Arthurs, et al., 1988: 57).[5] Otherwise, the Canadian labor law paradigm has been completed at labor and management's initiative by means of collectively bargained agreements and grievance arbitration.

The Canadian labor law paradigm differs in some significant ways from its North American neighbor's. Labor law is not based on a single federal statute, but, as noted above, upon both federal and provincial legislation. Yet "[t]he various Canadian [provincial] statutes are sufficiently similar to allow us to speak of a distinctive Canadian model of representation" (Weiler, 1983: 1806, fn. 134). Canadian labor laws are more supportive of union labor because they do not contain a Taft-Hartley type provision which qualifies a union's right to exclusive representation and treats the union as "a third force" in the workplace. Nor does Canadian federal legislation recognize the right of the provinces to enact "Right to Work" statutes (Rainsberger, 1989: 98). Other significant statutory provisions include stricter union security agreements, stronger unfair labor practices provisions, limited use of replacement workers, labor relations board-imposed first collective contracts when the parties do not agree, and more restricted judicial review of labor board decisions (Thornicroft, 1990: 846).

Canadian labor law contains more favorable procedures for union recognition and certification based upon the card system (Weiler, 1983: 1806–11).

Ontario's Labor Relations Act, for example, provides that if a union signs at least 50 percent of employees, the union can be automatically certified as the bargaining agent. A vote is necessary only if a union signs less than 50, but more than 30, percent (Ontario Labor Relations Act, Ch. 228, Sec. 7: 14). In addition, Canadian labor law does not clearly restrict the subjects of good faith bargaining to mandatory subjects and leaves all other bargainable (permissive) subjects to management's discretion. Instead, as H.W. Arthurs has found, Canadian labor arbitrators are divided between a "reserved rights [approach] premised on the assumption that management . . . does not surrender its traditional right to manage . . . [and one that] treat[s] the collective agreement as creating a new legal regime that puts the trade union and employer on an equal footing" (Arthurs, et al., 1988: 298). As a consequence, Canadian labor law may not be as wedded as the United States to protecting management's exclusive right to make strategic decisions and may instead be more open to organized labor's participation on the basis of a collectively bargained contract.

Canadian labor law, having created an NLRA structure for labor's organizing and contracting behavior, has allowed labor and management to complete the paradigm by creating a body of private law contained in their collectively bargained agreements. Within this framework, the Canadian auto workers, as members of the UAW's Canadian region, relied upon provincial labor law to develop the Canadian equivalent of the Fordist adversarial labor-management relations system, one also defined by highly formalized and detailed collective bargaining agreements modeled on the three major elements of the 1948 GM-UAW model. This labor relations system which defined life on the shop floor during the 'glory years' began to disintegrate during the era of capitalist industrial restructuring and double-digit inflation of the 1980s. The UAW's acceptance of the Big Three auto makers' demands for concessions and cooperation led to unbridgeable differences which forced the Canadian UAW to break away by 1985 and pursue a traditional adversarial collective bargaining and no concessions strategy (Gindin, 1989; and Yates, 1990). Thereafter, the Japanese transplants presented a new challenge to the separate labor-management visions of both unions.

The Lean Production Labor Relations Model

Japan has been the major force behind the global restructuring of the automobile industry, its organization of work, and its labor-management relations. In the space of one decade, six Japanese automobile firms built assembly plants across the North American industrial heartland and four Japanese firms—Mazda, Mitsubishi, Suzuki, and Toyota—established joint ventures with the Big Three auto makers. With them the Japanese brought their lean production methods and labor relations system which had made them a competitive force in the international automobile marketplace.

Lean production's principles and practices have created a crisis for the Fordist regime of industrial production, its labor relations system, and the NLRA paradigm and its Canadian variant, because lean production rejects the basic elements of the Fordist production model, its adversarial style of labor-management relations, and the legal rights of North American workers. Under lean production, wages, work rules, and jobs are not negotiated, because the workers do not belong to autonomous unions. Workers (or 'production associates') are paid essentially the same wage, except for a small supplement received by team leaders. Work rules are flexible and job classifications are minimal, because the team concept emphasizes multitask training, job rotation, and performance of housekeeping and maintenance duties (Holmes, 1989: 100). Since corporatist bargaining arrangements do not exist and labor has no independent legal basis for participation, lean production's cooperative labor-management relations mean that workers are integrated into the process of decision-making on management's terms.

Lean production and its labor relations system have challenged both the United States and Canadian labor-management relations systems and their legal paradigms in two settings (Drache and Glasbeek, 1989; Hertzenberg, 1992; Wells, 1992; and Yates, 1992). In a nonunion Asian transplant setting, lean production practices have subtly undermined their workers' NLRA right to organize and made it difficult, if not impossible, for the UAW and CAW to organize transplant workers. In a union setting at the Japanese-Big Three joint ventures and Saturn, lean production has not so much threatened union organizing or collective bargaining rights, as it has challenged the national UAW and CAW offices to design a labor-management strategy in cooperation with their union locals for collective bargaining and shop floor representation which effectively protects their members' interests.

North American Labor Law and Lean Production at Nonunion Japanese Transplants

The UAW and the CAW have faced their toughest challenge from the five nonunion Asian transplant firms: Honda, Hyundai, Nissan, Toyota, and Subaru-Isuzu. Operating outside the narrow regulatory confines of the NLRA and Canadian labor law paradigms and within the framework of the lean production labor-management relations, these transplant auto firms have avoided unionization by employing a two-part, union substitution and union suppression, strategy (Weiler, 1990: 110).

Japanese Transplant Union Substitution Strategy

The Japanese labor-management relations system has been transferred, in large part, to the North American nonunion Asian transplants (Florida and

Kenney, 1991). The transplant firms have relied upon a union substitution strategy which employs an interrelated set of lean production-based decisions about plant location, worker recruitment and training, and production practices to integrate their workers into the process of shop floor decision-making in a "decidedly subordinate way" (Turner, 1991: 14).

The transplant firms have selected greenfield sites for their lean production facilities, because these small town locations have permitted them to exercise virtually unqualified strategic control in selecting a work force with minimal union experience.[6] Honda drew upon an applicant pool composed of "young, inexperienced workers without previous manufacturing experience" (Shimada and McDuffie, 1987: 53). Nissan selected Smyrna, a small town in Tennessee, for this reason and because the auto maker believed that the state's Right to Work statute would discourage union organizing. As Mair, Florida, and Kenney report: "Nissan . . . in making its site selection decision avoided areas with strong traditions of labor union organization . . . [and] selected Tennessee where labor union organizing is hampered by a 'Right to Work' statute, largely to minimize the likelihood of worker representation by the United Auto Workers" (1988: 366; see also Kenney and Florida, 1993: 101).

Nissan and other transplants have also employed recruitment, training, and production processes which have screened in lean production team players and screened out prounion applicants. At Subaru-Isuzu, for example, the recruitment process included a questionnaire with statements on labor-management relations designed to eliminate applicants with prounion sympathies and group exercises to test an applicant's ability to perform as a team player (Graham, 1991: 68). SIA's worker training emphasized transmission of company values and its use of the team concept, *kaizen*, and just in time lean production practices to maximize managerial shop floor control. Of these the team concept was the most potent control mechanism, because SIA used the team concept not merely to reorganize and set the pace for work, but also to frustrate labor organizing by creating a management-defined shop floor culture (Graham, 1993: 161–62). SIA and the other transplants have been enormously successful. None of their assembly plants have been organized. Lean production, however it may be practiced, is firmly in place at the Asian transplants where management-defined employee participation is limited to the shop floor.

Labor Law Implications

The Asian transplant firms' location, recruitment, and training practices do not violate the NLRA and Canadian labor law which is largely limited to labor organizing, collective bargaining, and concerted action. The labor laws of both countries do not clearly extend to organized labor the right to participate in these strategic decisions, because they are managerial rights. Although lean production, as a production method, is unlikely to raise any NLRA or Canadian labor law issues, management's use of lean production teams in a nonunion setting may intrude upon their worker's right to organize an autonomous union. The team concept has become the subject of considerable legal contro-versy in the United States.[7] Whether the use of lean production teams by nonunion Asian transplants violates the National Labor Relations Act involves two related questions. First, is a lean production team a Section 2(5) labor organization? To be a labor organization, the employees must participate; the employee group must "exist for the purpose of dealing with the employer"; and it must concern itself with "grievances, labor disputes, wages, rates of pay, hours of employment, or conditions of work" (NLRA, Sec. 8(a)(2)). Second, if the team is a labor organization, the question is whether the employer has com-mitted a Section 8(a)(2) unfair labor practice by taking actions to "dominate or interfere with the formation or administration of any labor organization or con-tribute financial or other support to it" (NLRA, Sec. 8(a)(2)).

These questions cannot be answered in the abstract, because it is not clear how Asian transplant firms may use production teams, nor is there any judicial consensus on whether these production teams violate the NLRA. The federal appellate courts are divided over whether the central purpose of the NLRA (to prevent industrial strife) can be best furthered by an interpretation of the statute which promotes an adversarial or a cooperative style of labor-management relations.

The United States Supreme Court in *NLRB v. Cabot Carbon* (1959) interpreted Section 2(5) to provide the widest opportunity for workers to orga-nize autonomous unions and bargain at arms-length with management. A feder-al court applying *Cabot Carbon* would give a broad reading to Section 2(5)'s "dealing with" language and, thereby, leave very little room for a lean produc-tion team to qualify as anything other than a labor organization. If an employee group made proposals or recommendations, had discussions, asked questions, or offered information involving "grievances, labor disputes, wages, rates of pay, hours of employment, or conditions of work [which] an employer could simply accept or reject without discussion," the employee group would be a Section 2(5) labor organization, because it would be "dealing with" the employer (Datz, 1992: 4; and Schmidman and Keller, 1984: 773–74). The federal court would then turn to Section 8(a)(2), give a broad reading to its "dominates" language, condemn a firm's conduct if it merely created a potential for domination of the transplant team, and, thereby, impose a comprehensive ban on any employer involvement in the formation of a labor organization (Note, 1983: 1663; and Lee, 1987: 216).

The Supreme Court's *Cabot Carbon* analysis has, however, lost favor with the NLRB and the federal courts of appeal which prefer instead an interpreta-tion which promotes a cooperative style of labor-management relations. The

NLRB or a federal court, following the Board's decision in *General Foods* (1977) and the Sixth Circuit's decision in *NLRB v. Streamway Division of Scott and Fetzer Co.* (1982), would focus on the concept of representation, not mentioned in Section 2(5), and conclude that a transplant team was not Section 2(5) labor organization because it did not "represent" other employees, but instead involved mere "participation" by all members of the plant (Datz, 1992: 6; Hogler, 1984). Alternatively, the NLRB or a federal court could turn to the Supreme Court's decisions in *NLRB v. Bell-Aerospace Co.* (1974), *NLRB v. Yeshiva University* (1980), and *NLRB v. Health Care & Retirement Corporation of America* (1994) and conclude that a lean production team is not a Section 2(5) labor organization because it is composed of managerial employees (Menard and Morrill, 1979; and Note, 1981).

If a federal appellate court did find that a lean production team was a labor organization, it would turn to Section 8(a)(2) and rely upon the Seventh Circuit's decision in *Chicago Rawhide Manufacturing Co. v. NLRB* (1955) which held that the NLRA did not proscribe mere cooperation, but only employer conduct which overrode the employee's free choice and constituted actual domination, interference, or support of a labor organization (221 F.2d at 167). A federal court, relying upon *Chicago Rawhide*, would also find support from the Sixth Circuit's decisions in *Federal Mogul Corporation v. NLRB* (1968) and *NLRB v. Homemaker Shop v. NLRB* (1984) and the Ninth Circuit's decision in *Hertzga and Knowles v. NLRB* (1974).

These Sixth, Seventh, and Ninth Court of Appeals decisions are extremely relevant, because all the Japanese transplants, the Big Three-Japanese joint ventures, and Saturn are located in these three circuits. As Thomas J. St. Antoine observed, these "courts of appeal have departed from a strict reading of Section 8(a)(2) on such avowed policy grounds as rejection of a purely adversarial model of labor relations and acceptance of a cooperative arrangement [where it] reflects a choice freely arrived at and where the organization is capable of being a meaningful avenue for the expression of employee wishes" (1989: 52). In fact, the Sixth Circuit has said that the NLRA "must be construed to take into account modern industrial practices, such as employee participation programs" (Datz, 1992: 3). So these federal court decisions, unless reversed by the Supreme Court, have the potential to redefine labor relations at UAW organized auto plants, especially the joint ventures and Saturn, and to impair the union's ability to organize the transplants.

Asian Transplant Union Suppression Strategy

The UAW and CAW have encountered substantial difficulties in organizing the Asian transplants whose greenfield locations and team-based hiring, training, and production practices have allowed them to discourage union organizing efforts. The UAW and CAW have not made serious attempts to organize either the Georgetown or Cambridge Toyota plants (DeReyteur, 1990: B–6; and Chappell and Jackson, 1991: 2). The UAW initiated an organizing drive at Honda in Marysville, but discontinued the effort in 1985 while the CAW has attempted sporadically, but unsuccessfully to organize Honda in Alliston (Veltri, 1990: 2). Subaru-Isuzu also remains nonunion (Chappell and Jackson, 1991: 2). Only the Nissan and Hyundai plants have been objects of serious UAW and CAW organizing efforts.

UAW Organizing at Nissan. The UAW began its first major transplant organizing drive at Nissan where the union's principal issues were injuries and workloads (Slaughter, 1989: 1; and Kenney and Florida, 1993: 266). The UAW's effort was disadvantaged from the outset by Nissan's location in a Right to Work state—the unionization rate in Tennessee manufacturing was 13.5 percent—and by Nissan's recruitment methods which screened out any applicants with union sympathies or experience and by its worker training and team-based production methods which permitted the auto maker to control the workers' shop floor culture.

When the organizing drive began, Nissan took the typical antiunion position "that there [wa]s no need for [their] workers to be represented by 'third' parties," but then added a statement of formal neutrality: "If the employees choose to join a union at any time we will, of course, abide by that choice" (Kenney and Florida, 1993: 284). Then the auto maker proceeded to conduct a vigorous antiunion campaign, asserting its NLRA Section 8(c) free speech right to assure that their workers knowingly made that decision. "Nissan used its plant-wide video system and the daily work group meetings to hammer home its antiunion message . . . . The day before the vote, Nissan shut down the line for up to an hour on each shift for captive audience meetings" (Slaughter, 1989: 15; and Kenney and Florida, 1993: 284, 385). On July 26, 1989, Nissan workers voted 1,622 to 711, 69 percent to 31 percent against UAW representation. In the wake of the defeat, it appears that worker concerns about safety were not all that salient, nor was increased pay. In an antiunion culture, most employees were more concerned that the union's presence would create an adversarial atmosphere (Courier Journal, 1989: n.p.; and Gardner and Lupo, 1989: D–1, 7).

CAW Organizing at Hyundai. The CAW began its organizing drive at Hyundai's Bromont plant in 1990 where the central issues were the Korean auto firm's job rotation work rules and sliding-scale pension plan (Chappell, 1991: 6). Hyundai vigorously opposed the CAW's organizing efforts, but by December 1990, the union had acquired 350 signed union cards from the plant's 700 workers, enough to request the Quebec Department of Labor to hold a secret ballot on CAW representation. Still the union decided to seek another 100 signed union cards, because it believed that the auto maker had underreported the plant's employees "to lull the CAW into a false target that would prevent them from getting the minimum of signatures" (Shalom, 1990: C–1). The CAW's efforts were further complicated by a Hyundai employee-initiated petition against unionization said to be supported by 560 assembly line workers, but which the CAW and prounion Hyundai workers suspected was a fraudulent management-initiated effort (Shalom, 1990: C–1).

In spite of Hyundai's opposition, the CAW continued its organizing efforts, acquired a clear majority of signed union cards, and in March 1993 applied for certification, a process which could take "anywhere from a few months to two years" (Sinek, 1993: 37). Yet the CAW's success, so far, has to be seen against the backdrop of Hyundai's declining fortunes in the North American auto marketplace, rumors that it was contemplating moving its plant to Mexico, and in June 1993, an announcement that it would temporarily suspend its Bromont operations to convert and renovate the plant for the production of a new car, the Elantra (Dow Jones News, 1993: n.p.). Since the idled Bromont plant was officially closed in early 1995, it appears likely that the CAW's organizing efforts was at best a Pyrrhic victory.

Labor Law Implications

The UAW's and the CAW's mutual failure to organize the transplants raises important labor law questions. According to the ruling legal consensus, the Taft-Hartley's Right to Work Section 14(b) provision burdens United States labor unions because it provides a union-free environment for business while the absence of that provision in Canadian labor law allows business no safe haven. Labor law scholars also claim that Canada's union card procedure enables its unions to be more easily certified while United States unions must endure a lengthy and arduous organizing campaign followed by a secret ballot. The UAW's and CAW's mutual failure casts doubt on these asserted Canadian legal advantages and instead suggests that it is the similarities of the NLRA paradigm and its Canadian variant which do not intrude upon management's right to make strategic decisions about plant location, recruitment, training, and production practices: these better explain the ability of Asian transplant firms in both countries to avoid unionization.

On the American scene, the NLRA's Section 8(c)'s free speech clause, a Taft-Hartley provision, also helps explain Nissan's labor organizing victory. The United States Supreme Court decision in NLRB v. Gissel Packing (1969), and related NLRB decisions have broadly interpreted Section 8(c) to grant management considerable power during organizing campaigns, because the NLRB and the Supreme Court permit management to deliver "a message which would be received by a reasonable listener as a threat or promise . . . [including a] predict[ion] that dire consequences may result from a decision of workers to unionize, as long as those consequences are not within the direct control of the employer" (Rainsberger, 1989: 106–107). In Nissan's case, this probably means that if the UAW had brought a Section 8 unfair labor practice complaint against the auto maker the union would have been unlikely to prevail, since the NLRB would have found that Nissan's antiunion videos, T-shirts, and captive audience meetings held on company time were protected Section 8(c) speech. Nissan's statement implying that unionization could mean loss of two employee benefit plans would, however, have provided a closer case, because it was a consequence within the employer's direct control (Williams, 1982).

Summary

The Asian automobile manufacturers, using their lean production cooperative nonunion labor relations practices, have successfully challenged United States and Canadian auto workers unions, their adversarial labor-management relations systems, and their narrow job-control based labor law paradigms. The transplants have made plant locations choices and employed recruitment, training, and lean production practices which create a cooperative style of labor relations governed by management's commitment to the principles of flexibility and team-based work organization. At the same time, these lean production practices have been the basis for a two-part strategy which has frustrated their workers' NLRA right to organize and has made it impossible for the UAW and CAW to organize transplant workers. In fact, the transplants' task was made easier because the UAW was devastated by membership losses, the labor union movement was fragmented, corporatist bargaining arrangements were nonexistent, and organized labor lacked popular and political support.

North American Labor Law and Lean Production at UAW/CAW Plants

The UAW and the CAW represent workers at the Big Three North American assembly plants where the Fordist labor relations system and its legal foundations are largely in place. Collective bargaining is still based on an arms-length adversarial relationship, concerns itself almost exclusively with workplace matters, and produces nationally-defined wage scales, nationally and locally negotiated work rules, and a job-oriented shop floor. Now the Fordist collectively bargained contract, as the private legal dimension of the NLRA and Canadian labor law paradigms, is being reexamined by both management and labor. The Big Three auto makers have negotiated incremental lean production changes at most of their North American operations, but the major changes which may foreshadow a paradigm change have occurred at one Canadian and three United States Big Three-Japanese joint venture assembly plants—CAMI (GM-Suzuki), AutoAlliance (Ford-Mazda), Diamond-Star (Mitsubishi-Chrysler), and NUMMI (GM-Toyota)—and at GM's Saturn.

Organized labor and management's willingness to redefine their relationship and the nature of their collective bargained agreements involves not merely the reorganization of work on the shop floor, but also extends to strategic level matters. Yet the form of these private agreements and their meaning for organized labor will be shaped by the public law component of the NLRA paradigm and its Canadian variant which largely limit labor's contractual rights to the shop floor, but otherwise recognize the continued preeminence of managerial power. In the United States, for example, whether labor's rights extended to strategic matters was unclear until the Supreme Court's *Borg-Warner* decision limited the Wagner Act's good faith bargaining to mandatory subjects. In Canada, labor law less clearly restricts good faith bargaining, because arbitrators are divided over whether there are limitations on bargainable subjects. In practice, management in both countries has the right to make strategic decisions and, unless restricted by labor contract provisions, to decide workplace governance matters. As a result, organized labor participates in management's strategic decisions only on management's terms.

The New Labor-Management Contracts

The UAW and CAW agreements with the Big Three-Japanese joint ventures and Saturn have been major departures from the 1948 GM-UAW model for adversarial labor-management relations at the bargaining table and on the shop floor. These interim labor-management agreements, also identified as 'Letters of Intent' or 'Letters of Understanding,' run counter to established NLRA and Canadian labor law principles governing union organizing which require that workers select a union. These interim agreements, negotiated by the UAW's and CAW's national offices and signed by union and auto maker officials before any workers were hired or any cars were built, provide that once a work force has been hired and employed, the UAW and CAW may hold representation elections and, if the union is selected as the bargaining agent, it will be entitled to negotiate a contract with the auto maker.

These interim agreements also strike at the core of the Fordist collectively bargained workplace contract. As high trust, cooperative exceptions to the Master Agreements the UAW and CAW have negotiated on behalf of workers at the Big Three's North American auto operations, these interim agreements alter wage scales, work rules, and a job control-based shop floor on the basis of Japanese lean production labor relations principles. The workplace contract provisions, written in very general terms, are governed by the principles of egalitarianism, flexibility, and the team concept. Instead of wage scales based on seniority and job assignments, workers receive a common base pay to which may be added a bonus based on quality, productivity and performance criteria. Work rules are flexible which means that seniority and job classifications are largely discarded for team-based work organization which emphasizes multitask training, flexible hours, job and shift rotation, and the performance of house-keeping and maintenance duties. Grievances are minimal, because conflicts on the shop floor are resolved through a consultation procedure. Finally, these agreements create a two-tiered work force with job security provisions—no lay-offs except for unforeseen or catastrophic events—that apply to 80 percent of the work force, the permanent workers, but not to the remaining temporary workers.

The UAW's interim cooperative labor-management agreements also contain provisions which go beyond addressing mandatory bargaining subjects regarding the reorganization of work on the shop floor. Unlike the CAW's CAMI labor agreement, the UAW's extend to permissive bargaining strategic level subjects, formerly management's exclusive domain, and involve union and worker participation in the recruitment and training of workers. The UAW agreements with Mazda, NUMMI, and Saturn provided that the auto makers would hire a percentage of their employees, often 50 percent, from GM or Ford auto workers, and that the recruitment process would involve both union and management participation in the evaluation and selection of workers which the Saturn labor agreement extended to employee training (Bluestone and Bluestone, 1992: 197). In fact, the Saturn agreement went even further by elim-inating Paragraph 8's management rights clause, a cornerstone of GM-UAW contracts since the 1930s, and then extending the principle of joint labor-man-agement participation in the operation of the firm to union involvement in the design of the automobile, the engineering of the plant, the relationships with suppliers and subcontractors, the selection of dealers, and the advertising, distri-bution, and sales of the Saturn.

In sum, these interim agreements and the contracts that union locals sub-sequently negotiated have changed the meaning of the NLRA paradigm as it is defined by the GM-UAW Fordist labor-management relations model. Except for Saturn, they have left undisturbed management's strategic level control of the firm while extending managerial control to the shop floor by providing for integration on the basis of management-defined lean production principles. The GM-UAW Saturn Labor Agreement also nominally discards the manage-ment rights concept and then on the basis of lean production and codetermina-tion principles provides for labor-management integration at all levels of indus-trial decision-making. So, taken together, these interim agreements suggest that labor-management integration, whether limited to shop floor or extended to the board room, would occur at management's discretion.

The New Labor-Management Contracts in Operation

What these interim agreements would mean in practice was far from clear, because they were written in the vague and high trust language of lean

178 *North American Auto Unions in Crisis*

production's cooperative approach to labor relations. As a result, their meaning would be shaped by the two unions' distinctive approaches to labor management relations: the UAW's commitment to cooperative labor-management relations and the CAW's attachment to an adversarial shop floor. The national office was labor's voice in worker recruitment and training, but once the union was recognized and local leadership elected, the national office's relationship with the union's local and its labor management views would shape subsequent contract negotiations, shop floor practices, and strategic level governance.

Recruitment and Training. The UAW's and CAW's distinctive labor management relations views were reflected in their approaches to worker recruitment and training. The CAW, given its adversarial shop floor view of labor-management relations, left worker recruitment and training to CAMI management while the UAW's commitment to labor-management cooperation, beginning at NUMMI, led to its active involvement in both of these managerial activities beginning with NUMMI (Staudohar, 1991). The NUMMI-UAW Letter of Understanding provided that the GM-Toyota joint venture would hire at least 50 percent of its 2,500 person work force from among laid off UAW workers at the former GM-Fremont plant. The interim agreement also created a joint Employee Assessment Plan for NUMMI and UAW personnel to evaluate and select workers on the basis of their "past attendance, disciplinary record, and attitude towards Toyota's production and labor relations standards" (McPherson, 1985: 1). As a consequence, the interim agreement did not permit NUMMI management to screen out prounion applicants, but it did permit the auto maker to screen in team players, because the former GM workers would be hired, not on the basis of their GM seniority, but on their "demonstrated ability and capacity and where those were equal, the job would go to the employee with the greater experience" (Slaughter, 1983: 16).

The NUMMI recruitment process served as the model for Mazda, Diamond-Star, and Saturn.[8] At Saturn, the interim agreement, the GM-UAW Saturn Labor Agreement, provided that GM would give preference to its UAW represented work force in hiring its employees. Saturn's Consensus Guidelines govern an extensive applicant screening and selection process conducted by the work unit which needs staff. Work unit members use jointly prepared employee application forms to "explore not only the applicant's skills but something about their leadership qualities and adaptability to Saturn culture" (Bluestone and Bluestone, 1992: 197) As a consequence, Saturn's cooperative employment process, like NUMMI's, permits GM to screen in team players and shape the shop floor culture. Once workers are hired the Consensus Guidelines also govern the joint administration of all training programs. One of the most extensive and innovative training programs among the Japanese-Big Three joint ventures and Asian transplants, Saturn provides workers with ninety-two hours of training yearly. In spite of the appearance of equal labor-management influence, however, the training program is clearly biased against worker and union interests. Only a small portion, perhaps 30 percent, involves nontransferable technical training while the remaining 70 percent focuses upon cultural or attitudinal training: i.e., indoctrination into the Saturn corporate ideology (Yanarella and Green, 1994).

Contractual Reality on the Shop Floor. A collectively bargained contract is not completely understood by its own terms, but, as the document itself contemplates, it will be defined as it is applied and interpreted on the shop floor and through the process of grievance arbitration. Unlike the precise language of the Fordist labor contracts which define a job control shop floor, the general terms of the Saturn and joint ventures' lean production labor contracts cede job control to management's discretion. As a consequence, the lean production shop floor has provided a wider arena for labor-management conflict over contract application. In this setting, the meaning of the contract has been shaped by the national leadership's continuing involvement and by the local union's internal struggles, its relationship with its national office, and its daily encounters with management on the shop floor and in corporate offices.

The UAW's and CAW's continuing involvement in their union local's activities reflects their distinctive approaches to labor-management relations. While the UAW downplayed "any problems or discontent because they're trying to get recognition [at] . . . Honda, Nissan, and Toyota's plant in Kentucky" (Slaughter, 1987: 3), the CAW has openly confronted lean production. The CAW's "Statement on the Reorganization of Work" outlined the national union's rejection of lean production methods and guided its close cooperation with its CAMI Local 88 and their relations with CAMI management. As the CAW Research Group on CAMI observed: "The local occupies, or more accurately shapes, the space between a collective agreement that accommodates aspects of team concept and a policy statement of the national union which raises substantial questions about the implications of JPM" (Robertson, et al., 1992: 98).

At CAMI, the solidarity within Local 88 and between it and the CAW national office is missing at NUMMI, Mazda, and Saturn. At all three plants, the locals appear to be divided into rival caucuses which differ, not in their commitment to the team concept, but in terms of two views of labor-management cooperation. The Administration Caucus at NUMMI and USA Caucus at Mazda are willing to award substantial discretion to management, but the People's Caucus at NUMMI and New Directions Caucus at Mazda are less trusting of management, seek more effective union representation, and argue that for "true teamwork to take place . . . workers must have a strong and independent union to counter management's power" (Fucini and Fucini, 1990: 210; and

Parker, 1988: 12). Even at Saturn, the GM-UAW model of labor-management harmony, Local 1853's recent election revealed its internal divisions. In March 1993, Mike Bennett, its president, was challenged by three rival candidates who were committed to the Saturn labor-management partnership, but who found "considerable support for an agenda that called for putting more distance between union members and bosses" (Templin, 1993: A–4). A very divided Saturn local returned Bennett to office, but only by a bare majority in a run-off election (ibid.).

On the shop floor, management's lean production call for cooperation has restructured power against a viable autonomous local union in the most subtle ways. Management's quest for shop floor hegemony began with rules which require that all employees from the president to production associates share the same restrooms, parking spaces and cafeterias, and dress in the same outfits. So demanding is management's commitment to this pseudo-egalitarian culture that disputes have arisen over buttons, pins, and posies. In a more visible way, management, sometimes with the local union's assent, has further blurred labor-management distinctions by providing a common office space for the union's representatives and management's industrial relations personnel (Parker, 1991: 6). So successful was this approach at Mazda in the early years that many younger workers did not distinguish between labor and management representatives, because they wore the same uniforms and acted as a labor team, and, like their UAW counterparts at NUMMI, often counseled against filing grievances in the name of harmony (Fucini and Fucini, 1989: 119–121; and Parker, 1987: 3). Subsequently, UAW Local 3000 at Mazda, like CAW Local 88 at CAMI, has established separate offices and then faced the real struggle for control of the shop floor.

Shop floor control issues have been defined by the team concept and the common features of lean production labor relations. The spare outlines of the interim agreements have made the shop floor the setting for addressing management's lean production policies on absences from work, the replacement of sick or injured workers on the line, shift rotation, a two-track work force, and grievance and arbitration procedures.[9] The shop floor has also become the venue for defining the meaning of the team-based workplace and the critical role of the team leader. At CAMI, like Mazda, "[t]he position of team leader is a focal point of tension and conflict between the union and the company" (Robertson, et al., 1992: 97). Here the shop floor control issue is whether the team leader is part of the management team or the union team. At Mazda, this struggle may now favor the union local, because the 1991 Collective Bargaining Agreement provides that team leader will be elected and subject to recall by team members (Babson, 1993: 19).

After the vague and high trust language of these interim agreements met the crude reality of the shop floor, contract negotiations have focused on the unions' efforts to reduce management's discretion on the shop floor and to resist management efforts to create an even tougher lean production workplace. Contract negotiations have also addressed the union concessions contained in the interim agreements, but enjoyed by UAW and CAW employees of the Big Three auto makers: wage parity, overtime pay, health and pension benefits, and no strike clauses on health, safety, and work standards (Chappell, 1992: 8). The UAW and CAW have largely prevailed. Collective bargaining agreements have become much thicker and more detailed documents and have begun to address the interests of workers in lean production auto plants.

In sum, the Saturn and joint venture's interim labor agreements, framed in lean production's vague language, have provided management with the opportunity to define the shop floor on their own terms. Management has, however, met with limited success from both the CAW's well-defined adversarial unionism and from UAW locals' whose commitment to the team concept and lean production have not prevented them, in spite of their internal divisions, from humanizing the shop floor on which their members toil.

Labor Law Implications

The Saturn and joint ventures' interim labor agreements have the capacity to fundamentally alter the meaning of the NLRA paradigm and its Canadian variant. Whether these agreements, as private law, will lead to a paradigm shift will depend upon their surviving legal challenges before the courts and labor relations boards.

NLRB and the Saturn Labor Agreement. The NUMMI "Letter of Understanding" was the model for the interim labor agreements at CAMI, Diamond-Star, Mazda, and Saturn, but it was the GM-UAW Saturn Labor Agreement which became a test case. The National Right to Work Legal Defense Foundation (NRWLDF) challenged two Saturn agreement provisions: the GM-UAW decisions to grant preferential hiring rights to GM's UAW-represented employees and to recognize the UAW as the bargaining agent for the Saturn employees. The NRWLDF claimed that GM and the UAW in agreeing to the preferential hiring clause and in agreeing to the bargaining agent clause had violated NLRA Sections 8(a)(1), 8(a)(2), 8(a)(3), and 8(b)(1)(a).

The NLRB's general counsel dismissed both claims. The preferential hiring rights clause did not discriminate against non-GM employees, because "GM's need for a ready supply of skilled labor was 'a legitimate and substantial business justification' for preferring its own employees" (Powers, 1988: 94). Moreover, the clause was "the lawful byproduct of mandatory effects bargaining: the duty of an employer to bargain with a union over the economic effects that a management decision will have on union-represented employees, including a duty to bargain over preferential hiring treatment" (Powers, 1988: 94). The bargaining agent clause did not grant pre-hire recognition of the UAW, but future recognition if the UAW acquired majority support from Saturn employees. Subsequently, the NLRB Office of Appeals affirmed the decision, even though it might be "inconsistent with both Supreme Court precedent and previous Board decisions" (Powers, 1988: 96). In sum, the NLRB's Saturn case has bestowed approval on paradigm change by means of interim agreements.

Three Labor-Management Pre-Paradigms. The UAW and CAW's interim agreements and collective contracts with CAMI, Mazda, NUMMI, and Saturn management contain elements of Fordist adversarialism, Japanese lean production cooperation, and German codetermination. The agreements anticipate union worker participation which may range from integration into a lean production-defined shop floor to codetermination-based involvement in all strategic actions of the firm. How these agreements have operated in practice has depended upon the national union and its locals whose responses reflect a spectrum of acceptance and resistance to adversarialism, lean production cooperation, and codetermination. These agreements and labor's experiences with them may be expressed in terms of three pre-paradigms which foreshadow the creation of a new labor management relations system and its legal paradigm.

Pre-paradigm I is based on an CAMI-type agreement which establishes a management rights-based labor-management relationship at the strategic level. At CAMI, management has an unqualified right to recruit and train workers and, subject to the terms of a vaguely worded collective contract, to otherwise operate the firm. The general language of the agreement provides management with the opportunity to extend its control to the shop floor on the basis of lean production labor relations principles. But this effort has been resisted by the CAW and Local 88 who are committed to the major principles of the GM-UAW Fordist adversarial labor-management relations model. Thus, pre-paradigm I limits labor's integration to the shop floor where it is defined as a blend of lean production and adversarial labor-management relations and thus provides an arena for a shop floor struggle between adversarialism and cooperation in their purest form.

Pre-paradigm II is based on a NUMMI or Mazda-type collective contract which establishes a minimally qualified management rights-based labor-management relationship at the strategic level that has permitted the UAW to participate in worker recruitment. Otherwise NUMMI and Mazda management have an unqualified right, subject to the terms of high trust and vaguely worded collective contracts, to operate their firms. The collective agreement, as in pre-paradigm I, also provides management with the opportunity to extend its control to the shop floor by employing lean production labor relations practices, but the struggle which occurs on the shop floor, over time, will be a mixed response by contending local union caucuses about how best to accomplish the objectives of lean production's cooperative labor management relations. Thus, pre-paradigm II limits labor's integration, except for its worker recruitment role, to the shop floor where it is defined in lean production's cooperative labor-management relations terms and provides an arena for a struggle between contending local union caucuses over the meaning of cooperation.

Pre-paradigm III is based on a Saturn-type collective contract which discards the management rights clause and extends union joint participation beyond the shop floor to strategic level involvement in worker recruitment and training and in the design of the Saturn and the plant, the selection of suppliers and subcontractors, and the advertising, distribution, and sales of the automobile. The collective agreement, thereby, provides management with an even greater opportunity to exercise its control by applying lean production and codetermination labor relations principles to all aspects of industrial decision making. As a consequence, the shop floor struggle between contending local union caucuses about how best to accomplish the objectives of lean production's cooperative labor-management relations is framed in terms of the wider pressures for labor's strategic cooperation on management terms. Thus, pre-paradigm III nominally extends labor's integration to all levels of industrial decision making from the shop floor to the board room where it is defined in lean production and codetermination labor-management relations terms and provides an arena for a struggle between contending local union caucuses over the meaning of cooperation. Yet the union's almost complete integration makes the task of maintaining its independence more difficult, because jointness is practiced on management's terms.

Summary

The NLRA and its Canadian variant may not be defined in the years to come by the Fordist adversarial labor-management collective agreements which largely prevail at the Big Three's North American operations, but by an agreement defined in terms of one of the three pre-paradigms. Which one might it be? Lowell Turner (1991) argues that if unions are to survive and prosper in a competitive international arena, they need to be integrated into a firm's managerial decision-making. In this case, pre-paradigm I and II would not appear to be acceptable, because the CAW and UAW locals at CAMI, Mazda, and NUMMI do not "substantially participate with management regarding plans to reorganize work before actual decisions are made" (Turner, 1991: 16). Saturn's Consensus Guidelines suggest GM's labor-management jointness would satisfy Turner's criterion of "substantial participation," but Saturn's pre-paradigm III approach to cooperative labor-management would be an unwise choice, because union participation is not supported by national legislation which provides a legal framework for labor's independent status in managerial decision-making. As a consequence, Saturn seems to be merely a model for union subordination to management and a prescription for further decline into enterprise unionism.

If labor law reform will be difficult because corporatist bargaining structures are weak and organized labor's political strength is limited, then organized labor might be well advised to pursue an adversarial collective bargaining strategy. In this case, an otherwise dismal prediction for the UAW's future may be brightened by considering the CAW's pre-paradigm I adversarial approach to CAMI shop floor labor-management relations. Here the question is whether CAMI will serve as the basis for a Model 2 labor relations system. In fact, Turner has observed that whether his thesis is "flawed or at least in need of modification" may turn on the Canadian experience which may provide an alternative road for unions to explore in addressing the challenges of work reorganization (Turner, 1991: 234–35). Canadian labor does enjoy popular support and plays an active role in the New Democratic Party, but there is room for doubt that Canada will be able to acquire Model 2 characteristics, because corporatist bargaining structures are too weak, its labor federation is fragmented, and collective bargaining is not well coordinated.

The NLRA in a Post-Fordist Era

The NLRA paradigm continues to serve as the legal foundation for a Fordist model of adversarial labor relations. At the same time, the NLRA paradigm and its Canadian variant have permitted the UAW to negotiate pre-recruitment interim agreements with the Japanese-Big Three joint ventures and Saturn which have provided for labor-management cooperation on a wide range of strategic and shop floor matters. The NLRA paradigm has even allowed the Japanese transplants to screen out employees with pro-union sympathies and to create a nonunion workplace to discourage labor organizing.

These labor relations developments have occurred, in part, because the NLRA is a limited labor-management relations paradigm which contemplates that labor and management will define the paradigm's private law dimension in their collective agreements. Operating inside the NLRA's public law framework, the parties first established the Fordist adversarial labor relations system defined in terms of the 1948 GM-UAW model and then in the 1980s created three labor relations pre-paradigms which may suggest the existence of a post-Fordist order. At the same time the Japanese transplants, operating outside the paradigm's limited regulatory scope, have institutionalized a nonunion lean production labor relations model.

If Turner is correct and cooperative labor-management relations is the wave of the future, then organized labor needs to play an active role in a post-

Fordist world by strengthening its hand in truly cooperative actions from the strategic level to the shop floor and by organizing the nonunion transplants. Yet the redefinition of the NLRA paradigm by collective bargaining agreements at Saturn and the joint ventures and the practice of lean production labor relations at the Asian transplants do not bode well for the UAW, CAW, and North American auto workers' prospects. Advancing transplant labor organizing activities and promoting real labor-management cooperation will require alteration of the NLRA paradigm's public law dimension.

The UAW and CAW both have an ongoing interest in labor law reform. But the need is clearly more urgent in the United States, because Canadian labor law is more supportive of organized labor. In the United States, the fundamental question is: can the NLRA be altered to provide organized labor with the opportunity to play an active role in labor-management relations in a manner that protects and advances its interests? In answering this question, this section will explore the extent to which the prospects for labor law reform can be accomplished by judicial action or will require a legislative solution (Hogler and Grenier, 1992: Ch. 5).

Judicial Change

The NLRA has been defined by NLRB and federal court of appeals decisions, but these administrative and judicial actions do not provide an encouraging avenue for labor law reform. NLRB and federal court decisions have increasingly made it more difficult for auto workers and the UAW to exercise their NLRA rights to organize, bargain with management, and to take concerted action. To rectify this situation, there are at least two judicial actions which would advance the ability of labor to organize the transplants and bargain with management over a really cooperative labor contract.

The Supreme Court needs to reaffirm its commitment to its *Cabot Carbon* (1959) decision by overturning the Sixth, Seventh, and Ninth Court of Appeals decisions which "have departed from a strict reading of Section 8(a)(2) on such avowed policy grounds as rejection of a 'purely adversarial model of labor relations' and acceptance of a 'cooperative arrangement'" (St. Antoine, 1989: 52). The NLRB's recent decision in the *Electromation* case may provide the Court with the opportunity to make a definitive statement about the use of lean production teams in a nonunion setting (Labor Relations Week, 1992, 1993; and Scholossberg and Reinhart, 1992). A Supreme Court decision which found that the Japanese transplants' teams violated the NLRA Section 8(a)(2), because they impinged upon their employees' Section 7 rights would clearly strike a heavy blow at the Japanese labor relations model (Model 3) and in favor of union organizing and a pre-paradigm collective contract outlined above, because it would overturn the decisions of the courts of appeal in which all the transplants are located.

The Supreme Court also needs to overturn its decision in the *Borg-Warner* case and eliminate its "rigid and unrealistic dichotomy" between mandatory and permissive collective bargaining subjects (St. Antoine, 1989: 52). Since the Wagner Act did not explicitly make this distinction, overturning *Borg-Warner* and eliminating this judicially-imposed distinction would expand the NLRA's scope beyond its judicially-narrowed shop floor focus and grant labor an independent legal basis for strategic level participation. Since the Saturn Labor Agreement involves mandatory provisions, eliminating the mandatory-permissive dichotomy will threaten management's "entrepreneurial sovereignty" (St. Antoine, 1989: 51), but will ensure that management will not be able to have it both ways: speaking the language of cooperative labor-management relations but practicing the politics of managerial hegemony. Overturning *Borg-Warner* will provide the opportunity to make cooperative codetermined labor-management relations a reality.

If the Supreme Court reaffirmed its commitment to *Cabot Carbon* and overturned *Borg-Warner* decision and, thereby, judicially expanded labor's right to organize and extended its right to bargain over strategic level subjects, the Court would clearly advance employees' Section 7 rights to cooperative code-termined labor-management relations. Yet these judicial changes are only half of the equation. The other half which has the capacity to provide a comprehensive answer is labor law reform. Without labor law reform, organized labor has much to fear from labor-management cooperation and from the advocates of cooperation on the shop floor and adversarialism at the bargaining table. The Supreme Court's decision in *Yeshiva University* (1980) and more recently in *Health Care & Retirement Corp.* (1994) suggest that adversarial bargaining may be a moot point if a federal appellate court would decide that auto workers are managers when they cooperate in deciding matters that have traditionally involved strategic level subjects. So the UAW may be well advised not to abandon its adversarial tradition and cooperate in managerial decision-making until Congress seriously grapples with and resolves fundamental legal issues which have been brought into focus by the conflict between labor law paradigms.

Legislative Change

Since Congress failed to pass the Carter administration's labor legislation in 1978, one of the most provocative proposals for labor law reform was outlined by Barry and Irving Bluestone in their *Negotiating the Future* (1992) which proposes to move beyond Fordist collective bargaining's narrow shop floor level to a German codetermination-inspired 'Enterprise Compact' most closely embodied in the Saturn labor agreement and its Consensus Guidelines (see also Adams, 1992; and Bonanno, 1985). Consistent with pre-paradigm III, their Enterprise Compact would eliminate management's exclusive right to direct the firm and "herald joint labor-management action on all decisions of the firm, both workplace and strategic" (1992: 219). To create this new labor-management relations paradigm, the Bluestones do not believe it will be "absolutely necessary" to amend the NLRA, but they argue that "rewriting it . . . to give participatory management a government imprimatur would have the salutary effect of encouraging management and labor to consider adopting the spirit, and perhaps the provisions of the Enterprise Compact" (1992: 253).

The Clinton administration, enamoured of the German codetermination model (Model 1) and attracted to the Bluestones' *Negotiating the Future*, put labor law reform back on the political agenda in March 1993 when the Secretaries of Labor and Commerce, Robert Reich and Ronald Brown, appointed a Commission on the Future of Worker-Management Relations (Clark, 1993; McNamee, et al., 1993; and *Wall Street Journal*, 1993). Chaired by John Dunlop, a former Secretary of Labor and Harvard law professor, the Commission addressed three questions about what could be done to increase productivity through "labor-management cooperation and employee participation" and changes in the "legal framework and practices of collective bargaining" and to increase workplace problem solving by labor and management rather than by the courts or government agencies (Dunlop, 1994: x).

To explore these questions, the Commission held public hearings in Washington, D.C. and throughout the country which focused on both non-union and union plant issues largely defined in terms of contending labor law paradigms (Rothstein, 1993; and Estreicher, 1993; 51–52). The Commission's report, released on January 9, 1995, found that workplaces were "far too adversarial . . . for the good of the American economy" and that cooperative labor-management relations were "the best way to compete in the marketplace and secure both profits for the firm and good jobs for workers" (Dunlop, 1994: 2, 3). To this end, the Commission offered a set of legislative recommendations to remove "the legal uncertainties affecting some forms of employee participation [and labor-management partnerships] while safeguarding and strengthening employees' rights to choose a union and engage in collective bargaining" (Dunlop, 1994: xvii).

The Commission examined the variety of employee participation programs and, finding that there was a national interest to promote their expansion, recommended that NLRA Section 8(a)(2) be clarified to ensure that "nonunion employee participation programs should not be unlawful simply because they involve discussion of terms and conditions of work or compensation where such discussion is incidental to the broad purposes of these programs" (Dunlop, 1994: 8). At the same, the Commission, concerned about the rebirth of company unions, recommended that Section 8(a)(1) be amended to make it an unfair labor practice under Section 8(a)(1) "for an employer to establish a new participation program or to use or manipulate an existing one with the purpose of frustrating employee efforts to obtain independent representation" (Dunlop, 1994: 8). Legislation was also needed to address the Supreme Court's expansion of the "managerial employee exclusion" since its *Yeshiva* decision, because this judicial creation failed to ensure that workers who engaged in labor-management partnership programs would not be stripped of the NLRA right to organize a union and engage in collective bargaining (Dunlop, 1994: 11). Then the Commission turned to the issue raised by the GM-UAW Saturn contract and recommended that the NLRB reconsider its interpretation of Section 8(a)(2) and permit an employer who wants to move to a new location to negotiate a pre-hire agreement with the union which would represent workers at that operation (Dunlop, 1994: 11).

The Dunlop Commission then addressed the failure of labor law to protect workers' right to organize a union and to encourage collective bargaining. Accordingly, the Commission recommended that representation elections be held within two weeks after the NLRB determines employees have expressed an interest in a union and that employer challenges be resolved after the elections. The Commission believed that these changes would help minimize conflict in representation elections and the tactical advantages management derives from the current "lengthy political-style election campaign" (Dunlop, 1994: 18–19). In fact, the Commission encouraged employers and unions to consider the "card check" as "a non-conflictual way to determine . . . representation" (Dunlop, 1994: 20). During the election campaign, union representatives, excluded from the workplace, have a very limited opportunity to communicate with workers. To increase employee access to union organizers, the Commission recommended the passage of legislation to reverse the Supreme Court's decision in *Lechmere* v. *NLRB* (1992) and NLRB action to ensure that employees have "a fair opportunity to hear a balanced discussion of the relevant issues" (Dunlop, 1994: 23). Then the Commission turned to the problem of employer discrimination against employees during organizing campaigns and recommended that Congress amend Section 10(1), currently applicable to unions, to provide for swift and automatic injunctive relief for employer discrimination against employees during organizing campaigns or first contract negotiations (Dunlop, 1994: 21).

If the Dunlop Commission Report recommendations were enacted, a revised NLRA would strengthen labor organizing by shortening representation elections, by allowing union organizers greater opportunities to communicate with workers, by permitting courts to swiftly issue injunctions to address the problems of employer discrimination against workers during organizing campaigns, and by resolving employer challenges after elections as would eliminating the *Yeshiva's* managerial exclusion. The great cause for concern is, as Douglas Fraser observed in his Dunlop Commission dissent, the Commission's proposed revision of Section 8(a)(2) to permit "incidental discussion" by employee participation groups of "terms and conditions of work or compensation," because it would be "an invitation to abuse" (Fraser, 1994: n.p.). Employer abuse would also be enhanced by the Commission's failure to restore a more labor-oriented focus to the NLRA paradigm by recommending legislation which would reaffirm *Cabot Carbon*, overrule *Borg-Warner*, and, thereby, "encourage democratic participation and cooperation *between equals*" (Fraser, 1994: n.p.).

But the prospects for labor law reform are dim, because the Bluestones' Enterprise Compact and the Dunlop Commission Report fail to appreciate the critical support a legal infrastructure provides for paradigm change. Rewriting the NLRA is unlikely to happen, as Lowell Turner has observed, because labor-management jointness is only possible where there is a cohesive labor movement backed by corporatist bargaining and supported by a political party and labor laws which provide the basis for independent labor participation in industrial decision-making. In the United States, however, the labor movement is divided over the virtues of adversarialism and cooperation, corporatist bargaining and political party support is weak, and the NLRA does not provide the legal foundation for organized labor's independent participation. Or to put it succinctly: business opposition is too great; union power is too weak; "the United States . . . is not Germany" (Frank, 1993: 312).

The prospects for labor law reform, inspired by the Enterprise Compact and based on the Dunlop Commission Report, are also dim because the complexion of national politics has changed dramatically since the Dunlop Commission was created. With the 1994 election and the Republican takeover of Congress in 1995, rewriting the NLRA, along the lines suggested by the Enterprise Compact and the Dunlop Commission Report, is highly unlikely. The prospects are considerably brighter for congressionally-initiated legislation which would legalize nonunion employee involvement programs and further limit union organizing and collective bargaining in order to allow business to be more competitive in the global marketplace (Pearl, 1995: n.p.; and Sands, 1995: B6).

But in an era of international capital mobility, it seems appropriate to ask: will it make any real difference whether the Clinton administration or the Congress amends the NLRA and whether the legislation advances organized labor's interests? After all, labor-management relations law is defined in terms of the vector of national political forces while business operates in a highly mobile manner on an international economic stage. American business can leave the NLRA paradigm behind when it moves its manufacturing operations to Mexico and other overseas sites. Given these political, legal, and economic realities, how can organized labor meaningfully negotiate the future from a position of strength? A hopeful answer may lie in strategies that widen labor's agenda, including international alliances with unions and workers in other countries such as the cooperative efforts of the UAW AutoAlliance and CAW CAMI local and the worker-to-worker delegations that link UAW locals with workers in Mexico's maquiladora auto plants.

Notes

* Earlier drafts of this chapter appeared as "Negotiating the Future: The NLRA Paradigm and the Prospects for Labor Law Reform," *Ohio Northern University Law Review*, 21 (1995) 417–454; and "The UAW, Lean Production, and the Future of the National Labor Relations Act," *Labor Law Journal* 45 (1994) 167–181.

1. Diamond-Star, originally a Chrysler-Mitsubishi joint venture, became a wholly-owned Mitsubishi plant in October 1991 (See Chandler and Stertz, 1991: 4). Mazda's Flat Rock plant, was a nominally sole venture by the Japanese auto maker. Ford, which owns 25 percent of Mazda, was the silent partner (Parker, 1986: 13). In June 1992, Mazda became AutoAlliance International, a 50/50 Ford/Mazda joint venture. Ford also has a joint venture with Nissan at Avon Lake, Ohio, which has recently begun to produce the Ford Villager/Nissan Quest minivan (see Jensen, 1992: G–1).

2. The term 'Japanese transplants' will be used to describe the Japanese auto plants in the United States and Canada which have never operated as joint ventures with an American Big Three auto firm; they are the Honda plants in Marysville, Ohio and Alliston, Ontario; the Toyota plants in Georgetown, Kentucky and Cambridge, Ontario; the Nissan plant in Smyrna, Tennessee; and the Subaru-Isuzu plant in Lafayette, Indiana. The wider term, 'Asian transplants,' will be used to describe the Japanese transplants and Hyundai, the South Korean auto firm whose North American plant was located in Bromont, Ontario.

3. The Supreme Court subsequently affirmed and explained its *Borg Warner* decision in *Fiberboard Paper Products Corp.* v. *NLRB* (1964) and *First National Maintenance Corp.* v. *NLRB* (1981). See Leslie, 1992: 193–201.

4. Job control-focused collective agreements link a worker's pay to the wage rates for a specific job classification and job access to the worker's seniority.

5. All Canadian provinces, except Quebec, have a labor relations statute which establishes a labor relations tribunal for the private sector. "In Quebec, such functions are divided between a Labor Court/Tribunal du Travail and department officials called commissioners/commissaires" Arthurs, et al., 1989: 57.

6. See note 2 for the Asian transplants' greenfield sites.

7. NLRA, Section 8(a)(2), has been the subject of considerable scholarly discussion. See Brody, 1988; Clarke, 1987; Lipsky, 1992; Moberly, 1985; and Note, 1983, 1985.

8. For a brief discussion of the Mazda recruitment process, see Hill, 1989.

9. Lean production shift rotation requires workers to alternate day and night shifts every other week. The two-track work force is composed of regular employees and a cadre of temporaries who have no seniority or union rights.

New Dimensions for Labor in a Post-Fordist World

Donald M. Wells

A New 'Hegemony' in the Workplace?

Neo-liberalism is notoriously fulsome in its use of the language of 'freedom' to justify the privileging of the rights of capital while remaining silent about the condition of nonfreedom endured (Hayek, 1944; and Friedman, 1962) by most of those whose labor makes corporate capital 'competitive.' Workers in Canada, the United States, and other advanced capitalist economies are now experiencing attempts to deepen that condition of nonfreedom through the transplantation in hybrid forms of Japanese management practices often labeled 'lean production' and 'total quality management' (TQM).[1] These management practices are, at their core, an attempt to integrate production and culture into a unitarist "corporate culture" or "enterprise patriotism" (Binns, 1993: 11) that subordinates the class interests of workers to those of their employers.

It is difficult to assess management's success in creating such corporate cultures. These difficulties are compounded by the absence of a consensus about the definition of lean production. However, at a minimum, lean production is a management control system that seeks to enhance a firm's productivity objectives—particularly quality improvements—by means of three principles.

First, lean production enlists workers' commitment to improve the quality of the services and/or products they provide by defining all those who work in the labor process downstream from them, including fellow workers, as their 'customers.' Second, it encourages workers to use their tacit (i.e., experiential and informal) skills to improve continuously the quality and quantity of their work and to respond flexibly to changing requirements of production. Third, it gains worker participation in the process of breaking down the labor process into standardized, quantifiable specifications that are used continuously to refine jobs in order to produce to constantly higher specifications of quality and quantity.

With varying degrees of completion and coherence in their application, these principles are the basis of lean production, particularly in manufacturing. They are meant to achieve an increasingly hyperefficient use of production inputs, including labor; an integration of direct labor (e.g. assembly) and indirect labor (e.g. quality control); and a reduction of buffer stocks of inventories at each step of production. These principles of production also imply a parallel form of labor-management relations. Such a highly integrated, efficient system is fragile: the leaner the system, the fewer the buffers of time and resources, the more it is likely to be stressed and break down. Thus lean production requires worker commitment to respond to the threats of breakdown through greater flexibility and self-intensification of labor.

It is in this context that the unitarist logic of lean production and TQM can be understood. Analogous to the transition from management controls based on direct coercion to controls embedded in work technologies and bureaucratic rules (Edwards, 1979: 111–162), lean production is an attempt to move beyond the externalization of management power in technical and bureaucratic processes to the individual and collective internalization of managerial norms in the work force. This signifies a shift in emphasis from the control of bodies to the reshaping of psyches. Some critics see lean production as a new totalitarianism in the micropolitics of production that complements the rise of the New Right at the level of the state and society (Binns, 1993). For others it is a management system "dedicated to persuading the new laboring subject to become his or her own agency of hegemonic discipline and control" (Yanarella and Reid, 1996: 29). Still others suggest that such management practices are designed to get workers to participate in a "whole system of self-subordination" in a "brave new world of company-centered idealism" (Garrahan and Stewart 1992: 138).

At its core, lean production is an attempt to create a new form of what the Marxist theorist Gramsci (1971) termed "hegemony," a complex mobilization of consent within subaltern classes to the power of dominant social classes. In Canada and the United States during the 1980s and 1990s this new hegemony signifies the elimination of the limited adversarialism and limited union autonomy of the dominant Wagner model of industrial relations which grew out of the 1930s Depression and World War II (Wells, 1995b). It also implies a reconfiguration of more homogeneous 'modernist' worker identities structured around class and nation to a plurality of 'postmodern' worker identities centered on individual firms and workplaces (Harvey, 1989: 173–188).

This essay attempts to understand to what extent such a new hegemony is in the making by analyzing evidence from Japanese transplants and joint ventures in Canada, the United States, and Britain. The main thesis is that there is considerable evidence of worker behavior that is consistent with such a new hegemony, but it is premature to conclude that there has been extensive, enduring internalization of the ideology of lean production. Because of a lack of adequate evidence to support such internalization and because attitudinal changes are notoriously difficult to prove (Rinehart, 1978), compliant behavior by workers employed in lean production regimes is perhaps better understood as a rational adaptation to the coercion of external labor markets. The shaping of workplace labor-management relations is accomplished mainly, although by no means entirely, it is argued, through the interaction of internal and external labor markets. This explanation for worker compliance with management power places more emphasis on material constraints such as unemployment and the lack of 'good' jobs than it does on new ideological forces shaping the limits of worker and union resistance to management power. In effect, coercion rather than the internalization of management values through lean production is given greater explanatory prominence.

A Critique of Two Versions of Hegemonic Lean Production

There are two variants of the thesis that lean production is the basis of a new workplace hegemony. The first or 'harder' version posits a partial overcoming of the Taylorist division of labor. Thus, Womack et al. see workers in lean plants as "highly skilled problem solvers" (1990:102). Adler (1992) sees the development of a "learning bureaucracy" at the New United Motor Manufacturing Inc. (NUMMI) plant in California. Kenney and Florida discern "self-managing" work teams built around a "functional integration of tasks" in lean workplaces (1993:15–16). Kenney and Florida see such teams as a kind of collective technician lying at the heart of the new workplace hegemony.

> The team is the mechanism through which workers are mobilized to solve production problems and innovate for management. It becomes the source for overcoming production bottlenecks as workers use their own intelligence and knowledge to devise cooperative strategies to overcome such obstacles. The team is a simultaneous source of motivation, discipline and social control for team members, driving them to toil harder and more collectively (1993: 304).

The hegemonic capacity of this new model of production relations "lies in its ability to get workers to contribute ideas, offer suggestions and make continuous improvements in the products, quality and manufacturing process," even though this means they "are called upon to increase their own rate and pace of work" (270–271). In effect, this 'corporatist hegemony' entails the creation of an identity between worker and management goals by overcoming the alienation associated with deskilled labor.

This harder version of lean-production-as-hegemony is less than compelling for two reasons. First, it is not clear that any significant overcoming of the Taylorist division of labor is taking place, particularly in automobile assembly plants. The argument that lean production represents a shift away from Taylorism has been contradicted by major surveys of work at two joint ventures, CAMI (Robertson, et al., 1993; Rinehart, this volume) and Mazda (Babson, this volume). It is also contradicted by qualitative studies at Subaru-Isuzu (Graham, this volume), NUMMI and Nissan (Parker and Slaughter, 1988), Toyota and Saturn (Yanarella, this volume), Mazda (Fucini and Fucini, 1990), and Nissan (Garrahan and Stewart, 1992). A study of Japanese management at six manufacturing firms in Britain concluded that such methods sometimes "promoted a deskilling strategy" (Bratton, 1992: 130) and that increases in workers' technical competencies and autonomy only occurred in small batch, high value-added production (1992: 202)—precisely the kind of workplace that is least likely to have a Taylorist division of labor in the first place.

Such empirical research provides substantial evidence that lean production is organized around essentially Taylorist job structures with job cycles of between one and three minutes' duration. While job rotation within teams is found in some plants, it normally results in a combination of deskilled jobs, i.e., 'multitasking' rather than multiskilling and job enlargement rather than job enrichment. The critique of Kenney and Florida (1993) by Dassbach in the first chapter is especially cogent on this point.

Moreover, Williams et al., (1992) argue that characteristics that have been deemed definitive of lean production, including *kaizen* (continuous improvement) and just-in-time (or demand-pull) bufferless production were present at Ford in the early years. Similarly, Dassbach notes that "rigidities," such as detailed job descriptions, which are supposed to be specific to traditional labor processes in contrast to lean production, were in fact management concessions made during the 1950s. Since these features are not intrinsic to Taylorism, lean production and its predecessor are not qualitatively different. Thus, the argument is highly problematic if overcoming the Taylorist division of labor is a precondition for the new hegemony in lean production.

Secondly, the harder version of hegemony is methodologically weak in a fundamental sense. Kenney and Florida, for example, provide a comprehensive description of Japanese production mechanisms that are intended to internalize management goals. Yet the argument rests on the logic of such internalization with remarkably little evidence about the actual impact of such mechanisms on worker consciousness.

The other, 'softer' version of this new workplace hegemony is centered primarily on ideological conditioning rather than on the labor process. Binns, for example, argues in Weberian terms that TQM is part of an attempt by management to transfer its authority from a bureaucratic to a charismatic ethos that is almost religious in nature (1993: 51). In this second variant of hegemony, management control is based on an intimate authoritarianism that is constructed through socialization processes that subordinate workers within a form of 'cooperative Taylorism.' Socialization mechanisms include the rigorous recruitment of new hires focusing on selecting younger workers who are deemed inclined to cooperate effectively with management and fellow workers, extensive orientation and training, much of it ideological in content, *teian* (suggestion) programs, company recreation and sports events, peer counseling, work uniforms, group meetings, and corporate communications in the form of letters, newspapers, videos, all emphasizing the common interests workers and managers have in improving quality and productivity.[2]

This socialization is reinforced by worker surveillance of other workers (Garrahan and Stewart, 1992: 105–109 et passim) and by bonuses for productivity suggestions, for participation in quality circles (group meetings to deal with quality problems), and for keeping up attendance. Peer pressure is often stimulated by a failure to replace absentee workers and to make other workers bear the burden of the work that slower, older, weaker, or sick workers do not accomplish. Where workplaces are unionized, unions are often another mechanism of corporate socialization, sometimes to such an extent that workers find it difficult to distinguish the union from management (Kenney and Florida, 1993: 277–278). Even more than the NUMMI plant in California (Brown and Reich, 1989: 32–33), GM's Saturn plant in Tennessee may be the most extreme instance in the North American auto industry of such corporate-union integration (Yanarella, this volume; Bluestone and Bluestone, 1992: 191–201). In nonunion workplaces, these integrative mechanisms are usually directed against unionization (Green, this volume; Grenier, 1989; and Wells, 1993b).

As in the previous version of hegemony, teams and team leaders play a key role, but here the emphasis is less on production than on culture. Team leaders may perform the role of union stewards by settling disputes and thereby circumvent the grievance procedure, but at the same time, they also perform the coordination functions of first line supervisors and are sometimes involved in hiring decisions (Graham, this volume). Such mechanisms tend to obscure the lines between management and workers and are consistent with the unitarist ideology on which lean production is premised.

This softer version of hegemony is the more subtle and difficult to assess. One issue concerns management intentions: to what extent are these mechanisms designed to achieve ideological goals? Some managers at CAMI (a GM-Suzuki assembly plant in Ontario) claim that employee suggestions make a major contribution to cost-cutting (Rinehart, et al., 1993)[3] while others say that the suggestion programs are mainly meant to give workers a sense their ideas "are worth something" so they will "continue to participate and feel good" (Robertson, et al., 1993: 38). In any event, intentions are not the same as results.

Assessing the actual impact of these socialization mechanisms requires an understanding of workers' attitudinal responses. While the available evidence is not definitive, it is not very supportive of the effectiveness of this variant of hegemony. Kenney and Florida (1993) and Garrahan and Stewart (1992) show extensive worker compliance with management goals, but there is no evidence that management goals have been internalized in the work force. Indeed, Garrahan and Stewart report being "constantly surprised by the degree of skepticism expressed by line workers up to and including team leaders" (1992: 153). Similarly, a survey of thirteen firms employing TQM in Britain reported that there was worker resistance to management goals and cautioned against being definitive about cultural changes among workers (Hill, 1991). A study of Japanese management practices in British supermarkets found that: "behavioral realignment . . . denotes less internalization of management values of customer commitment than a perceivedly necessary response to increasing managerial surveillance and threat of sanction. Fear of job loss in a period of large scale unemployment is the bottom line of that perceived necessity" (Binns, 1993: 55).

The surveys of worker attitudes at CAMI and Mazda also suggest that most workers have not been successfully socialized into a commitment to managerial goals that is qualitatively different than those Walker and Guest (1952) described over forty years ago. Nine out of ten workers surveyed at CAMI felt the firm was no different than other firms (Robertson, et al., 1993: 44). Sixty percent reported that working in a team "gets us all pressuring one another"; 70 percent reported that teams were "a way to get us to work harder" (Ibid.: 29). Only 12 percent regarded CAMI as "special." Almost everyone saw innovations such as company uniforms as pseudo-egalitarian, and almost three quarters said CAMI is undemocratic (Rinehart, et al., this volume). At Mazda, four out of five said they could not maintain the current work intensity to retirement, a majority wanted the right to strike, and there were complaints about supervisory favoritism (Babson, this chapter).

Such attitudinal findings are supported by reports of worker behavior. The participant observation study by Graham (this volume) at Subaru-Isuzu found the kind of worker resistance typically reported in more conventional auto assembly plants. And at CAMI, teams demanded a series of reforms to make their jobs easier and safer, and the rate of grievances, slowdowns and work refusals has been growing (Rinehart, et al., this volume). Protesting CAMI and Mazda workers have refused to submit *teians* (Kenney and Florida, 1993: 107; Robertson, et al., 1993: 29). Less than 40 percent of those surveyed at CAMI take part in quality circles. Workers at some of these plants, including Mazda and CAMI, have elected militant leaders, as did NUMMI workers who listed line speed-up and managerial favoritism, among other grievances (Turner, 1991: 60).[4] There is also growing discontent at Saturn, where the union president who promoted closer collaboration with management won only 52 percent of the vote (Slaughter, 1993). At CAMI in 1992, a nearly unanimous strike vote and a five week strike led to gains in work standards, representation, and health and safety, as well as pay. In sum, this evidence suggests that it is premature to conclude that either the softer or harder version of hegemony has generally been successfully embedded in workplaces characterized by lean production.

Workers' Ambivalence to Lean Production

Despite the lack of evidence to support the use of lean production to construct a new hegemony of the workplace in either technical-structural terms or social-ideological terms, it is striking how stable labor-management relations seem to be at lean production auto plants. Although significant expressions of discontent have occurred, as noted above, strikes are rare, and there is evidence, as explained in the following section, that workers in lean workplaces are not calling for a reversion to more traditional labor processes. Nor do most workers support unionization of the lean plants in which they work. This latter point is manifested in the failure of both the CAW and the UAW to organize the transplants, except for joint ventures, such as CAMI, NUMMI, and Mazda, where the unions used their leverage in organized GM and Ford plants to pressure management into agreeing to unionize before workers had initiated the union certification process, indeed before most had been hired (Downs, 1989; and Wells, 1993a).

A widespread and strong desire to revert to nonlean production is also absent in union attempts to organize Japanese transplants. The CAW's campaign to organize the Hyundai assembly plant in Quebec was based not on any challenge to lean production but around demands to fulfill the promise of job rotation and to improve pensions (Yanarella, this volume). Furthermore, local unions at joint ventures and Big Three plants, participate with management in joint committees on health and safety, technological change, training programs, and cooperate with the introduction of various aspects of team ideology and practices. In such cases, the CAW and the UAW negotiate rather than reject such changes (Babson, this volume; Robertson, et al., 1993: 57; Wells, 1994a, 1994b; and Yanarella, this volume). Indeed, as a matter of policy, neither the UAW nor the CAW oppose lean production as such (Canadian Auto Workers, n.d.:10).

There is also evidence that workers themselves prefer to reform rather than to eliminate lean production. Workers at NUMMI, for example, blame many of their difficulties not on lean production itself but on the failure of American managers to understand the system, while workers at Mazda blame problems on the Japanese managers instead.[5] Similarly, workers at both Mazda and CAMI have called on management to fulfill the promise of lean production by improving access to job training and job rotation. At CAMI, nine out of ten of those surveyed said they liked working in teams (Rinehart, et al., 1993: 10; and this volume). And at Nissan in Britain "numerous interviewees revelled in the experience of 'group work' in the form of team-centered production units" (Garrahan and Stewart, 1992: 133).

Another Explanation for Worker Cooperation with Lean Production

At this point we are faced with a conundrum. Lean production does not lead to qualitatively higher skill levels or to greater worker influence over workplace decision-making, but it does lead to more intense work, more job stress and more workplace health and safety problems (Binns, 1993; Bratton, 1992; Fucini and Fucini 1990; Garrahan and Stewart, 1992; Kenney and Florida, 1993; Nomura, 1993; Parker and Slaughter, 1988; and Robertson, et al., 1993). At the same time, there is no substantial evidence of increasing worker or union resistance to lean production. The current explanation for this lack of worker resistance, a new hegemony in the workplace, is, however, insufficiently grounded in the available evidence to be persuasive. What, then, is the explanation for relative labor stability and widespread worker cooperation with lean production?

Most of the search for links between lean production and worker compliance has been focused on relations of production partly because of lean production's emphasis on the labor process and other microeconomic areas such as interfirm relations and product design. The focus on endogenous sources of hegemony in Japan is also explained by worker dependency on the internal labor markets of large firms, including worker expectations of long-term job security and pay bonuses tied to efficiency evaluations for a mostly male core of about one third of the labor force (Kumazawa and Yamada, 1989). This kind of job security, in the context of serious labor shortages in Japan, is largely absent in lean plants outside Japan. Nevertheless, an explanation for worker compliance in such plants in Canada, the United States, and Britain, that is based on weaker and more contingent forms of job and income security, and is sensitive to external labor markets, has a similar cogency.

In Canada, the United States, and Britain, the limited Keynesianism of the post-war period has been breaking down as globally competitive capital and the rise of neo-liberal political forces undermine its national and oligopolistic foundations. As a consequence, management power is being reinforced by a growing reserve army of labor. The 1980s witnessed increasing long-term unemployment and underemployment, the replacement of permanent, full-time jobs by part-time and temporary jobs, increasing wage polarization, cutbacks in the social wage, an increasing incidence of poverty, greater disparities between regional labor markets, and other indicators of labor market deterioration (Economic Council of Canada, 1990; Gaffikin and Morrissey, 1992; McBride,

1992; and Mishel and Bernstein, 1993). At the same time, falling union densi-
ties, the increasing segmentation of external labor markets, and the disintegra-
tion of internal labor markets (Noyelle, 1987), have all weakened the structural
basis of working class cohesion and politics (Esping-Anderson, 1991; and Offe,
1984).

The automotive sector was especially hard-hit during the late 1970s and
early 1980s. Japanese firms took an increasing share of the market while fourteen assembly plants owned by Big Three United States auto makers closed
down and a third of auto sector workers lost their jobs (Wells, 1994). Outside
the auto sector, there was a decline of wages in the manufacturing sector, a shift
to low-paying production jobs, and an increase in wage differentials based on
education (Mishel and Bernstein, 1993: 159–179, 425–431). These trends were
reinforced by newly build Japanese transplants, nearly all of which use large
numbers of temporary workers who are paid at much lower wage and benefit
levels. In this context, it is not overall unemployment in the economy that is
necessarily most important in explaining worker compliance. Rather, it is the
relatively high wages and better job security in lean production plants which
represent a last best hope for many to enjoy the 'middle class' lifestyle that forms
the basis of full citizenship in much of Canada and the United States.

As a consequence, there is fierce competition among workers for jobs in
lean workplaces: e.g., 100,000 applications for 3000 jobs at Toyota in Kentucky
(Yanarella, this volume). Transplants take advantage of unemployment and
wage pressures even more when they construct 'greenfield' sites in semirural
areas of border states of the United States South and Midwest where unemployment exceeds the average and in the 'rust belt' where deindustrialization has
been most severe. Garrahan and Stewart make a similar observation about the
location of the Nissan plant in Britain. They conclude that worker and community support for Nissan "stems directly from the company's willingness to put
capital and new technology into the vacuum created by industrial decline"
(1992: 34).

Perhaps more than anything else, job competition makes workers identify
with the 'competitiveness' of firms when the workers have been 'born again'
after enduring a 'significant emotional event,' such as major job loss. The GM
plant that would later become the NUMMI plant laid its work force off indefi-
nitely. Forty percent of those laid off were still unemployed a year and a half
later and those who found jobs took average pay cuts of about 40 percent.
NUMMI did not reopen as a lean production facility until three years after the
original plant had closed. And NUMMI did not rehire the "more troublesome"
workers (Brown and Reich, 1989: 29–31).[6]

Competition for well paid, relatively secure jobs is made even more fierce
because workers are increasingly forced to rely on corporate welfarism (company
pensions, health care, and dental care) thanks to the decline of state welfarism

in Canada, the United States, and Britain. This corporate welfarism is far less encompassing in Japanese transplants and joint ventures than in large firms in Japan (Dore, 1973), but it serves the same paternalistic purpose. In this context, the discourse of market liberalism in the 1980s and 1990s is understandably somewhat less compelling to many workers than its reality.

Lean production also reinforces the disciplining pressures of external labor markets in the way it shapes internal labor markets. The core-periphery relations of the external labor market have their counterpart in two-tier work forces. Most unionized transplants have contractual promises that the job security of core workers will be maintained for as long as the plant is economically viable (Kenney and Florida, 1993: 115). At Saturn, management guarantees 80 percent of the work force 'permanent' job security, barring "severe economic conditions." The remaining 20 percent are expendable (Bluestone and Bluestone, 1993: 195). Because the Saturn workers waived their right to transfer to other GM plants represented by the UAW, they are even more dependent on the economic success of the plant than other UAW members. Nonunion transplants informally assure job security for their core workers, too, by using a second tier of workers as a flexible supply of labor, as do Mazda and Diamond Star, where cheaper, part-time, temporary workers are a buffer against laying off core workers.[7] According to Kenney and Florida, temporary workers are "very intimidated" and effectively remind permanent workers in the transplants "how good they have it" (1993: 280–281).

This competition among workers and the ambivalence of many workers about lean production is thus more indicative of coercion rather than of voluntary consent. These conditions suggest that worker compliance with managerial quality and efficiency goals may be less the product of technical or social changes in the labor process than of growing differences in wages, benefits, and job security within internal labor markets and between internal and external labor markets. The significance of this may be understood by viewing lean production within a broader context in which corporate power is in the ascendancy, fortified by the pressures of increasing global competition. Any assessment of its implications for hegemony in the workplace needs to be made within a broader analysis of the ways political economies foster 'consent' within a framework of labor market coercion. Such pervasive coercion deserves greater weight than many analysts of lean production have given it.

The Contradictory Nature of Lean Production

Analysis of lean production as an agency of hegemony also needs to take account of its internal contradictions. As is widely recognized, lean production is a fragile production system based on the removal of buffers cushioning interruptions in the labor process. This fragility means that management depends on a continuous and higher level of worker cooperation in a lean production system than in traditional Fordist processes. If this cooperation derives less from the internalization of managerial norms in workers and more from their adaptation to external market forces, then lean production, or its key components, may prove to be more unstable than has generally been recognized. At CAMI, for example, where jobs have been somewhat more secure than at many other plants, the CAW has concluded that teams are "a terrain of contest." "For the most part . . . teams are not operating as management might like. Research results point to the presence of a growing team-based resistance to some of management's more excessive demands and policies" (Robertson, et al., 1993: 32).

Tight geographic integration in the context of 'just-in-time' production and single-sourcing has also made lean production vulnerable to coordinated worker resistance, as Ford workers have demonstrated in Europe (Wilkinson and Oliver, 1990).

While much attention has been paid to the dynamic and flexible qualities of lean production, less attention has been paid to its cost rigidities. One cost rigidity involves training. If continuous training is a necessary element of lean production, one must ask whether managers are likely to tolerate the costs of continuous training once public training subsidies are exhausted (see Yanarella, this volume). Another implication is the contradiction between training workers and transferring them to new teams where their skills are no longer applicable. In effect, management faces a choice between greater rigidity in allocating labor, in order to reduce costs of training, and more flexibility in allocating workers to jobs, as teams become more efficient (Babson, this volume).

Another contradiction is the cost increase associated with work intensification (e.g., higher rates of injury and more long-term disabilities). These costs are compounded because lean production systems are less able to reabsorb injured and worn out workers because they have fewer light, off-line jobs such as sweeping, repair, and quality control. This cost rigidity is most acute in unionized work forces where contract seniority provisions are more likely to protect older workers.

A final contradiction that may undermine the stability of lean production is its dependence on growth in consumer demand. In sectors such as the auto industry, with its massive overcapacity, lean production requires increasing market share in order to pay for the job security of its core workers. In Japan job security is seen to be critical to the success of labor relations (Aoki, 1990; and Dore, 1986). Such success can be costly. While lean firms may maintain the job security of core workers during short term downturns, this is more difficult when declines are protracted, as they are in several large firms in Japan.[8] Employment guarantees make the core work force a fixed cost of production. Everything else being equal, once the buffers of temporary contract labor have been laid off leaving the core workers, such labor force rigidity results in higher labor costs per unit as production volume declines. Meanwhile, competing nonlean firms at least those with flexible labor policies, are able to respond by cutting labor costs through further layoffs.

Lean Production and Enterprise Unionism

Several union-oriented advocates of lean production (e.g., Ephlin, 1988; and Bluestone and Bluestone, 1992) and critics (e.g., Babson, this volume), in addition to a number who are management-oriented or consider themselves above partisanship (e.g., Lawler and Mohrman, 1987; and Cohen-Rosenthal and Burton, 1987), maintain not only that coexistence between unions and lean production is possible but that unions are also needed to make these labor processes function more efficiently.

The most ambitious brief for a role, indeed a revitalization, of unions in supporting lean production is that made by Bluestone and Bluestone in their recent book, *Negotiating the Future* (1992). They present the Saturn plant in Tennessee as a model for the future of the labor movement. Organized labor would expand its role from co-managing the workplace to co-managing the enterprise. The union would hold a veto over almost every important corporate decision, including product pricing and finance issues. Labor and management would have a partnership based on equivalent power and a broadening of mutual interests. The main reason management would agree to such a role for the union is that workers' wages and benefits would be tied so directly to profit and productivity levels that management and workers would become, in effect, a collective entrepreneur at the level of the firm. Workers and managers would constitute a single team competing in a world of other teams of workers and managers.

In this framework the limited labor-management adversarialism of the postwar Wagner model of industrial relations in both Canada and the United States would be replaced by corporate (labor-management) teams. Industrial unions would be broken up into a series of plant or enterprise unions, each of which would become part of a corporate team and compete with the enterprise unions of other corporate teams. Such a framework would clearly be inconsistent with strategies based on solidarity among workers in the same industry, much less among workers as a class.

Saturn also appears to be an attempt to duplicate the UAW's "one party unionism" (Steiber, 1962) at the local level. Yanarella notes the "ebbing of local union democracy," pointing out that the president of the local "has buffered himself from the rank and file" with 350–400 appointed union officials (this volume).

Such enterprise unionism is an attempt to protect a core that remains of the UAW membership in the auto industry. This strategy is consistent with the declining power of unions, the job and income insecurity faced by many production workers, and the ambivalence that many rank and file UAW members have toward aspects of lean production, including teams. Yet it is precisely these weaknesses, together with the various contradictions in lean production noted above, that make it difficult to understand how enterprise unionism would be built upon anything but a junior partner status for labor. Not only would labor not be equal with management, but it would appear to have a role similar to a progressive human resource management department. Why would workers voluntarily agree to pay dues for this kind of union 'representation'? And if the union loses its legitimacy with its members, what value would the union have for management? Would not a company union similar to the 'employee associations' Nissan and Toyota created at their transplants be a logical next step?

Is There a Future for Organized Labor?

The main thesis of this chapter has been that, in lean production systems, worker compliance with managerial goals is profoundly conditioned by the coercive pressures of external labor markets. Accordingly, the employment and wage levels and the level of the social wage under Keynesian welfarism are at least as significant as innovations in production relations in fostering consent in such workplaces. This analysis takes us beyond the realm of the sociology of work where most study of this putative new hegemony of production has been focused. It centers on political economy, and increasingly on international political economy.

In part because the United States and Japan are the most powerful states in the international political economy, as well as the states in the OECD where organized labor and Keynesian welfarism are the weakest, lean production is being inserted into the globalization of capitalism in a context that is very favorable to management control of labor. At the same time, lean production systems are expanding when transnational trade and investment are growing in significance, particularly in low wage, high repression labor regimes in South Asia and Latin America. Such labor regimes constitute competitive constraints on less authoritarian labor regimes, and thereby diminish organized labor's room for maneuver.

Such circumstances not only go a long way toward explaining the limits of worker resistance in lean and traditional production systems, but also suggest a structural narrowing of the economic limits to that resistance. Certainly it could not reasonably be argued that such economic challenges are not the most formidable labor has faced, at least since the Depression of the 1930s. At the same time, as Polanyi (1957) argued so cogently, capitalist market relations cannot be understood separately from supportive political relations. Similarly, as in the 1930s, the future of unions remains highly indeterminate and politically contingent.

If organized labor is to have a real future apart from company unionism, labor movements in Canada, the United States and elsewhere will have to be transformed. Under current economic and political conditions, a new coordinative unionism will be very difficult to build. Yet there is an urgent need for such a unionism, and some efforts along these lines have already begun.

More than any other factor, the integration of production systems and the global political economy challenges unions to develop a heightened capacity for coordination. This coordination includes strategic planning among unions internationally, sectorally, and among the locals of the same union. It also includes linking unions with community and social movements around particular campaigns, such as the defense of social programs, to create a broader "movement politics" (Canadian Auto Workers, 1994: 13–20). It includes extending union organization horizontally to workers in other labor markets (especially in the private service sector and in smaller workplaces). It might also mean extending unions vertically to workers in nonunion segments of the same internal labor markets. For example, since lean production features the creation of closer collaboration among semiskilled workers, skilled trades workers, design technicians, and engineers and tends to reduce the status distinctions separating them, these changes in the labor process may be conducive to the unionization of more skilled strata of the work force. Finally, unions must strive to 'organize the organized' by creating new forms of worker participation in the union and the workplace. The following is a brief exploration of the rationale for, and meaning of, key aspects of this new coordinative unionism.

The Wagner model of industrial relations, which focuses on site-by-site collective bargaining, has created highly decentralized labor movements in Canada and the United States, and is thus conducive to enterprise unionism without the equal partnership envisioned by Bluestone and Bluestone (1992). Contract bargaining which gives priority to individual material benefits rather than to a collective voice has tended to reinforce individualism as workers are defined by their seniority privileges regarding job security, promotions, transfers, and shifts. Furthermore, Wagner-model contract bargaining, for the most part, focuses on a privatized politics of distribution that is disconnected from external labor markets, thereby reinforcing labor market segmentation and forfeiting the potential for broader class politics outside the union and the workplace. Wagner model unionism has thus contributed to workplace-centered politics of consumption that is consistent with the creation of a series of enterprise unions that compete with each other for job security and material benefits. This intraclass competition is reinforced by economic restructuring which polarizes labor markets between 'good' and 'bad' jobs inside and outside the workplace.

A critical challenge for unions in the workplace is to overcome the current limits of union representation and membership participation. Traditional contract bargaining means union leaders can influence workplace changes only during negotiations every few years, while lean production is based on continuous organizational change. At the same time, except for minimal participation in the contract ratification meetings, most workers are excluded from collective bargaining altogether. Except for grievance machinery, workers have few union mechanisms for taking part in workplace decisions. Wagner-model unions have generally avoided mobilizing their memberships around workplace issues, particularly if this might entail direct action in violation of no-strike and union security provisions in the contract. Efforts to overcome these limits need to include the development of an ongoing coordination of 'rank and file' participation through such innovations as task forces to identify work problems, educational campaigns, and continuous workplace-wide bargaining around issues such as job structures and working conditions (Banks and Metzgar, 1989; and Scannell, 1993: 109). Indeed, unions can attempt to use the language of participation articulated in lean production to promote their own agendas for participation in the workplace (Wells, 1987).

In the context of the imbalance of power between labor and management, however, such coordinated mobilization is unlikely to be sustained in isolation at the local level: indeed, it would make the local more vulnerable to whipsawing. Instead, coordination of rank and file mobilization at the level of the individual local needs to be complemented by a horizontal coordination of networks of locals to resist whipsawing. There are some signs that these horizontal links among locals are already emerging. Ties among activists at UAW's Mazda local and the CAW's CAMI local, for example, have been facilitated not only by visits between the locals but also by electronic networking. Beyond this, such networks need to be coordinated across whole economic sectors, such as automotive, however, if they are to offset whipsawing effectively. And so that unions themselves are not whipsawed (e.g., between the UAW and CAW), alliances will need to be coordinated among unions representing workers in the same firm or the same sector.

Because the growing global diversity of labor regimes encourages firms to compete by taking advantage of international variations in labor standards, coordinated union strategies at the firm and sectoral level will also increasingly require international union alliances.[9] Some unions in Canada and the United States are taking this direction. The United Electrical Workers in the United States and the Authentic Workers Front (an independent union) in Mexico are creating alliances in the electrical and machine manufacturing sectors (Johnson, 1993). International alliances are also emerging among unions in sectors such as communications, garments, and automotive (Rachleff, 1993: 106). The Japanese Auto Workers Union has called for "international coexistence" (Sengenberger, 1992: 18).

In order to reduce international whipsawing based on variations in labor standards, these international union alliances will need to negotiate a set of international labor standards among themselves and then push for international regulatory bodies to create an enforcable legal framework that incorporates the standards. A model for such a framework is the European Works Councils set up by the European Community. The Councils consist of union representatives from several countries who work for the same transnational firm (Macshane, 1993: 203).

Such a framework is harder to devise when there is considerable variation among labor standards, as in the case of North-South differences in labor regimes. Job competition among unions in different labor regimes tends to inhibit cooperation. Unions in high standard labor regimes are particularly prone to try to enhance the job security and wages of their members by using international labor standards as a form of trade protectionism. Labor in high labor standard regimes would be less likely, however, to simply adopt a protectionist posture when there is a threat of greater immigration from low labor standard regimes. Moreover, threats to labor standards are already apparent in the growing unevenness inside the high labor standard regimes, due in part to immigration from low labor standard regimes (Sassen, 1991). For pragmatic reasons such as these, union coordination across national boundaries is likely to increase.

If organized labor is to have a real future, a new coordinative unionism must be developed at the workplace, firm, sector and international levels. The likelihood of such a development may seem slim, particularly in view of the power of transnational capital. Yet the very fragility of lean production cautions against assuming that organized labor, even as it stands now, will be unable to grow in power. Since the evidence suggests that management strategies in lean production sites have not led to wholesale worker internalization of management's norms and values, the possibilities for a reinvigorated labor movement also remain more open than would have been the case under the lean-production-as-hegemony scenario. While the outcome, of course, is indeterminate, a transformed labor movement might allow workers to confront not only lean production but also key dimensions of power beyond the point of production. The shaping of workers' 'consent' is still contested terrain.

Notes

1. Other labels include 'toyotism,' 'synchronous manufacturing,' 'Japanese production management,' 'team concept,' 'innovation-mediated production,' and most recently 'the agile corporation.'
2. There is evidence that managers at some plants attempt to extend the training socialization of workers into the public education system as well by helping local school officials build a new emphasis on business-related group problem solving into the curriculum (Kenney and Florida, 1993: 108).

3. The limits on worker contributions to productivity increases through *teians* (suggestions) is emphasized by Nomura (1993) with respect to lean production in Japan where the key innovations in productivity stem from the engineers. Similarly, the CAW team of researchers at CAMI has concluded that productivity increases stem far less from team organization, etc., than from outsourcing, the design of the work process, etc.

4. Recently the adversarial local leadership at Mazda was voted out of office and replaced by another faction deemed to be less adversarial (interview with union leaders, UAW Mazda local, Flat Rock, Michigan, May 20, 1993).

5. Personal communication from Mike Parker, January 21, 1994. Kenney and Florida argue that management at Nissan and Mazda in the United States has not used job rotation because of productivity pressures (1993: 268–269).

6. Brown and Reich argue that plant closings do not by themselves produce cooperative labor relations in the longer run, and point to another GM plant in California where workers did not cooperate with lean production. They note the importance of a no-layoff pledge by management, however (1989: 34), and say that "for the workers to be convinced that working both harder and smarter will not cost them their jobs, they must be given job security" (1989: 41). For an analysis of the reasons why workers at the second plant were able to maintain their jobs through a militant campaign, see Mann (1987).

7. Interview, local union leaders, Mazda plant, Flat Rock, Michigan, May 1993; Kenney and Florida, 1993: 112.

8. Japanese firms in Japan may have at least two million excess employees on their payrolls, a number that is equivalent to three percent of the labor force (Crook, 1993). According to *The Economist*, "cleverer Japanese firms know that life-time employment is finished" (September 18, 1993).

9. For an overview of the interplay between class power within states and hegemonic state power within the international system, see Martin (1994).

Bibliographic References

Books, Book Chapters, and Articles

Adams, R. (1989). North American industrial relations: Divergent trends in Canada and the United States. *International Labor Review, 128*, 47–64.

―――. (1992). Efficiency is not enough. *Labor Studies Journal, 17*, 18–27.

Adler, P. (1993). Time and motion regained. *Harvard Business Review, 71*, 97–108.

―――. (1992). The learning bureaucracy: New United Motor Manufacturing Inc. In B. Straw and L. Cummings (Eds.), *Research in organizational behavior*. Greenwich: JAI Press.

―――― & Cole, R. (1993). Designed for Learning: A Tale of Two Auto Plants. *Sloan Management Review, 34*, 85–94.

Aglietta, M. (1976). *A theory of capitalist regulation: The U.S. experience*. London: NLB.

Allen, J. (1991). Making lifetime employment a U.S. reality: The Toyota experience. *Employment Relations Today, 18*, 185–92.

―――. (1992). Toyota's Camry, Toyota's training. *Technical and Skills Training*, October, 41–45.

Albert, L. (1988). *Call me Roger*. New York: Contemporary Books.

Aoki, M. (1984). Aspects of the Japanese Firm. In M. Aoki, (Ed.), *The economic analysis of the Japanese firm* (pp. 3–43). Holland: Elsevier.

Arthurs, H. W., Carter, D. D., Fudge, J., and Glasbeek, H. J. (1988). *Labor law and industrial relations in Canada* (3rd ed). Deventer, Netherlands: Butterworths.

Automotive News. (January 7, 1991). Read all about it: It's the machine that ate Detroit. *Automotive News*, p. 12.

Babson S. (1993). Lean or mean: The MIT model and lean production at Mazda. *Labor Studies Journal, 44*, 3–24.

Barth, C. (1917). Preface. In Babcock, G. *Taylor system in franklin management*. Easton: Hive Publishing.

Bartik, T. (1984). Business location decisions in the United States. *Journal of Business and Economic Studies, 3*, 14–22.

Beaumont, P. B. (Winter 1991). Trade unions and HRM. *Industrial Relations Journal, 21*, 300–308.

Bennett, T. (1986). The politics of the 'popular' and popular culture. In T. Bennett, C. Menger, and J. Woolscott, (Eds.), *Popular culture and social relations* (pp. 6–21). Philadelphia, PA: Open University Press.

Bennett, D. A. & King, T. D. (May 1991). The Saturn school of tomorrow. *Educational Leadership, 48*, 41–44.

Berggren, C. (1992, 1993). *Alternatives to lean production: Work in the Swedish auto industry.* Ithaca, NY: ILR Press.

————, Bjorkman, T., & Hollander, E. (1991). *Are they unbeatable?* Unpublished paper, University of New South Wales, Australia.

Binns, D. C. (Ed. and Comp). (1991). *A shared struggle: A Local 88 communications committee special report on the meetings with UAW Local 3000 Mazda unit in Flat Rock, Michigan.* Mimeo.

Blauner, R. (1964). *Alienation and freedom: The factory worker and his industry.* Chicago: University of Chicago Press.

Blount, J. (January 1990). Behind the Lines. *Canadian Business,* 62–67.

Bluestone, I. (1972). The next step toward industrial democracy. UAW paper.

Blair, J. P., Endres, C., & Fichtenbaum, R. (1990). Japanese automobile investment in West Central Ohio. In E. J. Yanarella and W. C. Green, (Eds.), *The politics of industrial recruitment* (pp. 117–136). Westport: Greenwood Press.

———— & Premus, R. (1987). Major factors in industrial location. *Economic Development Quarterly, 1*, 72–85.

Bluestone, B. & Bluestone, I. (1992). *Negotiating the future.* New York: Basic Books.

Bonanno, J. B. (1977). Employee codetermination: Origins in Germany, present practice in Europe, and applicability to the United States. *Harvard Journal on Legislation, 14,* 947–1012.

Bradbury, J. (1989). Strategies in local communities to cope with industrial restructuring. In G. J. R. Linge & G. A. van der Knaap (Eds.), *Labour, Environment and Industrial Change* (pp. 167–185). New York: Routledge.

Brauchle, P. S. & Pendleton, C. (Spring 1992). Providing customized training for a transplant auto manufacturer. *Journal of Industrial Teacher Education, 29,* 80–91.

Braverman, H. (1974). *Labor and monopoly capital.* New York: Monthly Review Press.

Brecher, J. & Costello, T. (Eds.). (1990). *Building bridges: The emerging grassroots coalition of labor and community*. New York: Monthly Review Press.

Briggs, P. (1988). The Japanese at work: Illusion of the ideal. In M. Parker & J. Slaughter, *Choosing sides: Unions and the team concept* (pp. 60–64). Boston: South End Press.

Brody, D. H. (1988). The future of labor–management cooperative efforts under Section 8(a)(2) of the National Labor Relations Act. *Vanderbilt Law Review, 41*, 545–575.

Brown, C. & Reich, M. (1988). When does union–management cooperation work? A look at NUMMI and GM–Van Nuys. *California Management Review, 31*, 26–44.

Buchele, R. & Christiansen, J. (1993). Industrial relations and relative income shares in the United States. *Industrial Relations, 32*, 1.

Burawoy, M. ((1979). *Manufacturing Consent*. Chicago: University of Chicago Press.

———. (1985). *The politics of production*. London: Verso.

Business Week. (July 24, 1989a). The UAW vs. Japan: It's showdown time in Tennessee. *Business Week*, pp. 64–65.

———. (1989b). Shaking up Detroit. *Business Week*, August 14, 74–81.

Canadian Auto Workers. (n.d.). *CAW–Canada organizing report*. Willowdale, Ontario: CAW/TCU.

———. (n.d.). *Workplace issues: Work reorganization: Responding to lean production*. Willowdale, Ontario: CAW/TCU.

———. (1990). *CAW statement on the reorganization of work*. Willowdale, Ontario: CAW/TCU.

———. (1990). Technology and training. In CAW, *A new decade: Challenging the corporate agenda: Our response*. Willowdale, Ontario: CAW/TCU.

———. (1993). *The CAMI Report: Lean Production in a Unionized Auto Plant*. Willowdale, Ontario: CAW/TCU.

Calvert, J. (1988). The divergent paths of Canadian and American labor. In M. Davis & M. Sprinker (Eds.). *Reshaping the U.S. left* (pp. 213–228). New York: Verso.

CAMI–CAW. (1989). *Agreement between CAMI Automotive Inc. and CAW Local 88*, January 23, 1989–September 14, 1992.

Carnevale, A. P., Gainer, L. J., & Meltzer, A. S. (1990). Resource a: A new plant perspective: Case study of Mazda. *Workplace Basics Training Manual* (pp. A.1–A.10). San Francisco: Jossey–Bass.

Carroll, W. K. (1990). Restructuring capital, reorganizing consent: Gramsci, political economy, and Canada. *Canadian Review of Sociology and Anthropology, 27*, 390–416.

Chandler, C. & Stertz, B. A. (October 31, 1991). Mitsubishi buys Chrysler's 50% stake in their Diamond–Star joint ventures. *Wall Street Journal*, p. 4.

Chappell, L. (May 8, 1989). Worker screening gives edge. *Automotive News*, pp. 3, 49.

———. (August 27, 1990). Culture clash results in rocky start for Mazda's U.S. plant. *Automotive News*, p. 16.

———. (February 21, 1991a). CAW tackles Hyundai Canada: Work rules and pensions cited. *Automotive News*, p. 6.

———. (May 20, 1991b). GM flocks north to learn from lean, mean CAMI. *Automotive News*, pp. 1, 44.

———. (September 21, 1992). CAMI strike wilts transplant rose. *Automotive News*, p. 8.

———. (May 31, 1993). UAW beats the drums for war on Saturn labor rules. *Automotive News*, p. 8.

——— and Jackson, K. (January 14, 1991). UAW again targets transplants. *Automotive News*, p. 2.

——— and Gadacz, O. (May 31, 1993). Hyundai joint venture near. *Automotive News*, pp. 1, 37.

——— & Pinto, L. (May 24, 1993). Saturn eyes Corvette plant. *Automotive News*, pp. 1, p. 8.

——— & Sinek, J. (June 14, 1993). Hyundai recoups, revises Canada plant. p. 4.

Chernow, R. (1979). The rabbit that ate Pennsylvania: Governor Shapp builds Volkswagen a $70 million hutch. *Mother Jones*, 2, 19–24.

Clark, G. L. (1989). *Unions and communities under siege: American communities and the crisis of organized labor.* New York: Cambridge University Press.

Clark, L. H. Jr. (April 6, 1993). Yet another Clinton commission on unions. *The Wall Street Journal*, p. A–14.

Clarke, S. G. (1987). Rethinking the adversarial model in labor relations: An argument for repeal of Section 8(a)(2). *Yale Law Journal*, 96, 2021–2050.

Clarke, S. (1990). The crisis of Fordism or the crisis of social democracy? *Telos*, 83, 71–98.

———. (1992). What in the f___'s name is Fordism. In N. Gilbert, R. Burrows, and A. Pollert (Eds.), *Fordism and flexibility: Divisions and change* (pp. 13–31). New York: St. Martin's Press.

Clawson, D. & Fantasia, R. (1983). Beyond Burawoy: The dialectics of conflict and consent on the shop floor. *Theory and Society*, 12, 671–680.

Clegg, S. & Wilson, F. (1991). Power, technology and flexibility in organizations. *A sociology of monsters: Essays on power, technology and domination* (pp. 223–273). New York: Routledge.

Cockburn, A. (May 17, 1993). Clinton and labor: Reform equals rollback. *The Nation*, pp. 654–55.

Cohen–Rosenthal, E. & Burton, C. (1987). *Mutual gains: A guide to union-management cooperation.* New York: Praeger.

Cole, R. (1979). *Work, mobility, and participation: A comparative study of American and Japanese industry.* Berkeley: University of California Press.

Confederation of Japanese Automobile Workers' Unions. (1992). *Japanese automobile industry in the future.* Tokyo.

Cooke, W. (1990). *Labor–management cooperation.* Kalamazoo: W.E. Upjohn Institute.

Cotrell, D., Davis, L., Detrick, P., and Raymond, H. (1992). Sales training and the Saturn difference. *Training and Development, 46* (December), 38–43.

Crook, C. (March 6, 1993). The Japanese economy: From miracle to mid–life crisis. *The Economist.*

The Courier Journal. (July 29, 1989). Free ride at Smyrna. *The Courier Journal*, n.p.

Cusumano, M. (1985). *The Japanese automobile industry.* Cambridge: Harvard University Press

———. (1988). Manufacturing innovation and competitive advantage: Reflections on the Japanese automobile industry. Cambridge, MA: International Motor Vehicle Program.

Daily Labor Reporter. (June 9, 1986). Advice memorandum issued by NLRB on GM–UAW Saturn agreement. *Daily Labor Reporter*, E–1.

Dassbach, C. H. A. (1986). Industrial robots in the American automobile industry. *The Insurgent Sociologist, 13*(4), 53–61.

———. (1991). The origins of Fordism: The introduction of mass production and the five dollar day. *Critical Sociology, 18*(1), 77–90.

Datz, H. J. (1992). Employee participation programs—Are they lawful under the National Labor Relations Act? Unpublished manuscript.

Davis, M. (1984). The political economy of late imperial America. *New Left Review, 123*, 6–38.

Daw, J. (August 27, 1986a). GM, Suzuki to build car plant in Ingersoll. *Toronto Star*, E1.

———. (August 28, 1986b). GM–Suzuki plant includes $85 million aid package. *Toronto Star*, A1.

———. (July 24, 1988a). Japanese–style hiring hall knocks auto workers' boots off. *Toronto Star*, F1.

———. (September 18, 1988b). Not your ordinary job interview: Japanese carmakers are spending big bucks to find workers who fit the corporate culture of their Canadian plants. *Toronto Star*, G1.

———. (May 23, 1991). Hyundai workers sign up for union. *Toronto Star*, B4.

Derber C. & Schwartz, W. (1985). Toward a theory of worker participation. In F. Hearn and L. Belmont, (Eds.), *The transformation of industrial organization*. Belmont: Wadsworth.

DeReyteur, R. (November 21, 1990). CAW targets Toyota in Cambridge drive. *Kirchner–Waterloo Record*, B–6.

Danger rises in new auto jobs. (July 7–9, 1990). *Detroit Free Press*, 2.

DiLorenzo, T. (1988). *Lessons from abroad: Japanese labor relations and the U.S. automobile industry*. St. Louis: Center for the Study of American Business.

Dohse, K., Jurgens, U., & Malsch, T. (1985). From 'Fordism' to 'Toyotism'? *Politics & Society, 74*, 141–178.

Dore, R. (1973). *Japanese factory, British factory*. Berkeley: University of California Press.

Dow Jones News. (June 6, 1993). Hyundai Canada plant to shut down October 1993 to Spring 1995. *Dow Jones News*, n.p.

Doyle, K. (1992). Can Saturn save GM? *Incentive, 166* (December), 30–37.

Drache, D. (1991). The systematic search for flexibility: National competitiveness and new work relations. In D. Drache and M. S. Gertler (Eds.), *The new era of global competition* (pp. 3–25). Montreal: McGill–Queen's University Press.

——— & Glasbeek, H. (1989). The new Fordism in Canada: Capital's offensive, labour's opportunity. *Osgoode Hall Law Journal, 27*, 517–560.

Dubnick, M. (1984). American states and the industrial policy debate. *Policy Studies Journal, 4*, 22–27.

Dunlop, J. (1994). *Report and recommendations, commission on the future of worker-management relations*. Washington, D.C.: U.S. Department of Labor.

Eaton, A. E. (1990). The extent and determinants of local union control of participative programs. *Industrial and Labor Relations Review, 43* (July), 604–620.

Economic Council of Canada. (1990). *Good jobs, bad jobs*. Ottawa: Minister of Supply and Services.

Editorial. (September 4, 1992). Labor's day at GM. *Wall Street Journal*, A8.

Edwards, R. (1979). *Contested terrain*. New York: Basic Books.

Elder, Ann H., & Lind, N. (1987). The implications of uncertainty in economic development: The case of Diamond–Star motors. *Economic Development Quarterly, 1,* 30–40.

Ephlin, D. F. (1986). United auto workers: Pioneers in labor–management partnership. In J. Rosow, (Ed.), *Teamwork: Joint labor–management programs in America* (pp. 133–145). New York: Pergamon.

Epstein, B. (1990). Rethinking social movement theory. *Socialist Review, 20,* 1.

Estreicher, S. (1993). Employee voice in competitive markets. *The American Prospect,* 48–59.

Farnsworth, Clyde H. (August 9, 1991). Free trade accord is enticing Canadian companies to U.S. *New York Times,* pp. A1, C3.

Ferman, L. A., Hoyman, M. & Cutcher–Gershenfeld, J. (1990). Joint union management training programs: A synthesis in the evolution of jointism and training. In L. A. Ferman, M. Hoyman, J. Cutcher–Gershenfeld (Eds.), *New developments in worker training: A legacy for the 1990s.* Madison, WI: Industrial Relations Research Association.

Fiori, G. (1970). *Antonio Gramsci: Life of a revolutionary.* New York: Schocken Books.

Flint, J. (1989). Constant improvement? Or speedup? *Forbes, 143,* 93.

Florida, R. & Kenney, M. (1991). Transplanted organizations: The transfer of Japanese industrial organization to the U.S. *American Sociological Review, 56,* 381–398.

Ford, H. with Samuel Crowther. (1922). *My life and work.* Garden City: Doubleday, Page.

Foster, J. B. & Woolfson, C. (1989). Corporate restructuring and business unionism: The lessons of Caterpillar and Ford. *New Left Review, 147,* 51–66.

Fox, W. F. (1990). Japanese investment in Tennessee: The economic effects of Nissan's location in Smyrna. In E. J. Yanarella & W. C. Green (Eds.), *The politics of industrial recruitment* (pp. 175–187). Westport: Greenwood Press.

———— & Neel, C. W. (1987). Saturn: The Tennessee lessons. *Forum for Applied Research and Public Policy, 2,* 7–16.

Frank, D. (March 8, 1993). Sleeping with the enemy. *The Nation,* 310–313.

Fraser, D. A. (1994). Dissenting opinion of Douglas A. Fraser. In J. Dunlop, chair, *Report and recommendations, commission on the future of worker-management relations.* Washington, D.C.: U.S. Department of Labor.

Friedman, A. (1977). *Industry and labor: Class struggle at work and monopoly capitalism.* London: Macmillan.

Freeman, R. B. & Rogers, J. (March 19, 1993). A new deal for labor. *New York Times*, p. A–7.

Froiland, P. (1993). Training as bait. *Training, 30*, 45–49.

Fucini, J. & Fucini, S. (1990). *Working for the Japanese: Inside Mazda's American auto plant*. New York: Free Press.

Fulton, J. L. (1991). *Special report: A communications committee follow–up report on UAW–Mazda agreement 1991–1994*. Mimeo.

Gardner, G. & Lupo, N. (July 30, 1989). UAW stung by loss in Tennessee. *Lexington Herald–Leader*, pp. D–1, 7.

Garon, S. (1987). *The state and labor in modern Japan*. Berkeley: University of California Press.

Garrahan, P. & Stewart, P. (1992). *The Nissan enigma*. New York: Mansell.

———. (1993). Work organizations in transition: The human resource management implications of the 'Nissan Way'. *Human Resource Management Journal, 2*, 46–62.

Geber, B. (1992). Saturn's grand experiment. *Training, 29*, 27–35.

———. (1993). Because it's good for you: Bill Clinton's training tax. *Training, 30*, 17–25.

Gelsanliter, D. (1990). *Jump start: Japan comes to the heartland*. New York: Farrar, Straus, Giroux.

Gindin, S. (1989). Breaking away: The formation of the Canadian auto workers. *Studies in Political Economy, 29*, 63–89.

Glaberman, M. (1983). Building the Japanese car. *Canadian Dimension, 17*, 17–19.

Glickman, N. J. & Woodward, D. P. (1989). *The new competitors: How foreign investors are changing the U.S. economy*. New York: Basic Books.

GM–Suzuki plant to employ 2000. (August 28, 1986). *Ottawa Citizen*, p. D9.

Goll, I. (1991). Environment, corporate ideology, and employee involvement programs. *Industrial Relations, 30*, 138–149.

Goodman, R. (1979). *The last entrepreneurs: America's regional wars for jobs*. Boston: South End Press.

Grady, D. O. (1987). State economic development incentives: Why do the states compete? *State and Local Government Review, 19*, 86–94.

Graham, L. (1991). Screening for a union free environment, Unpublished PhD dissertation.

————. (1993). Inside a Japanese transplant: A critical perspective. *Work and Occupations, 20*, 147–173.

Gramsci, A. (1970). *Selections from the prison notebooks*. Ed. and trans. by Q. Hoare & G. N. Smith. New York: International Publishers.

Green, W. C. (1990). Constitutional dimensions of state industrial recruitment. In E. J. Yanarella and W. C. Green (Eds.), *The politics of industrial recruitment* (pp. 53–84). Westport: Greenwood Press.

Grenier, G. J. (1988). *Inhuman relations: Quality circles and anti–unionism in American industry*. Philadelphia: Temple University Press.

Grinspun, R. & Cameron, M. (Eds.). (1993). *The political economy of North American free trade*. New York: St. Martin's.

Halberstam, D. (1986). *The reckoning*. New York: Avon.

Hampton, W. J. (June 4, 1988). How does Japan Inc. pick its American workers? *Business Week*, pp. 25–26.

Hansen, S. (1990). Industrial policies in the American states. In E. J. Yanarella and W. C. Green (Eds.), *The politics of industrial recruitment*, (pp. 3–22). Westport: Greenwood Press.

Harp, J. (1991). Political economy/cultural studies: Exploring points of convergence. *Canadian Review of Sociology and Anthropology, 28*, 206–224.

Harper, M. C. (1982). Leveling the road from *Borg–Warner* to *First National Maintenance*: The scope of mandatory bargaining. *Virginia Law Review, 68*, 1447–1503.

Hartz, L. (1964). *The founding of new societies*. New York: Harcourt, Brace, and World.

Harvey, D. (1989). *The condition of postmodernity*. New York: Blackwell.

Helm, L. & Edad, M. (September 30, 1985). Toyota: A job for life but a grind. *Business Week*, p. 77.

Hertzenberg, S. (1993). Whither social unionism? Labor and restructuring in the U.S. auto industry. In J. Jenson & R. Mahon, (Eds.), *The challenge of restructuring* (pp. 314–336). Philadelphia: Temple University Press.

Hiam, A. (1992). *Closing the quality gap: Lessons from America's leading companies*. Englewood Cliffs: Prentice–Hall.

Hilman, R. & Pratt, J. (July 26, 1985). Spring Hill gets Saturn. *The Tennessean*, pp. 1, 8.

Hinkle, D. (March 10, 1993). Saturn election may impact economic growth in county. *Columbia Daily Herald*, pp. 1, 3.

————. (March 9, 1993). Challenger blasts Saturn's union head [interview with Bob Hoskins, nominee of Members for a Democratic Union]. *Columbia Daily Herald*, pp. 1, 3.

Hill, R. C. (1989). Comparing transnational production systems: The automobile industry in the USA and Japan. *International Journal of Urban and Regional Planning*, 13(3), 462–480.

———, Indergaard, M. & Fujita, K. (1989). Flat Rock: Home of Mazda: Social impact of a Japanese company on an American community. In P. J. Arnesan, *The auto industry ahead* (pp. 69–131). Ann Arbor: Center for Japanese Studies.

Historical background leading to GM–Suzuki site selection. (n.d.). Compiled by T. Hunt. Town of Ingersoll. Mimeo.

Hogler, R. L. (1984). Employee involvement programs and *NLRB v. Scott & Fetzer Co.*: The developing interpretation of Section 8(a)(2). *Labor Law Journal*, 35, 21–27.

——— and Grenier, G. (1992). *Employee participation and labor law in the American workplace*. Westport: Quorum Books.

Holmes, J. (1988). Industrial restructuring in a period of crisis: An analysis of the Canadian automobile industry, 1973–1983. *Antipode*, 20, 19–51.

———. (1989). New production technologies, labour, and the North American auto industry. In G. J. R. Linge & G. A. van den Knaaf (Eds.), *Labor, environment and industrial change* (pp. 87–106). New York: Rutledege.

———. (1991). The globalization of the production and the future of Canada's mature industries: The case of the automotive industry. In D. Drache & M. S. Gertler (Eds.), *The new era of global competition* (pp. 153–180). Montreal: McGill- Queen's University Press.

——— & Rusonik, A. (1990). *The breakup of an international union: Uneven development in the North American auto industry and the schism in the UAW* [Working paper 90–1]. Kingston, Ontario: Industrial Relations Centre, Queen's University.

Horowitz, G. (1968). *Canadian labour in politics*. Toronto: University of Toronto Press.

Hull, F. & Azumi, K. (1988). Technology and participation in Japanese factories: The consequences for morale and productivity. *Work and Occupations*, 15, 423–48.

Huxley, C., Kettler, D. and Struthers, J. (1986). Is Canada's experience 'especially instructive'? In S. M. Lipset (Ed.), *Unions in transition* (pp. 113–132). San Francisco: Institute for Contemporary Studies.

Imai, M. (1988–89). *Kaizen Communique*, 2(3) Winter.

Inagami, T. (1985). *Japanese workplace industrial relations series, 14*. Tokyo: Japan Institute of Labor.

Institute of Social Science. (1990). *Local Production of Japanese Automobile and Electronic Firms in the United States: The Application and Adaptation of Japanese Style Management*. Tokyo: University of Tokyo.

Ishi, T. (1988). Japanese automobile and television assembly plants and local communities: County demographic correlates. Berkeley: Japan Pacific Resource Network.

Jackson, K. (July 2, 1990). Transplant wages will rise to match any gains at Big 3. *Automotive News*, p. 2.

Jackson, N. (Ed.). (1992). *Training for what? Labour perspectives on skill training*. Montreal, Quebec: Our Schools/Our Selves Foundation.

Jensen, C. (June 11, 1992). Avon lake enters minivan war. *Cleveland Plain Dealer*, p. G–1.

Jenson, J. (1989). 'Different' but not 'exceptional': Canada's permeable Fordism. *Canadian Journal of Sociology and Anthropology, 26*, 69–94.

———. (1990). Representation in crisis: The roots of Canada's permeable Fordism. *Canadian Journal of Political Science, 23*, 653–683.

Jessop, B. (1990). Regulation theories in retrospect and prospect. *Economy and Society, 19*, 153–216.

Johnson, D. (September, 1993). U.S., Mexican workers are teaming up to organize. *Labor Notes*.

Junkerman, J. (August, 1982). We are driven. *Mother Jones*, pp. 21–40.

———. (1987). Nissan, Tennessee. *The Progressive, 51*, 17–20.

———. (1988). Nissan: Teams without unions. In M. Parker and J. Slaughter, *Choosing sides* (pp. 219–223). Boston: South End Press.

Kamata, S. (1982). *Japan in the passing lane: An insider's account of life in a Japanese auto factory*. Trans. by T. Akimoto. New York: Pantheon.

Katz, H. C. (1985). *Shifting gears: Changing labor relations in the U.S. automobile industry*. Cambridge, MA: MIT Press.

Keller, M. N. (1991). Where America beats Japan. *World Monitor, 4*, 22–25.

Keller, M. (1989). *Rude awakening: The rise, fall, and struggle for recovery of General Motors*. New York: HarperCollins.

Kendall, R. M. (1987). Safety management: Japanese–style. *Occupational Hazards, 49*, 48–51.

Kenney, M. & Florida, R. (1989). Japan's role in a post–Fordist age. *Futures, 21*, 136–151.

———. (1988). Beyond mass production: Production and the labor process in Japan. *Politics and Society, 16*, 121–168.

———. (1993). *Beyond mass production: The Japanese system and its transfer to the U.S.* New York: Oxford University Press.

Kertesz, L. (June 6, 1988). Transplant wages, benefits similar. *Automotive News*, p. 1.

Klare, K. E. (1990). Critical theory and labor relations law. In D. Kairys (Ed.), *The politics of law* (pp. 61–89). New York: Panetheon.

Klein, J. (March/April, 1989). The human cost of manufacturing reform. *Harvard Business Review*, pp. 60–66.

———. (1991). A reexamination of autonomy in light of new manufacturing practices. *Industrial Relations*, *44*, 21–38.

Kochan, T. A., Katz, H. C., & McKersie, R. B. (1986). *The transformation of American industrial relations*. New York: Basic Books.

——— & Mower, N. (1984). *Worker participation and American unions*. Kalamazoo, MI: W.E. Upjohn Institute.

Koike, K. (1984). Skill formation systems in the U.S. and Japan. In M. Aoki, (Ed.), *The economic analysis of the Japanese firm* (pp. 47–75). Holland: Elsevier.

Kondracke, M. (July 27, 1992). Apprentices' sorcerer. *The New Republic*, *207*, pp. 14, 16.

Kornbluh, H. (1984). Workplace democracy and quality of work life. *Annals of the American academy of political and social science*, *473*, 88–95.

Koshiro, K (1983). The quality of working life in Japanese factories. In Taishiro Shirai (Ed.), *Contemporary industrial relations in Japan* (pp. 63–87). Madison: University of Wisconsin Press.

Krafcik, J. F. (Fall 1988). The triumph of the lean production system. *Sloan Management Review*, *29*, 41–52.

Krafcik, J. F. (1989). A new diet for U.S. manufacturing. *Technology Review*, *92*, 28–36.

Kraus, E. E. (1992). Political economy: Policymaking and industrial policy in Japan. *Political Science and Politics*, *25*, 44–47.

Kumazawa, M. & Yamada, J. (1989). Jobs and skills under the lifelong nenko employment practice. In S. Wood (Ed.), *The transformation of work?* London: Unwin Hyman.

Labor Relations Week. (January 6, 1993). Labor and management assess impact of labor board *Electromation* ruling. *Labor Relations Week*, *7*, pp. 19–20.

———. (December 23, 1992). NLRB cites Electromation for illegal domination. *Labor Relations Week*, *6*, pp. 1229–30.

Laclau, E. & Mouffe, C. (1985). *Hegemony & socialist strategy: Towards a radical democratic politics*. New York: Verso.

Lauria, D. (1990). The future of Ford in the U.S. car and light truck market, 1990–1995. Ann Arbor: Industrial Technology Institute.

Lawler, E. & Mohrman, S. (1987). Unions and the new management. *Academy of Management Executive*, p. 14.

Lee, B. A. (1987). Collective bargaining and employee participation: An anomalous interpretation of the National Labor Relations Act. *Labor Law Journal*, 38, 206–219.

Lee, M. E. & Alston, J. P. (1990). Is Japanese management style exportable. *Advances in Comparative Management*, 5, 197–209.

Leslie, D. L. (1992). *Labor law in a nutshell* (3rd ed.). St.Paul: West.

Levin, D. P. (March 23, 1993). Back to school for Honda workers. *New York Times*, pp. C1, C9.

Lewis, G. (1986). *News from somewhere: Connecting health and freedom at the workplace.* New York: Greenwood Press.

Levine, S. B. & Kawada, H. (1989). *Human resources in Japanese industrial development.* Princeton: Princeton University Press.

Lichtenstein, N. (1988). The unions' early days: Shop stewards and seniority rights. In M. Parker & J. Slaughter, *Choosing sides* (pp. 65–75). Boston: South End Press.

Lincoln, J. & Kalleberg, A. (1985). Work organizations and work force commitment: A study of plants and employment in the U.S. and Japan. *American Sociological Review*, 30, 738–60.

———. (1990). *Culture, control, and commitment: A study of work organization and work attitudes in the United States and Japan.* New York: Cambridge University Press.

——— and McBride, K. (1987). Japanese industrial organization in comparative perspective. *Annual Review of Sociology*, 13, 289–312.

Lipietz, A. (1987). *Mirages and miracles: The crisis of global fordism.* Trans. by D. Macey. London: Verso.

———. (1992). *Towards a new economic order: Postfordism, ecology, and democracy.* New York: Oxford University Press.

Lippert, J. (January 19, 1991). Possible Flat Rock strike gets OK. *Detroit Free Press*, p. 1.

Lipset, S. M. (1989). *Continental divide: The values and institutions of the United States and Canada.* New York: Routledge.

———. (1990). *North American cultures: Values and institutions in Canada and the United States.* Orono: Canadian–American Center.

Lipskey, A. A. (1992). Participatory management schemes, the law, and workers' rights. *The American University Law Review*, 39, 667–720.

Lowery, D. (1990). The national level roots of the failure of state industrial policy. In E. J. Yanarella and W. C. Green, (Eds.), *The politics of industrial recruitment* (pp. 194–204). Westport: Greenwood Press.

McNamee, M. & Del Va'e, C. (April 12, 1993). Reich's return to those thrilling days of yesteryear. *Business Week*, p. 45.

McPherson, K. (July 1985). Contract talks at GM–Toyota plant may set new pattern for auto industry. *Labor Notes*, p. 1.

MacShane, D. (1993). Labor standards and double standards in the new world order. In J. Brecher et al. (Eds.), *Global visions*. Boston: South End Press.

Magaziner, I. & Clinton, H. R. (March 1992). Will America choose high skills or low wages? *Educational Leadership, 49*, 10–14.

Mahon, R.. (1990). Adjusting to win? The new tory training initiative. In Katherine A. Graham (Ed.), *How Ottawa spends 1990–91: Tracking the second agenda* (pp. 73–111). Ottawa: Carleton University Press.

————. (1987). From Fordism to ?: New technology, labour markets and unions. *Economic and Industrial Democracy, 8*, 5–60

————. (1991). Post–Fordism: Some issues for labour. In D. Drache and M. S. Gertler (Eds.), *The new era of global competition* (pp. 316–332). Montreal: McGill-Queen's University Press.

Mair, A., Florida, R. & Kenney, M. (1988). The new geography of automobile production: Japanese transplants in North America. *Economic Geography, 64*, 352–373.

Mann, E. (1987). *Taking on General Motors: A case study of the UAW campaign to keep GM Van Nuys open*. Los Angeles: UCLA, Institute of Industrial Relations.

Marsh, R. M. (1992). The difference between participation and power in Japanese factories. *Industrial and Labor Relations, 45*, 250–257.

Martin, A. (1994). Labor, the Keynesian welfare state, and the changing international political economy. In R. Stubbs & G. R. D. Underhill (Eds.), *Political economy and the changing global order* (pp. 60–74). New York: St. Martin's.

Martin, E. (February 1992). The end of the body? *American Ethnologist, 19*: 120–138.

Marsh, R. M. (January 1992). The difference between participation and power in Japanese factories. *Industrial and Labor Relations, 45*, 250–257.

Masami, N. (1985). 'Model Japan'? Characteristics of industrial relations in the Japanese automobile industry. *Discusssion Papers* (pp. 1–3). Berlin: International Institute for Comparative Social Research and Labor Policy.

Maskery, M. (April 3, 1989). Japanese workers stress reduced hours in contract talks. *Automotive News*, p. 6.

————. (January 28, 1991). Toyota, Mitsubishi try 4–day workweek in Japan. *Automotive News*, p. 43.

————. (February 17, 1992). Japanese auto union demands a better life. *Automotive News*, p. 82.

————. (December 21, 1992). Japan's reducing plan. *Automotive News*, p. 101.

Mazda Motor Manufacturing Corporation, Personnel Division. (1990). *Employee Handbook For Team Leaders and Team Members*. p. A–3.

Mazda Motor Manufacturing Corporation and UAW Local Union 3000. (1991). *Collective bargaining agreement between Mazda Motor Manufacturing (USA) . . . and [UAW] Local union 3000, March 4, 1991– February 27, 1994*.

Menard, A. P. and Morrill, A. R. (1979). Are faculty members scholars or managers? The *Yeshiva* Case. *Labor Law Journal, 30*, 754–62.

Meyer, S. III. (1981). *The five dollar day: Labor management and social control in the Ford Motor Company, 1908–1921*. Albany, NY: State University of New York Press.

Mid–America Project. (1991). *Keiretsu, America: A tale of Japanese power*. Versailles, KY: Mid–America Project.

Milkman, R. (1991). *Japan's California factories: Labor relations and economic globalization*. Los Angeles: UCLA, Institute of Industrial Relations.

Miller, R. (1988). *New locational factors in the automobile industry*. Boston: MIT International Motor Vehicle Program.

Milward, H. B. & Newman, H. H. (1988). The escalation of state incentive packages and Japanese automobile alley. *Review and Perspective, 12*, 2–5.

————. (1990). State incentive packages and the industrial location decision. In E. J. Yanarella & W. C. Green (Eds.), *The politics of industrial recruitment* (pp. 23–51). Westport: Greenwood Press.

Moberly, R. B. (1985). Worker participation and labor–management cooperation through collective bargaining. *Stetson Law Review, 15*, 99–121.

Molot, M. A. (Ed.). (1993). *Driving continentally: National policies and the North American auto industry*. Ottawa: Carleton University Press.

Monden, Y. (1983). *Toyota production system*. Norcross, GA: Institute of Industrial Engineers.

Moore, W. J. & Newman, R. J. (1985). The effects of right to work laws. *Industrial and Labor Relations Review, 38*, 571–85.

Morris, J. (1991). A Japanization of Canadian industry? In D. Drache & M. S. Gertler (Eds.), *The new era of global competition* (pp. 206–228). Montreal: McGill-Queen's University Press.

Mortimer, K. (1990). EDAP at Ford: A research note. *Industrial Relations Journal, 20*, 309–314.

Moskal, B. (January 15, 1988). Can you pass the muster? *Industry Week*, p. 20.

———. (August 7, 1989). Hybrid incubator hatches workers. *Industry Week*, pp. 27–28.

Muszynski, L. & Wolfe, D. A. (1989). New technology and training: Lessons from abroad. *Canadian Public Policy, 15*, 245–264.

The New York Times. (April 6, 1993). The same old song. *The New York Times*, p. A–14.

Nevins, T. (1984). *Labor pains and the caijin boss: Hiring, managing, and firing the Japanese.* Tokyo: Japan Times.

New Horzons. (October/November 1990). Kaizen—friend or foe. *New Horizons*, p. 3.

Nomani, A. Q. & Ingersoll, B. (April 29, 1993). Auto makers air gripes as White House tries to formulate policy for industry. *Wall Street Journal*, p. 4.

Nomura, M. (1993). The end of Toyotism? Paper delivered at Lean Workplace Conference, Port Elgin, Ontario.

Note. (1981). Collective authority and technical expertise: Reexamining the managerial employee exclusion. *New York University Law Review, 56*, 694–741.

Note. (1959). The impact of the *Borg–Warner* case on collective bargaining. *Minnesota Law Review, 43*, 1225–42.

Note. (1983). Collective bargaining as an industrial system: An argument against judicial revision of Section 8(a)(2) of the National Labor Relations Act. *Harvard Law Review, 96*, 1662–1682.

Note. (1985). Participatory management under Sections 2(5) and 8(a)(2) of the National Labor Relations Act. *Michigan Law Review, 83*, 1736–1769.

O'Boyle, T. F. (November 26, 1991). New neighbor: To Georgetown, Ky, Toyota plant seems a blessing and a curse. *Wall Street Journal*, A1+.

Okayama, R. (1987). Industrial relations in the Japanese automobile industry, 1945–70: The case of Toyota. In S. Tolliday & J. Zeitlen (Eds.), *The automobile industry and its workers: Between Fordism and flexibility* (pp. 160–189). New York: St. Martin's Press.

Oliver, N. & Wilkinson, B. (1988). *The Japanization of British industry.* New York: Blackwell.

Organization for Economic Co-operation and Development (OECD), Centre for Education Research and Innovation. (1986). New technology and human resource development in the automobile industry. Paris: OECD.

Palmer, B. (1994). *Capitalism goes to the backcountry.* Toronto: Between the Lines.

Panitch, L. & Swartz, D. (1988). *The assault on trade union freedoms.* Toronto: Garamond Press.

Parker, M. (January/February 1990). Transplanted to the U.S.A. *Multinational Monitor*, pp. 37–41.

————. (1985). *Inside the circle*. Boston: South End Press.

————. (February 1986). New union consensus in secret agreement between UAW, Mazda. *Labor Notes*, p. 13.

————. (December 1988). The permanent temporaries: Mazda moves toward two-tier wage system. *Labor Notes*, p. 5.

————. (May 1991). New Mazda contract eases 'management-by-stress' system. *Labor Notes*, pp. 5–6.

Parker, M. & Slaughter, J. (1988a). *Choosing sides*. Boston: South End Press.

———— & Slaughter, J. (December 4, 1988b). Management by stress: Behind the scenes at NUMMI motors. *New York Times*. III: 2.

————. (1992). *A union strategy guide for labor-management participation programs*. Detroit: Labor Notes Press.

Partridge-Ullrich, R. J. & Heeter, T. G. (1988). Positioned for partnership: Indiana's employment and training experience with the Subaru-Isuzu automotive, inc. project. *Perspective: Essays and Readings on Issues in Employment Security and Training Programs, 4*, 21–28.

Paterson, G. (April 17, 1990). Mazda–UAW's Michigan honeymoon is over. *Wall Street Journal*.

Pearl, D. (January 9, 1995). Panel recommends easing restrictions on worker groups. *Company News* [Dow Jones News Retrieval], n.p.

Pelletier, R. (February 1991). President's message. *Off the Line*, No. 7.

Perrucci, R. (1994). *Japanese auto transplants in the heartland: Corporatism and community*. New York: Aldine de Gruyter.

———— & Patel, M. (1990). Local images of Japanese automobile investment in Indiana and Kentucky. In E. J. Yanarella & W. C. Green (Eds.), *The politics of industrial recruitment* (pp. 137–152). Westport: Greenwood Press.

Peters, T. J. (1982). *In search of excellence: Lessons from America's best-run companies*. New York: Harper & Row.

Pinto, L. (December 9, 1991). Mazda, workers disagree on reason for drop in injuries. *Automotive News*.

Piore, M. J. & Sabel, C. F. (1984). *The second industrial divide*. New York: Basic Books.

Powers, M. R. (1988). The GM–UAW Saturn agreement: A new approach to premature recognition. *Virginia Law Review, 74*, 89–122.

Rainsberger, P. (1990). The constraints of public policy: Legal perspectives on the decline of the labor movement since world war II. In B. Nissen (Ed.), *U.S. labor relations, 1945–1989* (pp. 91–136). New York: Garland.

Rachleff, P. (1993). *Hard-pressed in the heartland: The Hormel strike and the future of the labor movement.* Boston: South End Press.

Rechtin, M. (February 13, 1995). Bromont stays closed, Hyundai says. *Automotive News,* p. 20.

Reich, R. B. (1992). *The work of nations.* New York: Vintage.

Rinehart, J., Robertson, D., & Huxley, C. (1993). Reunifying conception and execution of work under Japanese production management. Unpublished paper, University of Western Ontario.

Robertson, D. (1990a). Corporate training syndrome: What we have is not enough and more would be too much. A paper prepared for the OFL Conference on Training.

———. (1990b). Multi-skilling: A labour view. An address to the Institute for International Research Industrial Conference Division, Toronto.

———. (1992a). Corporate training syndrome: What we have is not enough & more would be too much. In N. Jackson (Ed), *Training for what? Labour perspectives on skill training* (pp. 18–28). Toronto: Our Schools/Our Selves Foundation.

———. (1992b). The meaning of multi–skilling. In N. Jackson (Ed), *Training for what? Labour perspectives on skill training* (pp. 29–42). Toronto: Our Schools/Our Selves Foundation.

———. (1992c). Technology, skill and the economy: A response to David Wolfe and Leon Muszynski. Unpublished manuscript.

——— & Wareham, J. (1987). *Technological change in the auto industry: CAW technology project.* Willowdale, Ontario: CAW/TCA.

———. (1989). *Computer automation and technological change: North Telecom: CAW technology project.* Willowdale, Ontario: CAW/TCA.

Robertson, D., Rinehart, J., & Huxley, C. (April 1991). Team concept: A case study of Japanese production management in a unionized Canadian auto plant. Paper presented to the Ninth Annual International Conference on Organisation and Control of the Labour Process, University of Manchester, Manchester, England.

——— & the CAW Research Group on CAMI. (1992). Team concept and kaizen: Production management in a unionized Canadian auto plant. *Studies in Political Economy, 39,* 77–107.

———. (1993). *Japanese production management in a unionized plant.* Willowdale, Ontario: CAW/TCA.

Robbins, S. P. (January 1983). The theory Z organization from a power-control perspective. *California Management Review, 25,* 67–75.

Robinson, I. (1993). *North American trade as if democracy mattered: What's wrong with NAFTA and what are the alternatives.* Ottawa and Washington, D.C.: Canadian

Centre for Policy Alternatives and International Labor Rights Education and Research Fund.

Rosenfeld, H. (1993a). Team concept at CAMI. *Canadian Dimension, 27,* 21–24.

———. (1993b). Gains at CAMI. *Tech Notes, 3,* 3–4.

Rothstein, R. (1993). New bargain or no bargain. *The American Prospect,* 14, 32–47.

Rowand, R. (May 30, 1983). GM teardown shows U.S. Honda quality equals Japanese. *Automotive News,* p. 8.

Rubenstein, J. (1992). *The changing U.S. auto industry.* London and New York: Routledge.

Russo, J. (Fall 1986). Saturn's rings: What GM's Saturn project is really about. *Labor Research Review, 5,* 67–77.

St. Antoine, T. J. (1989). The legal and economic implications of union-management cooperation: The case of GM and the UAW. *Law Quadrangle: Notes, 33,* 46–54. Ann Arbor: University of Michigan Law School.

Safizadeh, M. H. (Summer 1991). The case of workgroups in manufacturing operations. *California Management Review, 33,* 61–82

Sakolsky, R. (Winter 1992). 'Disciplinary power,' the labor process, and the constitution of the laboring subject. *Rethinking Marxism, 5,* 114–126.

Sands, D. R. (January 10, 1995). Business, labor have little good to say about the report on their relationship. *Washington Times,* p. B6.

Sassen, S. (1991). *The global city.* Princeton: Princeton University Press.

Saturn Corporation. (1992). *T3 process* [Course # 4531]. Spring Hill, TN: Saturn Corporation.

———. (1993). Saturn education tracking system, Tennessee training schedule. Saturn corporation training mission. (N.d.). Spring Hill, TN: Saturn Corporation.

Saturn mission. (N.d.). Spring Hill, TN: Saturn Corporation.

Saturn labor agreement approved by UAW in July (1985) [Text]. (June 4, 1986). Washington, D.C.: Bureau of National Affairs, pp. E.1–E.6.

Sayer, A. & Walker, R. (1992). *The new social economy: Reworking the division of labor.* Cambridge: Blackwell.

Scannell, R. (1993). Adversary participation in the brave new workplace. In G. Adler and D. Suarez (Eds.), *Union voices: Labor's responses to crisis.* Albany: State University of New York Press.

Scherer, J. (1988). The Canadian–American UAW controversy. A paper presented at the Midwest Association of Canadian Studies.

————. (1990). The Canadian Auto Workers: A study in Canadian–United States relations. A paper presented at the Midwest Association of Canadian Studies Conference, Lexington, Kentucky.

Schmidman, J. & Keller, K. (1984). Employee participation plans as section 8(a)(2) violations. *Labor Law Journal, 35,* 772–780.

Schlossberg, S. I. & Reinhart, M. B. (1992). Electromation and the future of labor–management cooperation in the U.S. *Labor Law Journal, 43,* 608–620.

Schurman, S. J., Hugentobler, M. K., & Stack, H. (1991). Lessons from the UAW–GM paid educational leave program. In L. Ferman, H. Hayman, & J. Crutcher-Gershenfeld (Eds.), *Joint training programs: A union–management approach to preparing workers for the future.* Ithaca, NY: ILR Press.

Sengenberger, W. (1992). Lean production: The way of working and producing in the future? Paper delivered at the Forum on Labor in a Changing World Economy, Geneva.

Serafin, R. (November 16, 1992). The Saturn story: How Saturn became one of the most auccessful new brands in marketing history. *Advertising Age, 63,* pp. 1–3.

Shalom, F. (December 20, 1990). Battle to form union at Hyundai heats up: CAW says it is close to having enough to hold vote. *Montreal Gazette,* p. C–1.

————. (May 24, 1991). Union claims victory at Hyundai plant. *Montreal Gazette,* p. E3.

Shaiken, H., Herzenberg, S., & Kuhn, S. (1986). The work process under more flexible production. *Industrial Relations, 25,* 167–183.

Shaiken, H. & Herzenberg, S. (1987). *Automation and global production: Automobile engine production in Mexico, the United States and Canada.* San Diego: University of California, Center for U.S.–Mexico Studies.

Shimada, H. & MacDuffie, J. P. (1987). *Industrial relations and 'humanware': Japanese investments in automobile manufacturing in the United States.* Boston: MIT International Motor Vehicle Program.

Shimokawa, K. (1987). Product and labor strategies in Japan. In S. Tolliday & J. Zeitlen (Eds.), *The automobile industry and its workers: Between Fordism and flexibility.* New York: St. Martin's Press.

Shook, Robert L. (Ed.). (1988). *Honda: An American success story.* Englewood Cliffs: Prentice–Hall.

Sinek, J. (March 29, 1993). Hyundai workers want CAW. *Automotive News,* p. 37.

Slaughter, J. (1983). *Concessions and how to beat them.* Detroit: Labor Education and Research Project.

————. (September 17, 1983). Fremont workers will be rehired at GM-Toyota plant—But not by seniority. *Labor Notes,* p. 16.

————. (September 1989). Behind the UAW's defeat at Nissan. *Labor Notes*, p. 1.

————. (April 1987). Dissent grows at California GM-Toyota plant. *Labor Notes*, p. 3.

————. (October 1992a). Auto union wins outsourcing protection after nine-day Lordstown strike. *Labor Notes*, p. 5.

————. (June/July 1992b). Shrinking auto union beats back reformers. *Autoworker Gazette: Newsletter of the Rank & File Coalition*, p. 3.

————. (May 1993). Champion of labor-management cooperation wins narrow re-election at GM's Saturn. *Labor Notes*.

Solo, S. (October 22, 1990). Japan's unhappy auto workers. *Fortune, 122,* 10–11.

Solomon, C. M. (1991). Behind the wheel at Saturn. *Personnel Journal, 70,* 72–74.

Sorge, M. (October 18, 1982). The Japanese worker: All may not be as well as it seems. *Automotive News*, p. E-4.

Staudohar, P. D. (1991). Labor–management cooperation at NUMMI. *Labor Law Journal, 42,* 57–63.

Storey, R (1991). Studying work in Canada. *Canadian Journal of Sociology, 16,* 241–264.

Streeck, W. (1985). Introduction: Industrial relations, technological change and economic restructuring. *Industrial Relations and Technological Change in the British, Italian and German Automobile Industry.* W. Streeck (Ed.). Berlin: Wissenschaftszentrum.

————. (1989). Skills and the limits of neo-liberalism: The enterprise of the future as a place of learning. *Work, Employment and Society, 3,* 89–104.

————. (1993). Training and the new industrial relations. *Economic restructuring and emerging patterns of industrial relations* (pp. 167–187). S. Sleigh (Ed.). Kalamazoo, MI.: W.E. Upjohn Institute.

Subaru–Isuzu Automotive Inc. (1989). *Subaru–Isuzu Automotive Inc.-Facts and information.* Produced in Cooperation With the Indiana Department of Employment and Training Services.

Tannenbaum, S. I. & Yukl, G. (1992). Training and development in work organizations. *American Review of Psychology, 43,* 399–344.

Templin, N. (April 5, 1993). UAW chief at GM's Saturn unit vows to back consensus-management pact. *Wall Street Journal*, p. A-14.

Thompson, B. L. (1991). Negotiation training: Win-win or what? *Training, 28,* 31–35.

Thompson, P. (1989). *The nature of work* (2nd ed.). Atlantic Heights, NJ: Humanities Press International.

Thornicroft, K. W. (1990). Unions, union dues, and political activity: A Canada/U.S. comparative analysis. *Labor Law Journal, 41,* 846–855.

Tomasko, E. S. & Dickinson, K. K. (1991). The UAW–Ford education, development and training program. In L. Ferman, M. Hoyman, & J. Crutcher–Hershenfeld (Eds.), *Joint training programs: A union–management approach to preparing workers for the future* (pp. 55–70). Ithaca: ILR Press.

Toyoda, T. (1987). Quality through teamwork. In P. Arnesen (Ed.), *The Japanese competition: Phase 2* (pp. 23–29). Ann Arbor: Center for Japanese Studies.

Toyota Motor Corporation. (N.d.). Education and Training [Manual]. Toyota City, Japan: Toyota Motor Corporation.

———. (N.d.). Production at Toyota: Our basic philosophy. Toyota City, Japan: Toyota Motor Corporation.

———. (N.d.). Toyota production training program: General information. Toyota City, Japan: Toyota Motor Corporation.

———. (1984). Labor/management relations. Toyota City, Japan: Toyota Motor Corporation.

———. Education and Training Department. (1985). Education and training. Toyota City, Japan: Toyota Motor Corporation.

———. (1988). Nissan training center. Toyota City, Japan: Toyota Motor Corporation.

Training—A top priority from start to finish. (October 5, 1988). *Lexington Herald- Leader* p. 3.

Treece, J.B. (April 15, 1985). How a powerless work force sharpens industry's edge. *Business Week*, p. 61.

Turnbull, P. (1988). The limits of 'Japanization'—Just–in–time, labor relations and the UK automotive industry. *New Technology, Work, and Employment, 3*, 7–20.

Turner, L. (1991). *Democracy at work: Changing world markets and the future of labor unions.* Ithaca: Cornell University Press.

Turner, L. (1992). Industrial relations and the reorganization of work in West Germany: Lessons for the U.S. In L. Mishel & P. Voos (Eds.), *Unions and economic competitiveness* (pp. 217–246). Armonk, NY: M.E. Sharpe.

UAW Local Union 3000. (1991a). Strike authorization vote of January 16, (1991). Flat Rock, MI: UAW Local Union 3000.

———. (1991b). Contract ratification vote. March 14. Flat Rock, MI: UAW Local Union 3000.

———. (1991c). Team leader selection process as of 9/6/91. Flat Rock, MI: UAW Local Union 3000.

UAW-Mazda Motor Manufacturing Corporation. (1991). Collective bargaining agreement between Mazda Motor Manufacturing (USA) Corporation and the International Union, United Automobile, Aerospace and Agricultural Implement Workers of America, UAW and its affiliated Local Union 3000.

U.S. Department of Labor, Bureau of Labor–Management Relations and Cooperative Programs. (1987). New United Motor Manufacturing, Inc. and the United Automobile Workers: Partners in training. *Labor Management Cooperation Briefing* [No. 10].

U.S. Department of Labor, Office of Work–Based Learning. (1990). Workforce quality: Perspectives from the U.S. and Japan. Washington, D.C.: U.S. G.P.O.

Veltri, T. (October 31, 1990). Push to unionize Honda workers. *The Herald* (Alliston, Ont.), p. 2.

Versical, D. (November 21, 1988). Squeezing turnips at Ford. *Automotive News*, p. 1.

Vogel, D. (1989). *Fluctuating fortunes: The political power of business in America.* New York: Basic Books.

Vogel, E. (1979). *Japan as number one: Lessons for America.* Cambridge: Harvard University Press.

Wagner, R. J., Baldwin, T. T. & Roland, C. G. (1991). Outdoor training: Revolution or fad? *Training & Development, 45,* 51–57.

Walker, C. & Guest, R. (1952). *The man on the assembly line.* Cambridge: Harvard University Press.

Wall Street Journal. (April 6, 1993). The same old song. *Wall Street Journal*, p. A–14.

Walsh, J. (July 18, 1983). Quality equal to Japan claimed for U.S. Nissan. *Automotive News*, p. 14.

Walt, A. & American Arbitration Association. (1990). In the Matter of Local 3000, UAW and Mazda Motor Manufacturing (USA) Corporation. *Award of Arbitrator,* Case No. 54 30 0339 90, 17.

Warren, A. S. (1986). Quality of work life at General Motors. In J. Rosow (Ed.), *Teamwork: Joint labor–management programs in America* (pp. 119–132). New York: Pergamon Press.

Wells, D. (1987). *Empty promises: Quality of work life programs and the labor movement.* New York: Monthly Review Press.

———. (1993a). Recent innovations in labour–management relations: The risks and prospects for labour in Canada and the United States. In J. Jenson & R. Mahon (Eds.), *The challenge of restructuring* (pp. 287–313). Philadelphia, PA: Temple University Press.

———. (1993b). Are strong unions compatible with the new model of human resource management? *Relations Industrielles/Industrial Relations, 48*, 1.

———. (1993c). Lean production: The challenges to labour. A paper presented at the Conference on the Lean Workplace, Port Elgin, Ontario.

———. (1995). Origins of Canada's Wagner Model of industrial relations: The United Auto Workers in Canada and the suppression of 'rank and file' unionism, 1936–1953. *Canadian Journal of Sociology, 20*, 20.

Weiler, P. (1983). Promises to keep: Securing workers' rights to self-organization under the NLRA. *Harvard Law Review, 96*, 1769–1827.

———. (1990). *Governing the workplace: The future of labor and employment law.* Cambridge, MA: Harvard University Press.

White, Bob. (1987). *Hard bargains: My life on the line.* Toronto: McCelland and Stewart.

———. (1991a). Presentation. *The Canadian Auto Industry.* Toronto, Ontario, pp. 54–63.

———. (1991b). An inquiry into the current situation of the Canadian auto industry. A Presentation to the Hearings before the Standing Committee on Industry, Science, Technology, Regional and Northern Development, Ottawa.

Wilkinson, B. & Oliver, N. (1989). Power, control, and the kanban. *Journal of Management Studies, 26*, 47–58.

Williams, G. A. (1960). Gramsci's concept of egemonia. *Journal of the History of Ideas, 21*, 586–599.

Williams, K., Cutler, T., Williams, J., and Hasham, C. (1987). The end of mass production? *Economy and Society, 16*, 405–439.

———, Haslam, C., & Williams, J. (1992). Ford versus Fordism": The beginning of mass production? *Work, Employment and Society.*

———. (1992). Against lean production. *Economy and Society, 21*, 321–354.

Williams, R. (1973). Base and superstructure in Marxist cultural theory. *New Left Review, 82*, 3–16.

Williams, S. D. & Brinker, W. J. (1985). A survey of foreign firms recently locating in Tennessee. *Growth and Change, 16*, 54–63.

Williams, S. A. (1982). Distinguishing protected from unprotected campaign speech. *Labor Law Journal, 33*, 265–81.

Wilson, R. B. & Schmoker, M. (1992). Quest for quality: What schools can learn from the Japanese. *Executive Educator, 14*, 18–22.

Witt, M. (April/May 1991). Mexico-US-Canada FTA: Free workers, not free trade. *Canadian Dimension, 25*, 28–31.

Wokutch, R. E. (1992). *Worker protection, Japanese style.* Ithaca: Cornell University Press.

Womack, J. (1987). The Japanification of the American automobile industry. Cambridge: MIT International Motor Vehicle Program.

————, Jones, D., & Roos, D. (1990). *The machine that changed the world.* New York: Rawson and Associates.

Wonnacott, P. (1987). *U.S. and Canadian auto policies in a changing world environment.* Toronto, Washington, D.C.: Canadian–American Committee.

Wood, S. (1986). The cooperative labour strategy in the U.S. auto industry. *Economic and Industrial Democracy, 7,* 415–447.

————. (1987). The deskilling debate, new technology and work organization. *Acta Sociologica, 30,* 3–24.

Woodruff, D. (1992). Where employees are management: Commitment equals empowerment at Saturn. *Business Week,* p. 66.

————. (February 8, 1993). Saturn: Labor's love lost? *Business Week,* pp. 122, 124.

Yamada, N. (1985). Working time in Japan: Recent trends and issues. *International Labor Review, 124,* 699–718.

Yanarella, E. J. (1993). Whither hegemony? Between Gramsci and Derrida. In J. P. Jones, W. Natter, & T. Schatzki (Eds.), *Reassessing modernity and postmodernity* (pp. 65–98). New York: Guilford Publishers.

———— & Green, W. C., (Eds.). (1990). *The politics of industrial recruitment: Japanese automobile investment and economic development in the American States.* Westport: Greenwood Press.

———— & Green, W. C. (1993). Community, labor, and environmental participation in industrial recruitment: East Asian automobile investment in Canada in comparative perspective. *Economic Development Quarterly, 7,* 140–159.

————. (1994a). The UAW and the CAW confront lean production at Saturn, CAMI, and the Japanese automobile transplants. *Labor Studies Journal, 18,* 52–75.

————. (1994b). Canadian recruitment of East Asian automobile transplants: Cultural, economic, and political perspectives. *Canadian Journal of Sociology, 18,* 359–81.

Yanarella, E. J. & Reid, H. G. (1996). From 'trained gorilla' to 'humanware': Repoliticizing the body-machine complex between Fordism and post-Fordism. In J. P. Jones, W. Natter, & T. Schqtzki (Eds.), *The social-political body.* New York: Guilford Publications.

———— & Reid, H. G. (1990). Problems of coalition building in Japanese auto alley: Public opposition to the Georgetown/Toyota plant. In E. J. Yanarella & W. C. Green (Eds.), *The politics of industrial recruitment* (pp. 153–173). Westport: Greenwood Press.

Yates, C. (1990). The internal dynamics of a union: Explaining Canadian autoworkers' militancy in the 1980s. *Studies in Political Economy, 31*, 73–105.

———. (1992). Driving through the new reality. *Canadian Dimension, 26*, 11–12.

———. (1993a). Curtains or encore: Possibilities for restructuring in the Canadian auto industry. In J. Jenson & R. Mahon (Eds.), *The challenge of restructuring* (pp. 337–357). Philadelphia: Temple University Press.

———. (1993b). *From plants to politics: The Canadian UAW, 1936–1984.* Philadelphia, PA.: Temple University Press.

Yoshida, K. (1992). New economic principles in America—Competition and cooperation. *The Columbia Journal of World Business, 26*, 30–44.

Zahavi, G. (1983). Negotiated loyalty: Welfare capitalism and the shoeworkers of Endicott Johnson, 1920–1940. *The Journal of American History, 70*, 602–620.

Zellner, W. (July 10, 1989). For auto workers, it's team spirit vs. suspicion. *Business Week,* pp. 60–61.

Zwerdling, D. (1980). *Workplace Democracy.* New York: HarperColophon.

Statutes

National Labor Relations Act, 29 U.S.C., 151–169.

Ontario Labor Relations Act, ch. 228, Sect. 7, p. 14.

Cases

Chicago Rawhide Manufacturing Co. v NLRB, 221 F2d 165 (7th Cir 1955)

Electromation, 309 NLRB 163 (1993).

Federal Mogul Corp. v NLRB, 394 F2d 915 (6th Cir 1968).

Fiberboard Paper Products Corp. v NLRB, 379 US 203 (1964).

First National Maintenance Corp. v NLRB, 452 US 666 (1981).

General Foods, 231 NLRB 1232 (1977).

Hertzga and Knowles v NLRB, 503 F2d 625 (9th Cir 1974).

Lechmere v NLRB, 112 Sct 841 (1992).

NLRB v Bell–Aerospace, 416 US 267 (1974).

NLRB v Health Care & Retirement Corp. of America, 114 Sct 1778 (1994).

NLRB v Wooster Div. of Borg–Warner Corp., 356 US 342 (1959).

NLRB v Cabot Carbon, 360 US 203 (1959).

NLRB v Gissel Packing, 395 US 575 (1969).

NLRB v Homemaker Shop, 724 F2d 535 (6th Cir 1984).

NLRB v Streamway Division of Scott Fetzer Co., 691 F2d 288 (6th Cir 1982).

NLRB v Yeshiva University, 444 US 672 (1980).

Interviews

Allen, John. (1993). Former manager of Toyota Motor Manufacturing training center. Interview, Lexington, KY, 6 July.

Grygorcewicz, Tom. (1991). Plant chair, CAW Local 88, CAMI plant, Ingersoll, Ontario, 30 July.

High, Gary. (1993). Manager, Human Resource Development, People Systems, Saturn Corporation. Interview, Northfield Training Center, Saturn plant, Spring Hill, TN, 16 March.

Hinton, Mary. (1993). Former trainer, Toyota Motor Manufacturing, Inc. Interview, Lexington, KY, 28 July.

Hunt, Ted. (1991). Chief Administrative Officer, Ingersoll, Ontario, 29 July.

Metic, Hemi. (1991). Director of Organizing, Canadian Auto Workers, Willowdale, Ontario, 1 August.

Pellerin, Ron. (1991). Director of Service, Canadian Auto Workers, Willowdale, Ontario, 1 August.

Rinehart, James. (1991). Professor of Sociology, University of Western Ontario, London, Ontario, 27 July.

Rose, Damaris. (1991). Associate Professor and Research Associate, Institute for National Scientific Research, Montreal, Ontario, 5 August.

Index